ANSWERS TO THE TOP 50 QUESTIONS ABOUT GENESIS, CREATION, AND NOAH'S FLOOD

Daniel A. Biddle, Ph.D.

Copyright © 2018 by Genesis Apologetics, Inc.
E-mail: staff@genesisapologetics.com

 GENESIS apologetics

www.genesisapologetics.com
A 501(c)(3) ministry equipping youth pastors, parents, and
students with Biblical answers for evolutionary teaching in
public schools.

The entire contents of this book (including videos) are
available online: www.genesisapologetics.com/faqs

Answers to the Top 50 Questions about Genesis, Creation, and
Noah's Flood
by Daniel A. Biddle, Ph.D.
Printed in the United States of America

ISBN-13: 978-1727870305

ISBN-10: 1727870301

Print Version November 2019

Download the FREE "Genesis Apologetics" Mobile App for Creation v. Evolution Videos!

GENESIS
apologetics

Dedication

To my wife, Jenny, who supports me in this work. To my children Makaela, Alyssa, Matthew, and Amanda, and to your children and your children's children for a hundred generations—this book is for all of you.

We would like to acknowledge Answers in Genesis (*www.answersingenesis.org*), the Institute for Creation Research (*www.icr.org*), and Creation Ministries International (*www.creation.com*). Much of the content herein has been drawn from (and is meant to be in alignment with) these Biblical Creation ministries.

"Guard what has been entrusted to you, avoiding worldly and empty chatter and the opposing arguments of what is falsely called 'knowledge'—which some have professed and thus gone astray from the faith. Grace be with you."
—1 Tim. 6:20–21

"This is the Lord's doing; it is marvelous in our eyes."
—Psalm 118:23

Contents

About the Author

Dr. Daniel A. Biddle is president of Genesis Apologetics, Inc., a 501(c)(3) organization dedicated to equipping youth pastors, parents, and students with Biblical answers for evolutionary teaching in public schools. Daniel has trained thousands of students in Biblical Creation and evolution and is the author of several Creation books and other publications. Daniel's experience and qualifications include a Ph.D. in Organizational Psychology from Alliant University in San Francisco, California, an M.A. in Organizational Psychology from Alliant, and a B.S. in Organizational Behavior from the University of San Francisco. Daniel has worked as an expert consultant and/or witness in over 100 state and federal cases in the areas of research methodologies and analysis.

About the Ministry

Genesis Apologetics is a non-profit 501(c)(3) ministry that equips Christian students and their parents with faith-building materials that affirm a Biblical Creation worldview. We are committed to providing Christian families with Biblically and scientifically accurate answers to the evolutionary theory that public schools propagate. Our doctrinal position on Biblical Creation aligns with Answers in Genesis and the Institute for Creation Research (ICR), which take Genesis at face value, including its testimony of a miraculous creation and Flood that occurred thousands, not millions of years ago. Genesis Apologetics offers the following free online training resources:

- *Mobile App:* Search for "Genesis Apologetics" in the iTunes or Google Play stores.
- *www.debunkevolution.com*
- *www.genesisapologetics.com*

- YouTube Channel (**Genesis Apologetics**). Our channel includes over 100 videos that promote Biblical Creation.

Introduction

Promoting Biblical Creation on Social Media platforms is likely to cause controversy. The same is true when mentioning God, the Bible, or Creation in secular education and social gatherings. That's why we wrote this book. After posting over 100 videos online through various Social Media platforms, Christians, seekers, and evolutionists bombarded our ministry with thousands of questions and comments. We started noticing several consistent themes. People were asking the same fundamental questions using different words.

This book distills those questions into the 50 most consistently-asked questions and provides biblically-based answers that generally agree with qualified Creation Apologists and scientists. The questions are arranged in alphabetical order and include both written answers and videos that answer each question succinctly and accurately. The entirety of this book (including videos and references) is available online here: https://genesisapologetics.com/faqs/.

How to Be Effective in Creation Apologetics

Apologetics refers to defending the faith, not apologizing. The word comes from 1 Peter 3:15, "always be ready to give a defense [απολογια (apologia), or answer]…" We offer eight *key strategies* for creation apologetics. These can transform an ineffective or even harmful influence on a seeker's journey toward the Lord and Savior Jesus Christ into effective use by God to open someone's eyes to the truth of Creation and the Gospel upon which it is based (see 2 Timothy 2:14–26 and 2 Timothy 3:17).

1. **Be grounded**. God's Word is true, period. Yes, there are things we don't fully understand in God's Word and things we don't understand about the natural world. However, we should not fall into "Scripture spinning" traps that try to fit man's changing ideas into the Bible. For example, some try to insert millions of years into the Genesis genealogies, or to stretch the creation days into vast periods. Many Scripture passages affirm this strategy of understanding and applying the Bible's plain meaning, just as written (e.g., 2 Peter 3:16, 1 Timothy 6:20, Colossians 2:8, and Jeremiah 23:36).

2. **Prepare**. Two key steps help us prepare. First, we *watch* our motivation. If love does not motivate us, then we are off track. Love is a decision to act on another's behalf regardless of how you feel. Love keeps our pride in check. Love often directs us to wait before someone is ready to hear certain ideas. Jesus didn't share everything with His disciples all at once. He loved them by revealing just what they needed to hear at just the right time. Remember, most people have been *soaked* in the lies of the world. It takes time to unlearn years of secular "training." Second, *study* the Bible. Second Timothy 2:15 advises, "Be diligent to present yourself approved to God, a worker who does not need to be ashamed, rightly dividing the word of truth" and 2 Timothy 4:2 states, "Preach the word! Be ready in season and out of season. Convince, rebuke, exhort, with all longsuffering and teaching."

3. **Be aware**. There are three things to be aware of when doing outreach to the unsaved community. First, their minds are hostile towards God (oftentimes both knowingly and unknowingly) and thus they are hindered from seeing the truth about Creation and Salvation: "But the natural man does not receive the things of the Spirit of God, for they are foolishness to him; nor can he know them, because they are spiritually discerned" (1 Corinthians 2:14). Second, while they internally know

about God because God has revealed himself through Creation, their thoughts have turned futile and their hearts hardened because they block out the obvious truth that He exists (Romans 1:21–23). Third, they have become *willingly ignorant* of Creation and the Flood according to 2 Peter 3:3–6. This causes them to teach and reinforce long ages and uniformitarianism (the idea that present processes and rates are the key to understanding the past, without global catastrophes such as the Flood), showing a strong bias against miracles. Sadly, many Christians today also live without a full understanding of just how true and accurate the Genesis Creation and Flood records are. This compromise takes its toll on confidence in Scripture and on God's greatness.

4. **Be filled and led by the Holy Spirit**. Scripture tells us that we should be continually filled with the Holy Spirit (John 15:1–11, Galatians 5:16–25). This simply means deciding to think and do what God wants us to think and do, based on what the Bible says we should think and can do in Christ. Scripture clarifies that we can *quench* or *grieve* the Holy Spirit (1 Thessalonians 5:19; Ephesians 4:30). Ephesians 4–5 lists several actions that can do this, such as "living like the pagans" (4:17–19), lying (4:25), being angry (4:26–27), stealing (4:28), cursing (4:29), being bitter (4:31), unforgiving (4:32), and being sexually immoral (5:3–5). If certain actions can grieve the Spirit, other actions can equip believers to be filled with the Holy Spirit. Prayer, bible study, fellowship, and worship all help. But the decision to live God's way lies at the core of walking in the Spirit. Ephesians 2:10 states that we are "His workmanship, created in Christ Jesus for good works, which God prepared beforehand that we should walk in them." To walk in these works, we need to pay attention to His living Word. We also need to be mindful of the Spirit's prompting towards certain activities. God's Word is full

of examples that support "being led" by the Spirit (e.g., Acts 8:29, 13:2, 15:28, Romans 8:14, and Galatians 5:25).

5. **Show wisdom**. Our ministry has corresponded with thousands of inquiries and comments from people across a wide spectrum of views. It would be quite easy to categorize all these inquiries into two groups: (1) people who are not genuinely interested in finding an answer. They just want to throw up an objection to the Christian faith; and (2) those who genuinely seek answers and have humble hearts to listen. Spend more time with this second group. If they are open, *pour* into them. If not, move on quickly. The seeds fall on all kinds of soil, and good farmers invest their time wisely by watering hearts that yearn for Truth.

6. **Focus**. Our ministry surveyed a broad cross-section of nearly 300 young people, ages 14 to 24, asking an open-ended question: "Regardless of whether you believe in evolution, what is the best evidence that evolution is true?" Respondents gave varied answers, but we were able to sort them into ten categories. We found that just four categories make up 72% of the reasons for belief in evolution: (1) arguments pertaining to human evolution (25%); Darwin's theory proper (mutations, natural selection, etc.) (21%); fossils and so-called transitions (15%); and the apparent consensus of scientists and science regarding the theory of evolution (11%).[1] When deconstructing the lie of evolution in conversation or in a group presentation, we focus on these four areas. Be stingy about spending time on esoteric, splintered questions.

7. **Know when and how to retreat**. When you don't know the answer to a question, say you don't know! Even when we know nothing, we can always ask them to give a reason for the statements they make. Try to ask a question to get them thinking about what they believe

and why. If the other party doesn't interact on that level, then retreat with as much grace as possible.

8. **Spend more time studying the truth than learning about counterfeits**. Several great websites showcase solid biblical and scientific resources (see the **Helpful Resources** section in the back).

Age of the Earth: Does the Bible Really Say That God Created Everything in Six Days Just 6,000 Years Ago?

> *Suggested Videos:*
>
> Six Days: https://youtu.be/pjx88K8JTY8
> Young/Old Earth: https://youtu.be/QzEzkrMdgIs
> The Bible and History: https://youtu.be/6okZJlw84lo
> Radiometric Dating: https://youtu.be/fg6MfnmxPB4

Overview

Determining the age of the earth using the Bible is a straightforward, two-step process: (1) Determine whether the six days in Creation Week were *ordinary days*. This leads us to Adam, who was spontaneously created by God (i.e., he didn't evolve) on the Sixth Day of Creation; (2) Determine how long ago Adam lived using the genealogies in Genesis.

We know that the six days in Genesis 1 were *ordinary days* (not six long ages) because the Hebrew word for day (*yom*) is qualified with "*evening*," "*morning*," and a *number* for each of the six days in the Creation Week. When *yom* is used with any of these qualifiers throughout Scripture, it always means an *ordinary day*. We'll take an in-depth look at this topic in this section.

Determining *how long ago* Adam lived is a straightforward process because Genesis records the **fathering**

age and total **lifespan** of Adam's descendants all the way to Abraham and his sons (most directly; in some cases indirectly).[2] Summing the lifespans in these genealogies leads to Creation Week either about 6,000 or 7,600 years ago (based on the Masoretic or Septuagint texts, respectively[3]). We'll take a closer look at these genealogies below.

In addition to these interlinking (and overlapping) genealogies, the Genesis account itself provides two clues that lead to our understanding that Adam and Eve were the first humans who were created immediately after God had created everything else. The first clue is God's commission given to humans to take *dominion* over (that is, to wisely manage) everything God made during Creation Week. The second is God bringing the animals to Adam "to see what he would call them" (at the animal *kind* level, not every species) (Genesis 2:20). Thus, the Genesis account itself forbids inserting millions of years of animal death and life (e.g., some "dinosaur era") before Adam and Eve were present to take dominion over Creation and name the animal kinds.

Significance of Believing in a "Young Earth"

Most students who have graduated from Christian colleges can name at least four different views of the Genesis Creation account: the literal/historical "young earth" view, the Day-age view, Progressive Creation, and the Gap Theory. Unfortunately, however, many of these same students would also likely say "we don't really know because we weren't there" and/or "it doesn't really matter what you believe."

Sadly, these couldn't be further from the truth. First, as we will see below, we *can* reliably know when God created because He's clearly told us in His Word. Second, it really does matter what we believe.

How we regard God's Word (authoritatively or only as a guide book) has a direct bearing on how we live our lives. Today's students want to know: If truth doesn't start on the first page, then how many pages do I need to turn in the Bible until I run into truth?" If truth doesn't start on the first page, the rest is up for grabs.

Honest readers will admit that the text clearly means what it says in Genesis 1: *God created in six normal days*. Readers who spend time investigating the genealogies listed in Genesis 5, 10, and 11 will also admit that it's a historical narrative with real people, real dates, and real lifespans that lead directly back to Adam, the first human who was miraculously created out of the dust by God.

They will also notice that there's certainly no way to insert millions of years between these genealogies. While scholars may quibble about hundreds of years and the ancient texts upon which our modern bibles are based may differ by a couple thousand years, honest readers will admit there's certainly not room for millions of years. Without filtering what's clearly written in Genesis through secular science textbooks, the reader is left with a young earth.

If one submits to the *authority* of Scripture, relying on Scripture to tell them about the basic framework of the history of the world, origins, and their purpose, their lives will radiate outward from these understandings. Their entire worldview will be different than one who does not believe. For example, to a Christian who holds that Genesis 1 is literal history:

- God is the all-powerful Creator who spoke Creation into existence (Psalm 33:9, Hebrews 11). Each person will give an account to this all-powerful Creator.
- God started out everything "very good" without bloodshed and disease, but man's sins brought death, corruption, bloodshed and disease. Cancer is man's fault, not God's.
- God did not use a slow, random, murderous process of natural selection and survival of the fittest to bring the many types of life on earth into existence.
- The fossil record reflects God's judgement on a world turned corrupt after the Fall.

- Racism has no foundation because there aren't millions of years for the human line to splinter off to various "races." A recent dispersion at the Tower of Babel means all people groups are closely related, separated by only hundreds of generations.

Submitting to biblical truth—beginning in Genesis—results in all these benefits and more. A person whose worldview is anchored to biblical foundations will also be constantly reminded that they are *in the world but not of the world*, and that the world has fallen into the deception of the enemy (1 John 5:19). They will see the lie of "deep time" espoused in the vast majority of secular schools, media outlets, and state parks. These two perspectives are very different: It's either death and suffering over millions of years before Adam or a perfect creation marred by original sin just thousands of years ago.

A person can be saved by the Blood of Jesus and still believe in deep time, so we're not talking one's salvation. But if they believe in long ages they can't grow fully in their faith because it undermines the authority of Scripture and erases the logical foundation for Christ on the cross. Just try to explain the Gospel to someone without referring to a *historical* view of Genesis. It is a difficult (if not impossible) task.

Many Christians feel pressured to be accepted by the mainstream and thus buy into the idea of millions of years. Some just haven't fully thought through why they believe the way they do. Most of the time they really don't know how much it's costing them and their families.

Because I "converted" to a Biblical Creationist late in life, my two older children were raised by Christian parents who had "undeclared" positions on origins. Their questions about the dinosaurs and cavemen were always prefaced with "if the earth is young, the answer is… but if the earth is old, the answer is…" With this type of conditional answer to many of life's very basic questions, what they were really hearing was "maybe dad doesn't know," or (even worse) "maybe the Bible, which is supposed to be the most definitive book for me to build my life upon, doesn't have an answer, or perhaps it even doesn't even have the correct answer." Fortunately, I had the opportunity to re-solidify their faith before they went to college.

Blessings will come to those who completely embrace the whole Scripture. For example, Jesus said, "For whoever is ashamed of Me *and My words*, of him the Son of Man will be ashamed when He comes in His own glory, and in His Father's, and of the holy angels" (Luke 9:26).

The Book of Psalms is likely one of the most frequently read books of the Bible. The very beginning of this book starts out by stating those who believe in and meditate on the Torah (the first five books of Bible, led by Genesis) will be blessed in every way:

> Blessed is the man who walks not in the counsel
> of the ungodly, nor stands in the path of sinners,
> nor sits in the seat of the scornful; But his delight
> is in the law [Torah] of the Lord, and in His law
> he meditates day and night. He shall be like a
> tree planted by the rivers of water, that brings
> forth its fruit in its season, whose leaf also shall
> not wither; and whatever he does shall prosper.
> (Psalms 1:1–3).

The Bible presents the unchangeable, perfect, and true Words of God Himself, including what God says about the history of our world—history that occurred before the Great Flood of Noah's time thousands of years ago. And, since the Bible says that God cannot lie and that He even honors His Word along with His own name, we ought to treat Scripture with the reverence it deserves.[4]

The Days in Genesis 1

The Hebrew word for "day" (*yom*) is used over 2,000 times in the Old Testament. In some instances, it means a period of time or an era, but in the vast majority of instances it means an ordinary day.

In the first chapter of Genesis, it's clear that *yom* means an *ordinary day*. The first time *yom* is used in the Bible is Genesis 1:5: "And the **evening** and the **morning** were the **first day**" (v. 5). Notice that day (*yom*) is qualified by "evening," "morning," and a number (day one). This pattern— evening/morning/number—repeats for each of the six days in Genesis 1, so the entire Creation Week is described by days that are qualified as ordinary days.

The word *yom* is used over 400 times in the Old Testament when it's used with a number, like "first day." In every case, it always means an ordinary day. *Yom* is used with the word "evening" or "morning" 23 times, and "evening" and "morning" appear together without *yom* 38 times, and in all 61 instances the text refers to an ordinary day. God seemed to want to make it clear to us. He said "evening" and "morning," then a day, and a number.

Because God is all-powerful, He could have just created everything in an instant, but He didn't. He chose to take six days because He was setting up a *system of days* and a context for our lives and how the world works.

Genesis 1:14 states that God established "lights in the firmament of the Heavens to divide the day from the night" and that they would be used for "signs and seasons, and for days and years." This shows that God began the measurement of time using days and years: Two well-known units of time—days and years—are *linked* in Genesis 1:14, their duration being determined by the fixed movements of the earth in reference to the sun.

If we need to be convinced further, consider that God wrote the Ten Commandments with His own hand (Exodus 31:18, "He gave Moses two tablets of the Testimony, tablets of stone, *written with the finger of God*."). When God wrote the Fourth Commandment, he stated:

**For in six days the Lord made the heavens
and the earth, the sea, and all that is in them,
and rested on the seventh day. Therefore, the
Lord blessed the Sabbath day and hallowed it.**
(Exodus 20:11).

Here are the six days again—this time in the Ten
Commandments no less—and *written by the hand of God*. What
do you think God wanted the Israelites to believe when He said
this? Long ages or real days? God was talking about the
Sabbath, which is one day a week. If God meant "thousands of
years" when he said "day," then that would make for a really
long work week! It seems from this passage that *God told us
what to believe*, and how to model our lives: six days of work
followed by a day of rest.

Our weeks have been like this ever since the beginning.
After all, we don't have a five-day week, do we? Back in the
1920's the Soviets tried a five-day week and a six-day week,
but it was a major failure. So they went back to a seven-day
week. The seven-day week seems to be hardwired into human
existence—as if God designed us to work six days and take a
rest on the seventh.

Taking a careful look at the context of the Ten
Commandments, it wouldn't make much sense if nine out of the
Ten Commandments were literal and one was figurative. How
could lying, adultery, and stealing be figures of speech? They
are rather black and white—just like the days of Creation. We
certainly don't work for six long ages, but six days, then we
rest. God gave us a day of rest to reset our internal clocks. God
didn't have to give us that seventh day, but He knew we needed
it.

James Marshall's gold discovery in Coloma (1848) was
a catalyst that led to the California gold rush. Marshall's diary is
on display in a museum in Coloma, open to a page where he's
discussing the fact that people were caught up in a feverish gold
frenzy—mining gold *seven days a week* with no rest. They were
driven by the idea that the next "big nugget" was likely in the

very next pan. He then remarks that most of these miners died between the age of 35 and 40. It seems like God knew what He was doing by setting up the "six days and a rest" pattern!

When fending off scholars who were developing the idea that God really didn't create everything in six days (but rather only a single day), the famous reformer Martin Luther warned: "When Moses writes that God created heaven and earth and whatever is in them in six days, then let this period continue to have been six days, and do not venture to devise any comment according to which six days were one day. But if you cannot understand how this could have been done in six days, then grant the Holy Spirit the honor of being more learned than you are."[5]

Doesn't the Bible Say That "a Day to the Lord Can Be like a Thousand Years"?

Many Christians ask, "Doesn't the Bible say that 'a day to the Lord can be like a thousand years.'" Second Peter 3:8 actually says that "one day is with the Lord *as* a thousand years, and a thousand years *as* one day." This passage is talking about God's judgment and His patience with man's rebellion. It's not talking about Creation Week.

Notice that the verse says one day is *as* a thousand years. It's a *simile* showing that God is *outside* of time, because He is the *Creator* of time. We know that those who use this verse to say that one day in Creation Week took one thousand years are forcing that view onto the Bible since they never assert the last part of the verse: that a thousand years of Old Testament history all happened in one day.

This passage is saying that God is outside of time and is unaffected by it, but to man, a day is still a day. It's not defining a day, because it doesn't say, "a day *is* a thousand years." It's not even talking about the days of Creation. Rather, both times—a day and a thousand years—are described from God's perspective because "with the Lord" these times are the same. The verse is saying that with God, time has no meaning, because He is eternal, outside of the dimension of time that He created. So a thousand years, a day, and a second all are the same to Him. He sees all of history *simultaneously*.

Because *yom* is used over 2,000 times in the Old Testament, it's important to look at the context in which it's used. In the passage in Peter, the writer is referring to Psalm 90:4, which says, "For a thousand years in Your sight are like yesterday when it is past, and like a watch in the night," yet a night watch does not last 1,000 years, does it? Here, 1,000 years is just a figure of speech, a comparison to make something more vivid. In context, 2 Peter 3 is saying that although it may seem like a long time to us, the Lord still keeps His promises.

If each day in Genesis 1 was a thousand years, on day three God made the plants, but on day four He made the sun. We know plants need the sun to survive, so if each day was a thousand years, the plants would have all died long before the sun rose on the fourth day.[6] Also, flying insects like bees were created on the fifth day to pollenate plants and trees that were created on the third day. It really makes more sense if all these components of creation were present for it to work as a whole.

How Do We Get a 6,000-Year-old Earth from the Bible?

Genesis 5 lists ten patriarchs that lived before Noah's Flood. For each of these patriarchs, their age **before** having the son named, the years they lived **after** having a son, and their **total** years are listed:

Genesis 5: The Family of Adam

And Adam lived **130** years, and begot a son in his own likeness, after his image, and named him Seth. After he begot Seth, the days of Adam were 800 years; and he had sons and daughters. So all the days that Adam lived were 930; and he died. Seth lived **105**, and begot Enosh. After he begot Enosh, Seth lived 807, and had sons and daughters. So all the days of Seth were 912; and he died. Enosh lived **90** years, and begot Cainan. After he begot Cainan, Enosh lived 815 years, and had sons and daughters. So all the days of Enosh were 905 years; and he died. Cainan lived **70** years, and begot Mahalalel. After he begot Mahalalel, Cainan lived 840 years, and had sons and daughters. So all the days of Cainan were 910 years; and he died. Mahalalel lived **65** years, and begot Jared. After he begot Jared, Mahalalel lived 830 years, and had sons and daughters. So all the days of Mahalalel were 895 years; and he died. Jared lived **162** years, and begot Enoch. After he begot Enoch, Jared lived 800 years, and had sons and daughters. So all the days of Jared were 962 years; and he died. Enoch lived **65** years, and begot Methuselah. After he begot Methuselah, Enoch walked with God 300 years, and had sons and daughters. So all the days of Enoch were 365 years. And Enoch walked with God; and he was not, for God took him. Methuselah lived **187** years, and begot Lamech. After he begot Lamech, Methuselah lived 782 years, and had sons and daughters. So all the days of Methuselah were 969 years; and he died. Lamech lived **182** years, and had a son. And he called his name Noah, saying, "This one will comfort us concerning our work and the toil of our hands, because of the ground which the Lord has cursed." After he begot Noah, Lamech lived 595 years, and had sons and daughters. So all the days of Lamech were 777 years; and he died. And Noah was **500** years old, and Noah begot Shem, Ham, and Japheth.

Let's take a closer look at this passage focusing on Adam, the first one listed in Genesis 5:

Age Before Having First Son	Years Lived After Having a Son	Total Years
And Adam lived **130** years, and begot a son in his own likeness, after his image, and named him Seth.	After he begot Seth, the days of Adam were **800** years;	So all the days that Adam lived were **930**; and he died.

Notice that three numbers are given for Adam: his age before having Seth (130), the years he lived after fathering Seth (800), and his total lifespan (930 years). Because these three sets of numbers are provided for all ten patriarchs before the Flood, it's easy to assemble an inter-connected, non-overlapping chain that we can use for summing up the years that go straight back to Adam, the very first man created:

Table 1. Genesis 5 Genealogies.

Order	Patriarch	Age at Birth of First Son	Years Lived After Son	Total Age	Sum of Years
1	Adam	**130**	800	930	130
2	Seth	**105**	807	912	235
3	Enoch	**90**	815	905	325
4	Cainan	**70**	840	910	395
5	Mahalalel	**65**	830	895	460
6	Jared	**162**	800	962	622
7	Enoch	**65**	300	365	687
8	Methuselah	**187**	782	969	874
9	Lamech	**182**	595	777	1056
10	Noah	**500**	450	950	1556

Notice that adding the ages in the "age at birth of first son" column sums to a total of 1,556 years (as shown in the far-right column). Because Noah was 600 years old when the Flood came (Genesis 7:6), adding 100 years to Noah's age in the table (500) places the Flood at 1,656 years after Creation. Genesis 10 and 11 provide the next set of genealogies that allow us to move up the timescale to Abraham who lived about 2,000 BC, as shown in the chart below.

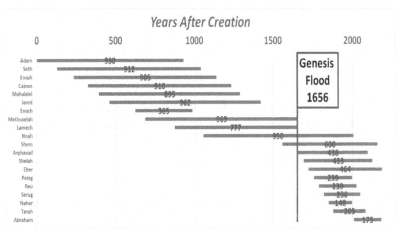

Figure 1. The First 20 Patriarchs since Creation.

Notice that the lifespans of the pre-Flood patriarchs overlapped. Plus, their lifespans declined in a systematic way. These give us confidence that Genesis records an accurate timeline (see **Lifespans Before the Flood: How Did People Live to Be 900 Years Old Before the Flood?**). Summing the time from Adam, the first man created on the Sixth Day of Creation Week, to Abraham is about 2,000 years, then from Abraham to the time of Christ is about another 2,000 years, then we have from Christ until now, another 2,000 years. So, the straight chronology from the Bible places Creation about 6,000 years ago.

Scholars have debated possible gaps in these genealogies for years, but even if there were gaps in these genealogies, we cannot insert them without basically rewriting the text to fit our own preferences. Further, such gaps may allow for hundreds of additional years, but certainly not thousands or millions!

Even many secular historians would agree with Christian scholars that Abraham lived about 2,000 BC, or about 4,000 years ago. If that's true, with Abraham being the 20th patriarch after Adam listed in the line-up provided in Genesis, we can't have tens of thousands of years' worth of missing genealogies based on the (evolutionary) idea that "modern" humans emerged from ape-like ancestors about 50,000 years ago.

For example, some creation views (e.g., Progressive Creation) agree with the evolutionary timeline that places the evolution of modern humans about 50,000 years ago.[7] With this position, there would be 44,000 years of "missing" genealogies in Genesis (4,000 genealogy years from Genesis, plus the 2,000 years from Christ to present)! Just how can one fit an extra 40,000+ years into the 4,000 years shown on Figure 1 (ten times the number of years accounted for in the Bible)? Under this model, the Bible's genealogies would not be a reliable record.

An additional consideration with the lifespans in Genesis is that many of them *overlap*, so there's not a lot of room for gaps. Further, the Genesis genealogies are repeated in other parts of the Bible, including the books of Ruth, Jude, Matthew, and Luke. This shows that the New Testament and Old Testament's human authors also believed in the Genesis genealogies as real history.

Finally, consider the fact that Jesus referred to the Old Testament over 40 times. Every single time He treated the Old Testament literally and historically. For instance, in Mark 10:6 Jesus mentioned that God created man and woman at the "beginning of Creation"—not long ages after Creation. Jesus also references other Old Testament accounts as true events, such as Noah's Flood, the destruction of Sodom and Gomorrah, Jonah and the great fish, and many others.

Aliens

Isaiah 45:18 states that God created (our) world to be inhabited: "For thus says the Lord, who created the heavens, who is God, who formed the earth and made it, who has established it, who did not create it in vain, who formed it to be inhabited: 'I am the Lord, and there is no other.'" Genesis 1 states that the other celestial bodies were created for signs, seasons, days, and years. Jesus came to earth to save us—not to another planet to save another race of beings. Romans 6:10 says "He died to sin once for all." If space aliens sinned, then He would have to go their planet and die for them, thus rendering this and similar verses incorrect. No scientific evidence supports space aliens. They probably don't exist at all. The fact that half of all Americans believe they do exist illustrates the power of movies and a dreadful lack of scientific and biblical knowledge.[8]

Antibiotic Resistance

Some evolutionists claim that bacterial survival in antibiotics is evidence of evolution in action. But drilling into the details reveals that specific, pre-engineered mechanisms already within bacteria allow them to "develop" resistance to antibiotics. In cases where genetic changes help bacteria survive in the presence of antibiotics, the genetic changes always also cripple the bacteria in some other way. No evolutionary processes are involved in either case.[9]

Archaeopteryx

Archaeopteryx used to be widely promoted by evolutionists as the prime example of an intermediate form or "missing link" between reptiles and birds. However, even this "trophy" does not qualify as a *transitional* fossil since its

27

socketed teeth, long bony tail, and wing-claws are all *fully-formed* structures of its alleged fossil representatives, showing no signs of *partial* evolutionary development.

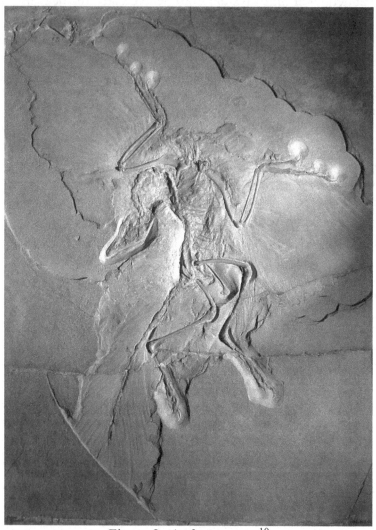

Figure 2. *Archaeopteryx*[10]

Archaeopteryx was originally discovered in 1861 and has since been widely used to promote evolutionary ideas. Alan

Feduccia, a paleontologist who led studies in the origins of birds stated: "Paleontologists have tried to turn *Archaeopteryx* into an earth-bound, feathered dinosaur. But it's not. It is a bird, a perching bird. And no amount of 'paleobabble' is going to change that."[11]

That statement illustrates a constant battle in the evolutionary camp about whether *Archaeopteryx* should be thrown out of the evolutionary lineup. Over the past several years, *Archaeopteryx*'s "perch" in the evolutionary tree has shifted up and down, going from being a bird to a dinosaur and then back to a bird depending on who does the analysis. *Archaeopteryx* was even further disqualified as an evolutionary ancestor for birds when scientists found what appears to be a crow-size bird and extinct four-winged birds in rock layers below (i.e., deposited earlier in earth's history than) those containing *Archaeopteryx*.[12]

Asteroids: Did a Massive Asteroid Kill off the Dinosaurs?

Most believe that an enormous impact caused an underground crater beneath the Gulf of Mexico, but impact craters are all round, and this feature is not. The impact theory also suffers from the fact that fossil frogs look the same as today's frogs. Frogs would have died before dinosaurs. The evidence is clear that a global, cataclysmic world-wide flood killed off the dinosaurs, burying them in certain vast sedimentary rock layers on all earth continents. There is, however, evidence that asteroids were involved in the Flood's destructive process, but Catastrophic Plate Tectonics were also involved. Violently moving continental plates (and resulting tsunamis) likely served as the Flood's primary burial catalyst for the demise of the dinosaurs.[13]

Babel Dispersion and Human Genetics

The Bible places the Genesis 10 Babel dispersion about 100 years after the Flood (around 2,250 BC or around 3,200 BC based on the Masoretic or Septuagint texts, respectively). This coincides with recent human genome research that found evidence for massive genetic diversification about that same time. One of the research papers stated, "The maximum likelihood time for accelerated growth was 5,115 years ago."[14] This places the beginning of the period of genetic diversification of humans close to the Genesis Flood and subsequent dispersion at the Tower of Babel, a point in time that the earth began to be repopulated through Noah's descendants.

Behemoth

> *Suggested Video:*
>
> Does Job 40 Describe a Sauropod?
> https://youtu.be/mEJENaCgq70

The ancient Book of Job[15] refers to Behemoth. What was it? Consider the description of this animal from Job 40:6–24:

> Then the Lord answered Job out of the whirlwind, and said: "Now prepare yourself like a man; I will question you, and you shall answer Me... Look at Behemoth, which I **made along with you** and which feeds on grass like an ox. What **strength it has in its loins**, what **power in the muscles of its belly**! Its **tail sways like a cedar**; the **sinews of its thighs are close-knit**. Its **bones are tubes of bronze**, its **limbs like rods of iron**. It **ranks first among the works of**

God, yet its Maker can approach it with his sword. The hills bring it their produce, and all the wild animals play nearby. Under the lotus plants it lies, hidden among the reeds in the marsh. The lotuses conceal it in their shadow; the poplars by the stream surround it. **A raging river does not alarm it; it is secure, though the Jordan should surge against its mouth**. Can anyone capture it by the eyes, or trap it and pierce its nose?

In Job, God describes 13 of His created animals, such as an ostrich, horse, and deer, then caps off the discussion by telling Job about His two grandest creations: Behemoth and Leviathan. God calls Behemoth the "first of all of His ways," using the Hebrew term (re'shiyth), which means *first in a rank*, the *chief*, the *most supreme* of His creative works.

When we scan through all land-dwelling creatures—both living and extinct—which one comes up as the "first in rank," the most colossal or the chief? Clearly the sauropod dinosaur. Pairing God's Word that Behemoth is the grandest creature He ever made with the fact that sauropods are the largest land creatures we've ever found should give us a clue to Behemoth's identity.

Sauropods were huge. The largest one found to date (named *Patagotitan mayorum*) was over 120 feet long—that's 10 freeway lanes across! At a weight of 76 tons, it's a wonder these creatures could even walk. Let's review some amazing sauropod anatomy, starting first by looking at one of their unique design features: their long necks.

The necks of the sauropod dinosaurs were by far the longest of any animal, six times longer than that of the world record giraffe and five times longer than those of all other terrestrial animals.[16]

Mamenchisaurus youngi
(Pi et al, 1996)

Figure 3. *Mamenchisaurus,* a Type of Sauropod Dinosaur.[17]

Researchers for years thought sauropod necks would be too heavy for their length. Leading sauropod researcher Dr. Matthew Wedel notes: "They were marvels of biological engineering, and that efficiency of design is especially evident in their vertebrae, the bones that make up the backbone."[18] After spending years studying the long necks of sauropods, Dr. Wedel revealed that the vertebrae of these massive sauropods had genius, weight saving air spaces.[19]

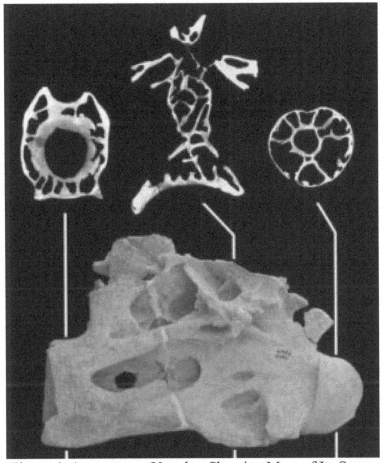

Figure 4. Apatosaurus Vertebra Showing Most of Its Space
Filled with Air Cavities.[20]

He wrote, "one of [a] Sauropod's four and a half foot
[long] vertebrae [sic] would have been surprisingly light and
could reach 90% air by volume!"[21]

Figure 5. Dr. Wedel with a 4-1/2-Foot Sauropod Vertebra That Could Reach 90% Air by Volume.

More exhaustive studies have revealed that the vertebrae of most sauropods were often 50–60% air by volume, with some as high as 90% (see Figure 4).[22] While Dr. Wedel estimates that this would only reduce the overall weight of some of these creatures by 8–10%, most of the weight would be removed from the critical areas of the neck, where extra weight would have been challenging for the creature to lift its head, eat, or turn around.

Yet there's more—these big creatures needed *lightweight* vertebrae to enable them to lift their heads—but these extra-long necks also needed *design* such that the animal could eat, drink, and move its head without its neck folding in half or pinching vital nerves, the trachea (for breathing), or esophagus (for eating). Having an extra-light structure was only part of the solution.

While their air-charged vertebrae may solve the puzzle of how they could lift and move their massive heads and necks, it doesn't solve the challenge of how they could possibly inhale enough oxygen through their tiny nostrils, which were only about twice the size of those on a living horse! How can a 140,000+ pound animal inhale enough oxygen through such tiny nostrils? Perhaps they thrived better in a world before Noah's Flood when the oxygen levels were likely higher.[23]

In Job, God describes Behemoth's diet: eating grass like an ox. In 2005 researchers found grass in sauropod coprolites in India, and some palaeobotanists are even saying that this will cause a "rewrite in our understanding of dinosaur evolution," because evolution holds that grass didn't evolve until millions of years after the dinosaurs had gone extinct.[24]

God describes Behemoth's strength in his hips and power in his stomach muscles. Again, we have a strong clue that Behemoth was a sauropod dinosaur because, while many animals have strong hips and stomach muscles, none were as strong or central as certain sauropods. The muscular and connective tissue structures around the hips and stomach were necessary for sauropods to move, walk, turn, and eat. For some sauropods, like the Diplodocus, its highest point of its core body was the hips and its whole body balanced on the hips, front-to-back. Diplodocus was able to rear up on its back legs and balance on its tail like a tripod, making use of the hips to support not just the back half of its body but the front half too. This required enormous strength in the hip and stomach muscles, considering they lifted tons of their own body into the air. Below the hips was an incredible weight distribution system that went from a massive femur (which in some cases was nearly eight feet long), to two shin bones, then five foot bones, and then five toes.

Behemoth's tail also closely matched those of sauropods. God describes that he "moves his tail like a cedar tree" and follows this by stating, "the sinews of his thighs are tightly knit." Paleontologists have learned from the muscle attachment locations in their bones that the tightly-knit structure of Behemoth's thighs and hips actually made his tail sway from side-to-side with each step, much as a cedar tree does when it sways in the wind![25] Tail drag marks are only rarely found behind sauropod footprints, indicating their tails were raised while they walked. It's difficult to think of a creature that fits this Biblical description better than a sauropod dinosaur.

God describes his bones "like beams of bronze." Most Bible versions translate this phrase as "tubes of bronze," "conduits of bronze," or "pipes of brass," which conveys both "strength" and being hollow like a channel or a tube. This matches the fact that that sauropods had the largest leg bones of any animal, and they are in fact just like tubes of metal, having a hard outer casing and spongy marrow and veins on the inside.

Then God says that its "ribs are like bars of iron." Unlike much of the sauropod's skeleton that was spongy and filled with air for weight savings, its ribs were *fully ossified*— they were made of solid bone![26] Again, we see a solid match between God's description of Behemoth and a sauropod dinosaur.

God even describes Behemoth's habitat: "He lies under the lotus trees, in a covert of reeds and marsh. The lotus trees cover him with their shade" and "The willows by the brook surround him." This was a creature that had to be near lots of green food—living in a lush, tropical environment. Large sauropods had to eat a half a ton of vegetation every day, and they likely had to eat all day long to consume this amount of food.

Next God says: "Indeed the river may rage, yet he is not disturbed; He is confident, though the Jordan gushes into his mouth." Why would God point out that this animal can stand in a rushing river? Lots of animals can do this, depending on the size of the rushing river. In this case, God said, "the river may *rage*, yet he is *not disturbed,*" and that Behemoth is confident even though this raging river should gush into his mouth. The Jordan river is the largest river in Palestine and it currently flows at only 15% of the rate it flowed in the past.[27] Even so, in the winter this river would be incredibly difficult to cross, and it would take a *very* sizable animal to stand *undisturbed* in the rushing current and, even more, let the current gush into its mouth! Some of the larger sauropods stood over 20 feet at the shoulders and weighed over 70 tons. Creatures of this size and mass could withstand a raging river better than any others.

Even with all this evidence, some say that Behemoth was just a mythical creature. Why would God try to display His awesome creative power by describing something that never existed? Anyone can do that. And why would God say that Behemoth was the "chief" of all His creations after describing 13 real, still-living animals in the same passage? Why go through all the trouble to describe Behemoth as a grass-eating animal that lies peacefully in the shadow of the river plants along with his physical description, diet, and habitat—all of which happen to fit a known creature: a sauropod dinosaur?

Table 2 lists 14 characteristics of this creature that are provided in Job 40, and a sauropod dinosaur seems to fit the description better than any other creature, alive or extinct. Certain Bible footnotes[28] state that Behemoth was a hippo, elephant, or crocodile but these do not come close to matching all 14 characteristics God used to describe Behemoth. They certainly are not the "first in rank" or "chief" of God's creations. Would God tell Job to "gird up his loins" to behold the "chief of his creations" just to show off a hippo? An elephant? These creatures were plentiful! They don't have tails that sway like cedar trees, and these animals have been captured and killed by man throughout history.

Table 2. Behemoth Description from Job 40

Behemoth Description (Job 40)	Sauropod	Hippo	Crocodile
1 - "made along with" man	YES	YES	YES
2 - eats grass like an ox	YES	YES	NO
3 - strength in hips/stomach muscles	YES	NO	NO
4 - he moves his tail like a cedar	YES	NO	NO
5 - sinews of his thighs are tightly knit	YES	YES	YES
6 - bones are like beams of bronze	YES	NO	NO
7 - ribs like bars of iron	YES	MAYBE	MAYBE
8 - "chief/first" in rank of all God's creations	YES	NO	NO
9 - mountains yield food for him, and all the beasts of the field play there	YES	MAYBE	NO
10 - lies under lotus trees, in reeds/marsh	YES	MAYBE	NO
11 - lotus trees cover him with their shade; willows by the brook surround him	YES	YES	YES
12 - The river may rage, yet he is not disturbed	YES	NO	NO
13 - He is confident, though the Jordan gushes into his mouth	YES	MAYBE	MAYBE
14 - unapproachable by anyone but its maker	YES	NO	NO

God says that only Behemoth's Creator can approach him, that he cannot be captured by humans when he is on watch, and that no one can use barbs to pierce his nose. These make sense for sauropod dinosaurs with their towering heads and huge size. Its long tail also makes him unapproachable. Based on fossils, some sauropods could cover a 200-foot circle with deadly force using their sometimes 50-foot-long tails.[29] Some sauropods could probably create sonic booms with their tails—just like a whip.[30]

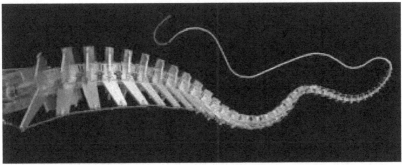

Figure 6. Study Demonstrated that Sauropod Tails Could Create Sonic Booms. (D. Sivam / P. Currie / N. Myhrvold)

Figure 7. Perhaps Behemoth's Tail Made Behemoth Unapproachable by Anyone but God, His Creator.[31]

It's not by chance that God says to Job that Behemoth can *only be approached by his creator*. To this day, elephants and hippos are surrounded by hunters and killed, but good luck even getting near this creature to put a snare in its nose.

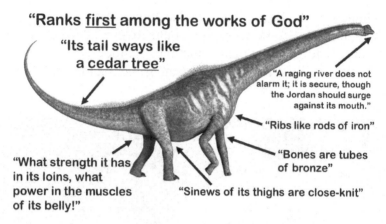

Figure 8. Behemoth in Job Chapter 40.

These features—weight-bearing hips, legs, feet, and toes, incredible air-filled vertebrae, and others—show up already formed in the ~300 sauropods that have been discovered in sedimentary layers laid down by the Flood. Yes, there is variability within the sauropod kind, but these animals have been grouped by these (and other) common design characteristics. If God Himself created these animals and placed them on the Earth, then no wonder they had every aspect of their essential design features already in place and fully integrated from the start.

Cain (mark of)

Suggested Videos:

What is the Mark of Cain?
https://www.youtube.com/watch?v=4Glg4RVHR68

Are Black People the Result of the Curse of Ham?
https://youtu.be/C1-6_FyUmDA

After Cain killed his brother Abel, God said to Cain, "Now you are under a curse and driven from the ground, which opened its mouth to receive your brother's blood from your hand. When you work the ground, it will no longer yield its crops for you. You will be a restless wanderer on the earth" (Genesis 4:11–12). To this, Cain replied, "My punishment is more than I can bear. Today you are driving me from the land, and I will be hidden from your presence; I will be a restless wanderer on the earth, and whoever finds me will kill me" (Genesis 4:13–14). God responded, "Not so; if anyone kills Cain, he will suffer vengeance seven times over." Then the Lord put a mark on Cain so that no one who found him would kill him" (Genesis 4:15–16).

So just what exactly was this "mark" that God put on Cain? The Hebrew word translated "mark" means a "mark, sign, or token," leaving many to speculate what the "mark" may represent in this context. At a minimum, we know from the text that it was some type of (likely external) visible sign so that others would identify and not kill Cain.

Some people (especially in the past) mistakenly believed this mark to be dark skin. Racists used this perspective to justify African slavery and discrimination against people with dark skin. But this position is completely unbiblical. Nowhere in the Scriptures is the Hebrew word for mark (*owth*) used to refer to skin color. Cain's curse was Cain's curse—not an entire people group. The text does not say that Cain's curse was passed on to his descendants. Whatever the mark was, it was certainly not generational, but applied only to Cain.

Cain (wife of)

Many people have asked, "Since Genesis 1–4 only records two children of Adam and Eve (Cain and Abel), and all humanity descended from Adam and Eve, then where did Cain's wife come from? Related to this, if Cain married a relative, then doesn't this indicate incest? And if Cain did marry a relative, wouldn't we expect their offspring to suffer degenerative effects?

Some try to answer this by saying that Cain's wife came from a race of Pre-Adamic humans who were around before Adam and Eve. This explanation doesn't fit within Scriptures, which are clear that Adam was the first man created (Genesis 2:7,18–19; 1 Corinthians 15:45). Eve was also given her name because she was the *mother of all living* (Genesis 3:20). These two facts rule out the idea of some Pre-Adamic race from which Cain chose a wife.[32]

The simple answer to this challenge is found in the very next chapter. Genesis 5:4 says, "After he begot Seth, the days of Adam were eight hundred years; **and he had [other] sons and daughters**." Because Adam lived a long life and God had promised Eve that he would greatly multiply her conception (Genesis 3:16), many people could have existed at the time when Cain killed Abel (a conservative estimate is that 32,000 people could have been alive at that time this event occurred). Jewish tradition states that Adam had 33 sons and 23 daughters!

But what about incest? If Cain married his sister, he did not commit incest because incest did not become a crime until thousands of years later. Intermarriages between brothers and sisters were permissible until God later gave the Book of Leviticus (chapter 18) which condemned these relationships. After all, Abraham married his half-sister with no problems. Since that time, mutations have accumulated exponentially in humans.

Carbon-14 Dating

Suggested Videos:

Does Carbon 14 Dating Go Beyond Biblical History?
https://youtu.be/60xe-aDNLxc

Carbon dating assigns ages to once-living materials such as wood, bone, teeth, and shells. Evolutionary researchers do not use it to age-date rocks. It begins by measuring the ratio of radioactive versus stable versions of an element. Carbon dating works by basing an age calculation on the ratio of radioactive carbon (^{14}C) to normal carbon (^{12}C) in the atmosphere before nuclear bomb testing to the same ratio in the sample. Carbon-14 decays to nitrogen. Using a formula that compares that ratio to a standard modern ratio produces a "percent modern carbon" (pMC) value that scientists use to estimate carbon ages for carbon-containing materials.

Carbon-14 (^{14}C) doesn't decay linearly, but instead decays fast at first, then more slowly later, according to a predictable pattern that can be expressed in units called a half-life. Given the relatively short ^{14}C half-life of 5,730 years, organic materials purportedly older than 100,000 years (nearly 18 half-lives) should contain absolutely no detectable ^{14}C. However, coal, diamonds, and even dinosaur bones contain amounts of ^{14}C at levels detectable by modern instruments.[33] Carbon dating of historical objects of known age is sometimes accurate back to about 1,000 BC, as verified by historical records.[34]

Carbon-14 dating begins with sound, repeatable science when researchers record isotope ratios. So the method itself is not the issue—it's the *assumptions* that are made when the raw isotope ratio gets converted to calendar years that carbon dating becomes unreliable and inaccurate, especially on very old artifacts. While carbon dating can in fact return somewhat accurate ages for items that are a couple thousand years old (see discussion and endnotes below), too many evolutionary assumptions accompany carbon dates for items into the deeper past. Several unknown factors can seriously impact carbon ratios. Just a partial list of these factors includes:

1. **Forest fires**. Massive forest fires can change ^{14}C/^{12}C ratios much in the same way that volcanic eruptions

have.[35] Do we have a complete record of forest fires dating back thousands of years?

2. **Atomic activity/releases**. Atomic bomb testing *doubled* the amount of ^{14}C in the 1950s and 1960s. Professor Nalini Nadkarni, an ecologist at The Evergreen State College in Washington stated that this testing caused: "a tremendous spike of ^{14}C — actually 100 percent more ^{14}C coming into the atmosphere than what we'd had previous to those atom bomb tests."[36] Researchers have found clever ways to normalize measurements to pre-bomb levels, but these extra complications may add more uncertainty to radiocarbon-based age assignments.

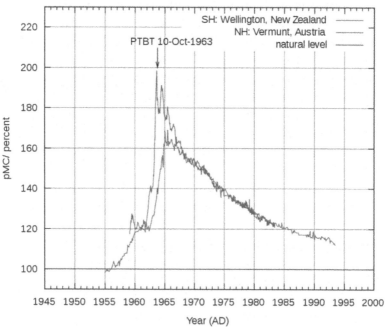

Figure 9. Effect of Atomic Bomb Testing on Carbon Dating.[37]

3. **Volcanic eruptions.** When volcanoes erupt, they eject enormous amounts of carbon into the air. Because geological carbon does not have much ^{14}C, the ^{14}C/^{12}C ratio in the area gets diluted. In one case, it even made *living* plants appear to be 1,000 years old![38] How would

a recent past of high volcanism, as shown by ancient lava fields, ash falls, and dead volcanoes, have affected ancient carbon isotope ratios?

4. **Industrialization (past burning of coal)**. It is widely accepted that the mass burning of coal during the industrial revolution released an enormous amount of ^{12}C into the air, which changed the $^{14}C/^{12}C$ ratio in the atmosphere. Tree-ring studies can give some insight into the $^{14}C/^{12}C$ ratio before the industrial revolution, and modern carbon dating takes this into account by running experimental measurements through a calibration formula.[39] But how do we know what the ratio was like thousands of years ago? We simply don't. The dating system hangs on these types of assumptions![40]

5. **Solar flares**. Several studies have shown: 1) significant solar flares have occurred in the past, and 2) these flares have an impact on carbon levels in the atmosphere. For example, in AD 774–775 there was an increase of 1.2% in the ^{14}C content of tree rings, which was about 20 times as high as the background rate of variation.[41] This "spike" was followed by a decline that lasted several years. The cause of this difference is thought to be a solar flare, as the same signal is found in ^{14}C in tree rings around the world, including Germany, Russia, the United States, and New Zealand.[42] Other researchers have noted similar findings.[43] Do we know whether other solar flares like this occurred thousands of years ago?

6. **The Reservoir Effect**. Heavy or light carbon atoms can become trapped, or at least concentrated, in "carbon reservoirs" where carbon isotopes do not quickly mix with the atmosphere.[44] As a result, some modern deep ocean organics show a carbon age of 1,500 carbon years, for example. Nearby limestone can also affect carbon isotope concentrations, giving false ages—or at least ages that need even more corrections.

7. **Partial pressure**. Geologic indicators show that atmospheric CO_2 levels were much higher in the past.[45] This would have diluted the apparent ^{14}C concentration, again making artifacts look older than they are.

8. **Magnetic field**. Several thousand years ago, Earth's magnetic field may have been twice as strong as today, assuming today's decay rate.[46] This would have slowed the rate at which cosmic radiation generates ^{14}C in the upper atmosphere, disrupting the basis for ^{14}C of very old objects.

9. **Fossil fuels (current and future)**. A research paper published in the *Proceedings of the National Academy of Sciences*[47] led to upheaval in the radioisotope dating field. The study's findings were spread by numerous science news outlets because they reveal emerging challenges to the reliability of ^{14}C dating based on the impact of *burning fossil fuels*. For example, Scientific American's take on the article was: "A T-shirt made in 2050 could look exactly like one worn by William the Conqueror a thousand years earlier to someone using radiocarbon dating if emissions continue under a business-as-usual scenario. By 2100, a dead plant could be almost identical to the Dead Sea scrolls, which are more than 2,000 years old."[48]

10. **Disequilibrium**. A critical assumption used in ^{14}C dating has to do with the ratio of ^{14}C to ^{12}C. To compute ^{14}C "ages" today, this ratio has to be stable and constant. If this assumption is not true, ^{14}C dating will give incorrect dates. If the amount of ^{14}C being produced in the atmosphere is equal the amount being removed, the atmosphere is in a *steady state* (also called "equilibrium"). If this is not true, the ratio is not steady, or in a state of *disequilibrium*. Dr. Willard Libby, the founder of the ^{14}C dating method, assumed the ratio of ^{14}C and ^{12}C to be constant. His reasoning was based on a belief in deep time and evolution. In his original work, however, he noted that the atmosphere did *not* appear to

be in equilibrium. His calculations showed that if the earth started with no ^{14}C in the atmosphere, it would take up to 30,000 years to build up to a steady state (equilibrium): "If the cosmic radiation has remained at its present intensity for 20,000 or 30,000 years, and if the carbon reservoir has not changed appreciably in this time, then there exists at the present time a complete balance between the rate of disintegration of radiocarbon atoms and the rate of assimilation of new radiocarbon atoms for all material in the life-cycle."[49] Dr. Libby's concern has turned out to be very real. Studies since Libby's original work have shown the ^{14}C / ^{12}C is *not* constant: "The Specific Production Rate (SPR) of ^{14}C is known to be 18.8 atoms per gram of total carbon per minute. The Specific Decay Rate (SDR) is known to be only 16.1 disintegrations per gram per minute."[50] If it takes about 30,000 years to reach equilibrium and ^{14}C is still out of equilibrium, the earth must not be very old.

When scientists attempt to stretch the results of carbon dating back many thousands of years, do they inadvertently violate any of the assumptions discussed above? How can we know without being there to measure the various factors to see if the assumptions hold true?

There is actually some solid evidence that many of the assumptions discussed above do *not* hold true. A key study conducted in 1989 by the British Science and Engineering Research Council (BSERC) arose over concern about the practice of carbon dating. Many results continued to come back with varying dates for various artifacts of known ages (i.e., artifacts which could be reliably dated using written history). So BSERC decided to conduct an *international blind test* on the practice of carbon dating itself. The test was conducted by sending dated artifacts of "known age" to 38 of the world's leading radiocarbon testing laboratories. The results of the study confirm that something is amiss:[51]

The British Science and Engineering Research Council (which funded the installation of the C14 apparatus at Oxford) ran a series of tests in 1989 with 38 laboratories involved worldwide. As a consequence, the council has insisted this year (1990) on new quality-control measures, by which checks are made with standard reference materials of known age. Of the mass spectrometry technique used at Oxford, Dr. Baxter reports: 'It came out very badly in the survey, even when dating samples as little as 200 years old.' **Only 7 out of 38 laboratories produced satisfactory results,** and the margin of error with **artefacts of known age was two or three times greater than the technique's practitioners claim.** *Nature* (the magazine which published details of the original C14 experiment) has now published a demonstration that **the radiocarbon technique is not only unsound but also outdated.** The Geological Observatory of Columbia University in New York has proved that the C14 results given in past years are in error by as much as 3,500 years in dating fossils, artefacts and events of the past 40,000 years, and **the further back we go in time, the greater the error.** Dr. Fairbanks of the observatory staff points out that since the C14 dating depends on the ever-variable quantity of C14 in the atmosphere produced by cosmic rays, any alteration of that production either by nature, or by the solar system, or by man-made interference (such as thermo-nuclear bombs) must cause a collapse of the whole hypothesis. He quotes the significant underestimation of the age of ancient objects and states that in a large number of tests C14 failed consistently, the samples being far older than the C14 findings showed. (emphasis added)

How can carbon dating be regarded as scientifically reliable and accurate when 0 of 38 laboratories "achieved a correct date, even with plus or minus tolerances, and many were off by *thousands of years*"? Do we know about all the forest fires and volcanic eruptions that have occurred in the distant past? Atomic activity? Solar flares and cycles? Earth's magnetic field? There are so many assumptions required to journey into the distant past—it's a better idea to trust the Creator, who was there, than the words of secular scientists.

A final factor to consider when it comes to carbon dating is the worldwide Flood described in Genesis 6–9, plus the recent Ice Age that followed right after the Flood. Noah's Flood would have uprooted and buried entire forest systems, decreasing the release of ^{12}C into the atmosphere through the decay of vegetation. Creation scientists have investigated this, and believe the Flood explains why most dinosaur bones typically cluster between 17,850 to 49,470 radiocarbon years.[52]

Civilizations before the Flood

YouTube is filled with videos that discuss "ancient civilizations" and "pre-flood civilizations." Many of these videos include a lot of speculation and inference. However, some of them attempt to draw realistic conclusions through a biblical framework. When viewing this type of evidence about supposed pre-flood civilizations, consider bracketing the information presented within a framework of the biblical "knowns":

1. There was a single worldwide flood between 2,348 BC (at the earliest) and 3,300 BC at the latest.
    a. The Flood devastated the globe, in keeping with God's promise to "… destroy man whom I have

created from the face of the earth" (Genesis 6:7). Ask yourself "how could a civilization/ancient structures" survive such a catastrophe (see our video that discusses the catastrophic nature of the Flood here: https://youtu.be/i8SCjn1hubc).

    b. If we find sedimentary layers with fossils under the structure (especially from the last few Flood-deposited Megasequences of deposition[53]), the structures were built after the Flood.

2. The Bible is clear that technologically advanced civilizations existed before and after the Flood. Many of these advanced civilizations built structures, and some of these structures likely required advanced building methods, some of which may not be known today.

3. Most Flood deposits contain grains of pulverized rocks, or remains of mostly crushed and sorted animal parts. Its violence would have pulverized ancient buildings.

Given the biblical knowns, it is *possible* but very unlikely that some parts of these structures (e.g., perhaps large foundation stones) still exist today.

Climate Change

Four primary factors help us to understand climate change from a biblical worldview. First, climate change has been occurring since creation (just thousands of years ago), but especially since the Flood. The world has been recovering since the global Flood and the single Ice Age that followed just hundreds of years afterwards. The world has also been winding down and "groaning" under the curse of sin brought by man after creation (Romans 8).

Second, God is in control (ultimately) and will sustain this planet for life until He returns. Genesis 8:22 reminds us: "As long as the earth endures, seedtime and harvest, cold and heat, summer and winter, day and night will never cease." God made the planet and made man. He will sustain them both under His plan.

Third, we are given the "dominion charge" by God to be good stewards of the planet, taking proper care of its resources and life. Many fail in this, for example with widespread dumping chemical waste into rivers. This poor stewardship carries consequences.

Fourth, earth's atmosphere includes a dizzying array of known and unknown factors. Thus, they speak prematurely who claim that one factor, such as pollution, warms the whole earth. These statements also ignore many studies that show how solar intensity changes affect earth's temperature more readily than human activity might.

Creation Days

The literal/historical view of Genesis that the six days in creation week are ordinary days and the genealogies in chapters 5 and 10 really do trace back to Adam just thousands of years ago reflects centuries of sound biblical interpretation and history. The Pharisees at the time of Christ held to this position unwaveringly. Jesus regarded Genesis as historical each of the 42 times He referenced the Old Testament. The Hebrew word for day (*yom*) *always* means an ordinary day when used with 'evening,' 'morning,' or a number (like yom is used for bracketing each of the six days of creation in Genesis 1).

Did God mince his words when he said (in the 4th commandment no less) that He created the heavens, the earth, the sea and everything in them *in six days* (Exodus 20:11)? [54] Did he want the receiver of this communication to believe anything but six ordinary days when he spoke it in context of the Sabbath, which is a real day? On Day Four God further

51

showed that these were literal days by telling us the purpose for which He created the sun, moon, and stars—so we could tell time: literal years, literal seasons, and literal days. The creation week days were plain days for the same basic reasons that any similarly structured passage, like the Israelites marching around Jericho, conveys ordinary days. See the **"Age of the Earth"** section for a more detailed discussion on the six days of Creation.

Dendrochronology (Tree Ring Dating)

Trees like the Bristlecone pine and the Giant Sequoias have rings that "date" as old as the Flood. The oldest Sequoia tree has rings that date it about 3,266 years old; the oldest Bristlecone is about 4,844 years old (using a one-ring-per-year counting method).[55] Also, several studies have established that trees can (and do) grow more than one ring per year.[56] Some dendrochronologies reach toward 10,000 years. To build these, workers place individual tree-based chronologies end-to-end toward the past in an effort to fill in imagined evolutionary time.

Dinosaurs: Were They on the Ark?

Suggested Videos:
www.genesisapologetics.com/dinosaurs

There are three factors to consider when answering this question. First, the Bible is clear that humans were alive at the same time as dinosaurs. We were created to take dominion over *all* that God had just created, and Adam *named* every kind of animal after they were created. Genesis 1 says God created the great beasts, and dinosaurs qualify. Behemoth, likely a sauropod, lived with Job (see Job 40:15). There was no "dinosaur era" millions of years before humans existed.

Second, dinosaur soft tissue and original organics including proteins provide strong evidence for the recency of dinosaurs as well as for the way in which the vast majority of them perished (see **Dinosaurs-Soft Tissue**).

Third, many dinosaurs have design features that give clues that the pre-flood world was much different than the world today (see **Pre-flood World**). Fewer than 1,000 species have been identified based on fossils, with fewer than 80 inter-fertile kinds. It would have been feasible for Noah to load juveniles on the Ark.

Dinosaur Soft Tissue

> *Suggested Videos:*
> *www.genesisapologetics.com/dinosaurs*

Over 50 scientific, peer-reviewed journal articles describe 14 bio-organic materials in dinosaur bones that simply should not exist if the dinosaurs died out 65 million years ago. Many of these, like collagen, have studied decay rates that establish maximum shelf-lives of between 10,000 and 100,000 (some studies) and 300,000 to 900,000 years (other studies). Both are far, far shorter than 65 million years.

Because the "expiration date" for these 14 bio-organic materials is well before 65 million years, they must be just thousands of years old. The science of protein decay fits the Bible's timeline of dinosaurs recently buried in Noah's Flood much better than it does evolutionary long ages.

For readers who would like to dive deeper into this line of research, we recommend the Spring 2015 issue of the *Creation Research Society Quarterly Journal*,[57] which includes a technical review of what's covered in summary form below.

Fresh Dinosaur Biomaterial #1: Blood Vessels

Blood vessels transport blood throughout the body. They include the tiny capillaries, through which water and chemicals pass between blood and the tissue. Bones include capillaries and larger vessels. Small, pancake-shaped cells loaded with long-lasting collagen protein comprise blood vessels.

The blood vessels shown in Figure 10 were discovered when Dr. Mary Schweitzer's team was attempting to move a gigantic *Tyrannosaurus rex* fossil by helicopter that turned out to be too heavy. They were forced to break apart the leg bone. When looking at the inside of the leg bone at the lab, they discovered that the inside of the bone was partially hollow (not mineralized), revealing the soft tissue shown in Figure 10 that was extracted after treatments to remove the minerals.[58]

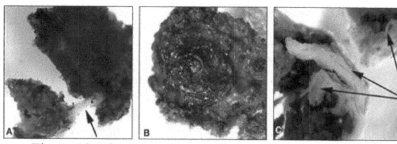

Figure 10. Tissue Fragments from a *Tyrannosaurus rex* Femur.[59]

The tissues that are shown on the left of Figure 10 show that it is flexible and resilient. When stretched, it returned to its original shape. The middle photo shows the bone after it was air dried. The photo at right shows regions of bone showing fibrous tissue, not normally seen in fossil bone.

Since this publication in 2005, blood vessels from several other dinosaurs and other extinct reptiles have been described and published in numerous leading scientific journals, including the *Annals of Anatomy*, *Science* (the leading journal of the American Association for the Advancement of Science),

Public Library of Sciences ONE, and the *Proceedings from the Royal Society B*, which focuses on the biological sciences.[60]

Fresh Dinosaur Biomaterial #2: Red Blood Cells

Red blood cells carry oxygen and collect carbon dioxide using hemoglobin protein—also found in dinosaur and other fossils. Dr. Mary Schweitzer was one of the first to discover and publish the discovery of red blood cells, which she shares in her own words: "The lab filled with murmurs of amazement, for I had focused on something inside the vessels that none of us had ever noticed before: tiny round objects, translucent red with a dark center. Then a colleague took one look at them and shouted, 'You've got red blood cells. You've got red blood cells!'"[61]

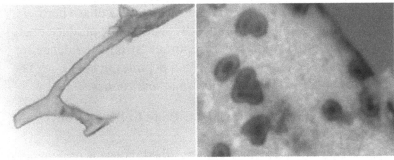

Figure 11. Red Blood Vessels and Cells from a *Tyrannosaurus rex* Bone.

These two photos in Figure 11 are from a 2005 discovery from Dr. Schweitzer that clearly show blood vessels from a *T. rex* bone (left) and red blood cells (right). How could these cells last for 65 million years? At least five peer-reviewed scientific journals have published accounts of red blood cells in dinosaur and other fossil bones.[62]

Regarding this discovery, Dr. Schweitzer remarked, "If you take a blood sample, and you stick it on a shelf, you have nothing recognizable in about a week. So why would there be anything left in dinosaurs?"[63] That's certainly a good question, and one that has an easier answer if dinosaurs are only thousands of years old!

After this discovery, Dr. Schweitzer ran into challenges when trying to publish her work in the scientific literature. Dr. Schweitzer remarks, "I had one reviewer tell me that he didn't care what the data said, he knew that what I was finding wasn't possible." Dr. Schweitzer wrote him back and asked, "Well, what type of data would convince you." The reviewer replied, "None."

Fresh Dinosaur Biomaterial #3: Hemoglobin

Hemoglobin protein contains iron and transports oxygen in red blood cells of most vertebrates. Some invertebrates, including certain insects and some worms, also use hemoglobin. In vertebrates, this amazing protein picks up oxygen from lungs or gills and carries it to the rest of the body's cells. There, oxygen fuels aerobic respiration by which cells produce energy.

Scientific studies have reported "striking evidence for the presence of hemoglobin derived peptides in the (T-rex) bone extract"[64] and several other dinosaur "era" bones.[65]

Fresh Dinosaur Biomaterial #4: Bone Cells (Osteocytes)

Secular scientists have described dinosaur proteins like hemoglobin, even though no experimental evidence supports the possibility that they can last for even a million years. But dinosaur bones hold more than just individual proteins. They sometimes retain whole cells and tissue remnants. An osteocyte is a bone cell that can live as long as the organism itself. Osteocytes constantly rebuild bones and regulate bone mass. Figure 12 shows highly magnified blood vessels, blood products, and osteocytes that were found on the inside of a brow horn of a Triceratops.

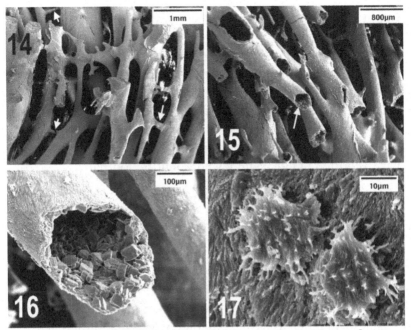

Figure 12. Soft Bone Material from a Brow Horn of a
Triceratops horridus from Montana.[66]

Figure 12 shows blood vessels linked together (white
arrows in frame 14). Frame 15 shows possible blood products
lining the inner wall of a hardened vessel (white arrow). Frame
16 is enlarged from frame 15 and shows crystallized nature of
possible blood products lining inner wall of hardened vessel.
Frame 17 shows two large oblate osteocytes lying on fibrillar
bone matrix.

At least four scientific studies have established
osteocytes in dinosaur bones. One study even found nucleic
acid signatures consistent with ancient DNA right where the
nucleus would have been in dinosaur osteocytes.[67]

Fresh Dinosaur Biomaterial #5: Ovalbumin (Proteins)

Another protein found in fossils that microbes don't make is called ovalbumin. It makes up 60–65% of the total protein in egg whites. Ovalbumin has been found in exceptionally preserved sauropod eggs discovered in Patagonia, Argentina, a dig site that included skeletal remains and soft tissues of embryonic titanosaurid dinosaurs. These findings were reported in a peer-reviewed scientific journal.[68]

Fresh Dinosaur Biomaterial #6: Chitin

Chitin is a biochemical found in squid beaks and pens, arthropod exoskeletons, and certain fungi. If chitin was meant to last for millions of years, then it might have filled Earth's surface as dead insects, krill, and fungi left their remains over eons. Chitin is tough, but no known experiment supplies any reason to so much as suspect that it could last a million years, let alone hundreds of millions, as at least two scientific studies report finding in fossils.[69] Our Creator equipped many microbes with unique enzymes that digest chitin, so what could have kept those microbes away from all that chitin for millions of years?

Fresh Dinosaur Biomaterial #7: Unmineralized Bone

Fresh-looking, un-mineralized dinosaur bones pop up in dig sites around the world. In Alaska, for example, a petroleum geologist working for Shell Oil Company discovered well-preserved bones in Alaska along the Colville River. The bones looked so fresh that he assumed these were recently deposited, perhaps belonging to a mammoth or bison. Twenty years later scientists recognized them as Edmontosaurus bones—a duck-billed dinosaur.[70]

Figure 13. Unfossilized Hadrosaur Bone from the Liscomb
Bone Bed.[71]

Mineralized bones can look darker than bone and
typically feel quite heavy. Un-mineralized bones retain their
original structure, often including the tiny pore spaces in spongy
bone, as shown in Figure 13. One study includes an interesting
section that states:

> Finally, a two-part mechanism, involving first
> cross-linking of molecular components and
> subsequent mineralization, is proposed to explain
> the surprising presence of still-soft elements in
> fossil bone. These results suggest that present
> models of fossilization processes may be
> incomplete and that *soft tissue elements may be
> more commonly preserved, even in older
> specimens, than previously thought.*[72]
> Additionally, in many cases, osteocytes with
> defined nuclei are preserved, and may represent

an important source for informative molecular data (emphasis added).

Numerous other studies published in scientific journals have described these un-mineralized dinosaur bone findings.[73]

Sometimes evolutionists are surprised by the fact that many dinosaur bones contain "fresh," original bone. It seems that decades of conditioning that "dinosaur bones become solid rocks" and ideas of "millions of years" have framed assumptions that are frequently being broken today.

However, researchers out in the field—actually digging up bones—oftentimes have a different viewpoint. Take Dr. Mary Schweitzer's testimony for example, where she notes that many "fresh" dinosaur bones still have the stench of death:

> This shifting perspective clicked with Schweitzer's intuitions that dinosaur remains were more than chunks of stone. Once, when she was working with a *T. rex* skeleton harvested from Hell Creek, she noticed that the fossil exuded a distinctly organic odor. "It smelled just like one of the cadavers we had in the lab who had been treated with chemotherapy before he died," she says. Given the conventional wisdom that such fossils were made up entirely of minerals, Schweitzer was anxious when mentioning this to Horner [a leading paleontologist]. "But he said, 'Oh, yeah, all Hell Creek bones smell,'" she says. To most old-line paleontologists, the smell of death didn't even register. To Schweitzer, it meant that traces of life might still cling to those bones.[74]

Experienced dinosaur fossil collectors have developed similar opinions. Take experienced dinosaur hunter and wholesaler, Alan Stout, for example. Alan Stout is a long-time fossil collector and has collected and sold millions of dollars' worth of dinosaur specimens to collectors, researchers, and museums worldwide.[75] After collecting in the Montana Hell Creek formation (and surrounding areas) for over a decade Alan states that many of the dinosaur bones he finds in the Cretaceous layers are only 40% mineralized, with as much as 60% of the bone being original material. He even notes that some of the fossils "look just like they were buried yesterday after scraping off just the outside layer of mineralization."[76]

Fresh Dinosaur Biomaterial #8: Collagen

Collagen is the main structural protein found in animal connective tissue. When boiled, collagen turns into gelatin, showing its sensitivity to temperature. In 2007, scientists discovered collagen amino acid sequences from a *T. rex* fossil that supposedly dated at 68 million years. Met with controversy, some suggested these proteins came from lab workers who accidentally contaminated the samples being studied. Or perhaps traces of ostrich bone proteins lingered in the equipment used in the study. Some even said, well perhaps "a bird died on top of the *T. rex* excavation site."[77] However, three separate labs verified collagen in dinosaurs in 2009[78] and again in January 2017.[79] The 2017 study even confirmed the collagen at the *molecular level*, and stated, "We are confident that the results we obtained are not contamination and that this collagen is original to the specimen."[80]

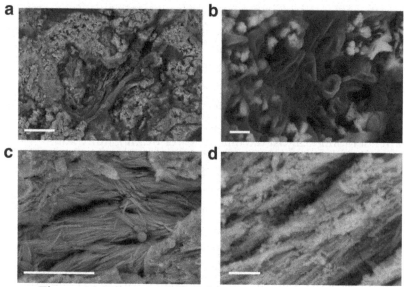

Figure 14. Fibers and Cellular Structures in Dinosaur Specimens.[81]

Experiments have projected that the absolute theoretical maximum life of collagen ranges from 300,000 to 900,000 years under the best possible conditions.[82] This shows that collagen proteins should not last one million years, but could (in the absence of microbes) last for thousands of years. This confronts millions-of-years age assignments for dinosaur remains, but is consistent with the biblical time frame.

But the "rescuing devices" being offered by evolutionists are not far behind. For example, in a recent article published in *Science*, Dr. Schweitzer tried to explain how the collagen sequences supposedly survived tens of millions of years: "… as red blood cells decay after an animal dies, iron liberated from their hemoglobin may react with nearby proteins, linking them together. This crosslinking, she says, causes proteins to precipitate out of solution, drying them out in a way that helps preserve them." Critical of this idea, however, Dr. Matthew Collins, a paleoproteomics expert at the University of York in the United Kingdom, stated that he doesn't think that the process described by Dr. Schweitzer could "arrest protein degradation for tens of millions of years, so he, for one, remains skeptical of Schweitzer's claim: 'Proteins decay in an orderly fashion. We can slow it down, but not by a lot.'"[83]

Fresh Dinosaur Biomaterial #9: DNA (Limited)

One measured decay rate of DNA, extracted from recently deposited fossil bird bones, showed a half-life of 521 years. DNA decays quickly. It should have spontaneously decayed into smaller chemicals after several tens of thousands of years—and it could only last that long if kept cool. A few brave secular scientists have reported DNA structures from dinosaur bones, although they did not directly address the question of its age.[84]

Fresh Dinosaur Biomaterial #10: Skin Pigments

In 2008, a group of paleontologists found exceptionally well-preserved Psittacosaurus remains in China and published images of dinosaur collagen fiber bundles. Other scientists published stunning skin color images from a separate Psittacosaurus, also from China, and found evidence of original, unaltered pigments including carotenoids and melanins. Nobody has performed an experiment that so much as suggests these pigments could last a million years. Still other studies have reported scale skin and hemoglobin decay products—still colored red as were some of Dr. Mary Schweitzer's *T. rex* and hadrosaurine samples—in a Kansas mosasaur.[85]

Fresh Dinosaur Biomaterial #11: PHEX (Proteins)

PHEX is a protein involved in bone mineralization in mammals. In 2013, Dr. Mary Schweitzer published detailed findings of the soft, transparent microstructures her team found in dinosaur bones. Because this discovery was so controversial, her team used advanced mass spectrometry techniques to sequence the collagen. Other methods demonstrated that proteins such as Actin, Tubulin, and PHEX found in osteocytes from two different dinosaurs were not from some form of contamination, but came from the creatures' remains.[86]

Fresh Dinosaur Biomaterial #12: Histone H4 (Proteins)

Bacteria do not make histone H4, but animals do. DNA wraps around it like a spool. Dr. Mary Schweitzer and her team found this protein inside a hadrosaur femur found in the Hell Creek Formation in Montana, which bears an assigned age of 67 million years. It might last for thousands of years if kept sterile, but no evidence so much as hints that it could last for a million years.[87]

Fresh Dinosaur Biomaterial #13: Keratin (Structural Protein)

Keratin forms the main structural constituent of hair, feathers, hoofs, claws, and horns. Some modern lizard skins contain tiny disks of keratin embedded in their scales. Researchers identified keratin protein in fossilized lizard skin scales from the Green River Formation that supposedly date to 50 million years ago. They explained its presence with a story about clay minerals attaching to the keratin to hold it in place for all that time. However, water would have to deposit the clay, and water helps rapidly degrade keratin. The most scientifically responsible explanation should be the simplest one—that this fossil is thousands, not millions of years old.[88] Other fossils with original keratin include Archaeopteryx[89] bird feather residue and stegosaur spikes.[90]

Fresh Dinosaur Biomaterial #14: Elastin

Elastin is a highly elastic protein found in connective tissue, skin, and bones. It helps body parts resume their shape after stretching or contracting, like when skin gets poked or pinched. Bacteria don't need it or make it, and elastin should not last a million years, even under the best preservation environment. Scientists reported finding this protein in a hadrosaur femur found in the Hell Creek Formation in Montana.[91]

Biomaterial Summary

Because these findings are game-changers, they are not without challenge by those who hold strongly to evolutionary ideas. Some of the "rescuing devices" that have been offered to attempt to explain these findings include iron in the blood acting as a preservative, the material being mistaken from a bird carcass mixed with the fossil, laboratory contamination, and even microbial biofilm (from bacteria in the bones). These explanations show an eagerness to attempt to dismiss the findings while clinging to the belief in millions of years. Rather than questioning the supposed long ages needed to prop up the evolutionary view, they seek other explanations to explain the presence of these materials.

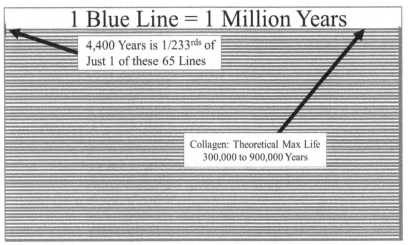

Figure 15. Dinosaur Biomaterials Time Comparison.

Figure 15 shows a simulated timeline to attempt to put these findings into perspective. Each of these 65 lines represents 1 million years. Showing 4,400 years (approximate date of the Flood) on this chart is difficult, but is represented by a tiny dot in the upper left, which is 1/233rds of just one of these lines, or less than one-half of 1 percent of one of these lines. While this assumption can never be tested, some studies have measured an absolute theoretical maximum life of between 300,000 and 900,000 years.[92] If these dinosaur bones are really 65 million years old (and older), this collagen lasted for *72 to 217 times longer than these measured and extrapolated maximum collagen shelf lives*. Does this require strong faith?

Is it really possible that all 14 of these biomaterials lasted for 65 million years? If they represent more recent deposits and were quickly sealed in Noah's Flood only thousands of years ago, then these finds fit fine. The fact that these materials lasted even this long is remarkable, but within measured age estimates. These 14 fresh biomaterials clearly fit a timescale of just thousands of years more accurately than millions of years.

Dragons

There are numerous ancient drawings and carvings of dinosaur-like creatures in almost every continent around the world. Dragon legends also exist in almost every culture around the world. Many of these describe creatures that are similar in size, shape, and features.

While many of these are likely fictional stories or exaggerations, it's quite surprising how many of these "dragon tales" are told by credible historians—historians that we trust for framing history as we know it today. Why do so many accept historical facts from these famous historians, but readily dismiss their accounts of dragon/dinosaur creatures? Are we selectively choosing only the parts of their accounts that fit our worldviews?

For example, in 1271 Marco Polo authored the *Travels of Marco Polo*. Marco was the first European (on record) to visit China and Asia and record it in *detail*. His work and maps popularized the 4,000-mile "Silk Road" trade route. Maps of Asia were based on his descriptions until the sixteenth century, and Christopher Columbus relied on these maps for finding a sea route to China (1492).

Marco recorded dragons living with man. Regarding the Province named Karajan, he wrote, "Here are found snakes and huge serpents, ten paces in length and ten spans in girth (that is, 50 feet long and 100 inches [about eight feet] in girth). At the fore part, near the head, they have two short legs, each with three claws, as well as eyes larger than a loaf and very glaring. The jaws are wide enough to swallow a man, the teeth are large and sharp, and their whole appearance is so formidable that neither man, nor any kind of animal can approach them without terror. Others are of smaller size, being eight, six, or five paces long (1961, pp. 158–159)." He continues by explaining how the "local citizens of the area hunted and killed the creatures."

In 330 BC, Alexander the Great invaded India and brought back reports of seeing a great hissing dragon living in a cave, which people were worshiping as a god.[93] Later Greek rulers supposedly brought dragons alive from Ethiopia.

Athanasius Kircher (lived AD 1601–1680) was a German Jesuit Scholar who published 40 major works and taught at Roman College for over 40 years. In his chapter on dragons in *Mundus Subterraneus*, Kircher records: "Of winged dragons, dispute has only arisen between authors, most of whom declare them to be fanciful, but these authors are contradicted by histories and eyewitnesses. Winged dragons—small, great, and greatest—have been produced in all times in every land." These could well refer to pterosaurs alive after the Flood.

Pliny the Elder (lived from AD 23–79), a well-known Roman scholar and historian was the author of *Naturalis Historia* ("Pliny's Natural History"). In this famous work, Pliny writes: "Africa produces elephants, but it is India that produces the largest, as well as the dragon." Less than two centuries later, Greek historian and philosopher Lucius Flavius Philostratus (AD 170– 247) wrote: "The whole of India is girt with dragons of enormous size; for not only the marshes are full of them, but the mountains as well, and there is not a single ridge without one. Now the marsh kind are sluggish in their habits and are thirty cubits long, and they have no crest standing up on their heads."[94]

Herodotus was a famous Greek historian who lived between 484 and 425 BC. He was the first Greek writer who succeeded in writing a large-scale historical narrative that has survived the passage of time, which contributed to Herodotus being known as the "father of history." Herodotus records: "Winged serpents are said to fly from Arabia at the beginning of spring, making for Egypt: but the ibis birds encounter the invaders in this pass and kill them…the serpents are like water snakes. Their wings are not feathered but very like the wings of a bat."

The above is only a selection of examples. Several more exist. The reader is encouraged to draw from the resources at _www.answersingenesis.org_ for books that discuss this topic thoroughly. The book by Vance Nelson titled, "Untold Secrets of Planet Earth: Dire Dragons" give the clearest evidence that dragons were dinosaurs.

Flat Earth

The earth is not flat. It is round, like a ball. Proper Biblical interpretation supports this and observational science proves it. The recent swell of flat-earth believers all derive from persuasive-sounding YouTube videos—not science or the Bible. For a balanced review of this topic, see "Does the Bible Teach That the Earth Is Flat?" by astronomer Danny Faulkner.[95]

Fossils—Do They Support Creation or Evolution?[96]

Suggested Videos:

The Fossil Record: Proof of Noah's Flood or Evolution
https://www.youtube.com/watch?v=qHRYnm_J4ts&t=7s

The fossils glaringly support the young earth Biblical history of the recent, special creation of our world followed by a single earth-covering Flood on our planet just thousands of years ago. Darwinists, however, interpret the fossil record, or the remains of past life found within the rocks of the earth's crust as circumstantial evidence that biological species originated by natural selection from a universal common ancestor. Do fossils really show the evolutionary "tree of life" preserved in stone? This Darwinian model should show the following three features:

1. **Ancestral Forms**: Lowest rocks contain few relatively "simple" ancestral life forms (i.e., *the less-evolved root organisms*).
2. **Intermediate Forms**: Life forms gradually display new organs and other body designs in an uninterrupted, increasingly advanced chain in higher rock layers (i.e., *the transitional trunk*).
3. **Divergent Forms**: Ever-increasing numbers of diverse organisms (i.e., *the more-evolved branches*) occupy the higher geological strata.

The fossil record falsifies *all three* evolutionary expectations. Instead, the fossil record biologically, paleontologically, and geologically supports *all* Creation and Flood expectations. We evaluate these three next.

Fossil Strike One—Evolutionary "Ancestral Forms" Never Existed

Rather than animal kinds coming about by natural selection somehow adding new genes and organs to pre-existent ancestors as Darwin's ideas predicted, the fossil record provides no hint in the lowest known fossil-bearing rocks (named "Precambrian" and "Cambrian") of single-celled organisms morphing into the multi-celled creatures. The "Cambrian Explosion" describes the sudden appearance of all the radically-different blueprint types of each animal all in one rock system. This gap—which occurs globally—should not even exist locally if evolutionism is true.

Jonathan Wells, in his eye-opening book entitled *Icons of Evolution: Science or Myth?—Why Much of What We Teach about Evolution Is Wrong* wrote:

> ...in Darwin's theory, there is no way phylum-level differences could have appeared right at the start. Yet that is what the fossil record shows... In other words, the highest levels of the biological hierarchy appeared right at the start. Darwin was aware of this, and considered it a major difficulty for his theory...Darwin was convinced, however, that the difficulty was only apparent.... Many paleontologists are now convinced that the major groups of animals really *did* appear abruptly in the early Cambrian. The fossil evidence is so strong, and the event so dramatic, that it has become known as "the Cambrian explosion," or "biology's big bang." (emphasis added).

This sudden appearance of all the major, complex body-plans of biology in the lowest fossil-bearing sedimentary rock layers without "simpler" forms gradually leading up to them fits creation according to kinds. Trilobites, for example, have eye structures that are even more complicated than humans! Some types of trilobites had eyes with over 15,000 individual lenses![97]

The fact that trilobites are prevalent in the lowest fossil layers is actually evidence that the first creatures to get rapidly buried in the Flood were those that were dwelling on the bottom of the ocean.

Fossil Strike Two—Evolutionary "Transitional Forms" Never Existed

If all living things are indeed related to each other through a gradual development of pre-existing organisms as Charles Darwin said and as is often illustrated by so-called branching "evolutionary tree" diagrams known as "phylogenetic charts," then we would expect to find countless intermediate species or transitional forms between major biological groupings. Transitional *creatures*, supposedly exemplified by such headliners as ape-to-man "hominids," the coelacanth fish,[98] and *Archaeopteryx* (an extinct bird that evolutionists believe possesses some reptilian-like features causing it to be classified as an evolutionary transitional form[99]) supposedly bridge classification boundaries by possessing transitional *features*. See the sections titled, *Archaeopteryx* and *Tiktaalik/Coelacanth* for details on these fossils.

Without true transitional structures, does the fossil record support or upsettingly contradict the Darwinian view of phyletic gradualism? Former Darwinists Percival Davis and Dean H. Kenyon ask in their book, *Of Pandas and People* (1989):

> Does Darwin's theory match the story told by the fossils? To find out, we must first ask, what kind of story would it match? His theory posited that living things formed a continuous chain back to one or a few original cells. If the theory is true, the fossils should show a continuous chain of

creatures, each taxon leading smoothly to the next. In other words, there should be a vast number of transitional forms connecting each taxon with the one that follows. The differences separating major groups in taxonomy [such as invertebrates and the first fish] are so great that they must have been bridged by a huge number of transitional forms. As Darwin himself noted in *The Origin of Species* (1859), "The number of intermediate varieties, which formerly existed on earth [must] be truly enormous." *Yet this immense number of intermediates simply does not exist in the fossil record.* The fossils do not reveal a string of creatures leading up to fish, or to reptiles, or to birds. Darwin conceded this fact: "Why then is not every geological formation and every stratum full of such intermediate links? *Geology assuredly does not reveal any such finely graduated organic chain.*" Indeed, this is, in Darwin's own words, "the most obvious and gravest objection which can be urged against my theory"[100] (emphasis added).

If evolutionary gradualism were true, then every organism's genetics would be evolving out of its inferior/past/ancestral code into a superior/future/descendant form. In short, *every life-form would be transitional* between its supposed past and its evolutionary future. However, the fossil record does not match this. Every distinct, self-bounded biological body plan appears suddenly. Fossils show no evolutionary intermediates with transitioning structures.

Instead, all preserved and present phyla demonstrate *stasis*—the dominant fossil trend of maintaining anatomical sameness. They show essentially no fundamental change in appearance over time, though some show a decrease in size. In addition, 95% of the fossil record phyla are comprised of marine invertebrates, some of which look the same throughout their entire vertical span through different rock layers.[101] The completeness of the fossil record deserves recognition after more than 150 years of fossil collecting and more than 200,000,000 fossils found. *Newsweek*'s 1980 admission of Darwin's elusive intermediate species being only imaginative is still embarrassingly accurate:

> The missing link between man and apes... is merely the most glamorous of a whole hierarchy of phantom creatures. *In the fossil record, missing links are the rule...* The more scientists have searched for the transitional forms between species, the more they have been frustrated.[102] (emphasis added)

In their journal disclosure, evolutionists Stephen Jay Gould and Niles Eldridge have honestly admitted the pseudo-scientific, philosophical origin of Darwin's view by their candid confession that *"Phyletic gradualism* [gradual evolution]... *was never 'seen' in the rocks* ... It [gradualism] expressed the cultural and political biases of 19th century liberalism" (emphasis added).[103] Thus, the "onward and upward" notion of evolutionary progress involving innovation and integration was a product of various social prejudices, not science.

Darwin had every hope that future research would reveal numerous transitional forms in the fossil record.[104] Now, after 150+ years of digging and millions of additional fossils identified and catalogued, do we have enough evidence to conclude whether transitional forms exist? Remember, if evolution is true, it would take numerous "prior versions" to move between forms—e.g., from a mouse to a bat.

To investigate this issue, Dr. Carl Werner and his wife Debbie invested over 14 years of their lives investigating "the best museums and dig sites around the globe [and] photographing thousands of original fossils and the actual fossil layers where they were found."[105]

After visiting hundreds of museums and interviewing hundreds of paleontologists, scientists, and museum curators, Dr. Werner concluded: "Now, 150 years after Darwin wrote his book, this problem still persists. Overall, the fossil record is rich—200 million fossils in museums—but the predicted evolutionary ancestors are missing, seemingly contradicting evolution."[106] He gives a series of examples:

- Museums have collected the fossil remains of 100,000 individual dinosaurs, but have not found a single direct ancestor for any dinosaur species.
- Approximately 200,000 fossil birds have been found, but ancestors of the oldest birds have yet to be discovered.
- The remains of 100,000 fossilized turtles have been collected by museums, yet the direct ancestors of turtles are missing.
- Nearly 1,000 flying reptiles (pterosaurs) have been collected, but no ancestors showing ground reptiles evolving into flying reptiles have been found.
- Over 1,000 fossil bats have been collected by museums, but no ancestors have been found showing a ground mammal slowly evolving into a flying mammal.
- Approximately 500,000 fossil fish have been collected, and 100,000,000 invertebrates have been collected, but ancestors for the theoretical first fish—a series of fossils showing an invertebrate changing into a fish—are unknown.
- Over 1,000 fossil sea lions have been collected, but not a single ancestor of sea lions has been found.
- Nearly 5,000 fossilized seals have been collected, but not a single ancestor has been found.

If this was not enough, one more key consideration should clearly convince. What if, after countless millions of hours spent by researchers mining the crust of the earth for fossil evidence, the fossil record is essentially *complete*? That is, it stands to reason that the millions of fossils we have collected over the last 150 years *exhaustively* record all basic life forms that ever lived, with only a few additional "big surprises" to be found. Given this, can we say that the question of transitional forms has been *asked and answered*?

One way to find out is to "calculate the percentage of those animals living today that have also been found as fossils. In other words, if the fossil record is comprised of a high percentage of animals that are living today, then the fossil record could be viewed as being fairly complete; that is, most animals that have lived on the earth have been fossilized and discovered."[107] Carl Werner provides a chart demonstrating the results of such an investigation:[108]

- Of the 43 living land animal *orders*, such as carnivores, rodents, bats, and apes, nearly all, or 97.7%, have been found as fossils. This means that at least one example from each animal order has been collected as a fossil.
- Of the 178 living land animal *families*, such as dogs, bears, hyenas, and cats, 87.8% have been found in fossils.

Evolution had its chance—over 150 years and millions of fossils—to prove itself, and it has come up wanting. The theory has been weighed, tested, measured, and falsified. Aren't 200 million opportunities and one and one-half centuries enough time to answer the issue that *confounded* Darwin himself?

> Why, if species have descended from other species by fine gradations, do we not everywhere see innumerable transitional forms? Why is not all nature in confusion, instead of the species being, as we see them, well defined?…But, as by this theory innumerable transitional forms must have existed, why do we not find them

embedded in countless numbers in the crust of the earth?…But in the intermediate region, having intermediate conditions of life, why do we not now find closely-linking intermediate varieties? This difficulty for a long time quite confounded me.[109]

Fossil Strike Three—Evolutionary "Divergent Forms" Never Existed

Darwinian evolution predicts that as phyla continue to diverge or branch out from their ancestral, evolutionary stock, their numbers should increase just as tree limbs radiate from a central trunk. According to Wells, "Some biologists have described this in terms of 'bottom-up' versus 'top-down' evolution. *Darwinian evolution is 'bottom-up,' referring to its prediction that lower levels in the biological hierarchy should emerge before higher ones. But the Cambrian explosion shows the opposite"* (emphasis added).[110] The fossil evidence indicates that the number of phyla in fact decreases from about 50–60 at the "Cambrian Explosion" to approximately 37 living phyla. Extinction—the opposite of evolution's required new phyla—have certainly occurred.[111] *"Clearly the Cambrian fossil record explosion is not what one would expect from Darwin's theory. Since higher levels of the biological hierarchy appear first, one could even say that the Cambrian explosion stands Darwin's tree of life on its head"* (emphasis added).[112]

Rather than a "bottom-up" continuum of ever-morphing divergent forms, the fossil record reveals definite gaps between, and "top-down" hierarchical variation within, phyla. In fact, these anatomical differences separating major design themes make biological classification of organisms (taxonomy) possible![113] Without these clear-cut gaps between organism kinds, biologists would not be able to divide plants and animals into their respective kingdoms, phyla, classes, orders, families, genera, and species.

Those familiar with the Bible will recognize that one would expect these gaps between biological kinds if all terrestrial life reproduces "after its own kind," a truth that the Scriptures declares *ten times* in its first chapter (Genesis 1:11, 12, 21, 24, 25). In fact, even the New Testament affirms that "All flesh is not the same flesh, but there is one kind of flesh of men, another flesh of beasts, another of fish, and another of birds" (1 Corinthians 15:39). Since God's written Word lists different creature groupings as separate kinds with anatomically unique "flesh," biological classification ultimately describes "a created arboretum" with an ancestral tree for each kind, not a single "evolutionary tree of life" that connects all organisms as Charles Darwin proposed.

Fossils in Sum: Gradualism Strikes Out While Creation Hits Home Run.

The fossil record bears witness that there are (1) *no ancestral roots*—no "primitive" organisms between microfossils and visible life, (2) *no transitional trunk*—no anatomically-intermediate creatures with structurally-transitional features (e.g., partially-evolved organs, limbs, etc.), and (3) *no divergent branches*—no new phyla being genetically descended from less-evolved "common ancestors."

If the fossil record does not support the evolutionary predictions of ancestral roots, transitional trunk, and divergent branches with regard to the major categories of life, then what does it show? Eight fossil observations confound evolution:

1. Separation from other phyla by definite, unbridgeable gaps with no ancestor-descendant/bottom-to-top transitional relationship.
2. All forms suddenly appear as unique body plans with fully-formed structures.
3. All phyla are represented from the beginning as fossils, demonstrating fossil-record completeness.

4. All are complex, functional, and were or still are able to survive.
5. All show no innovative change in their basic anatomical form after they first appear as fossils—only minor, top-down variation within a blueprint design.
6. Nearly all (95%) are phyla of marine invertebrates.
7. Many of these are found throughout the fossil record, not restricted to a certain vertical range of rock.
8. Extinction has decreased the number of phyla from 50–60 to nearly 37 —the opposite direction of evolution.

In addition, eight fossil observations *confirm* the Biblical Creation/global Flood history:

9. **Polystrate fossils** cut across multiple rock layers, supporting rapid sedimentation.
10. Over **1,000 documented massive fossil graveyards** around the world, the vast majority of which were deposited by various watery catastrophes.[114]
11. **Mass killing and the violent deaths** of creatures on all continents fits the global nature of Noah's Flood (e.g., the Morrison Formation in the U.S. which covers 13 states).
12. **Mixed groupings of organisms** from various ecological zones of different habitat and elevation fit the Bible's picture of Flood chaos.
13. Highly **energetic, destructive processes** capable of burying organisms alive, ripping rocks and creatures apart, and/or transporting their carcasses great distances calls for a flood of biblical proportions.
14. **Rock formations** with mostly ocean-dwelling creatures catastrophically fossilized, unlike today's ocean creatures that do not fossilize.
15. Fossils occur on **continentals**, not deep ocean bottoms.
16. Some geologic deposits cover **hundreds of thousands of square miles and spanning several continents**.

Gap Theory

The Gap Theory was introduced in the early 1800s as a way to compromise Scripture with the newly-emerging "deep time" ideas that Enlightenment thinkers began to associate with rock layers. Geology was trending toward uniformitarianism (the idea that present processes and rates were the key to understanding the past, without global catastrophes such as the Flood) and that the Earth was far older than the Bible-based flood geology would allow. The Gap Theory allowed religious geologists to insert a gap of deep time between the first two verses of the Bible (Genesis 1:1 and 1:2).[115] They imagined eons of rock and fossil deposition, all supposedly orchestrated by the devil.

In reality, however, this attempt to compromise Scripture failed to harmonize with *either* secular geology *or* the Bible. Uniformitarian geologists reject the idea of any global Flood, whether the biblical Noah's Flood, or a pre-Noachian Flood (some gap theorists call this "Lucifer's Flood"). The Gap Theory fails key tests from the Bible and reason.

The theological "fatal flaw" of the Gap Theory is that it places the fall of Satan, the existence of evil, death, suffering, bloodshed, and disease in a world that God had declared *"very good"* (Genesis 1:31) and a world that had *no death* (everything ate plants, see Genesis 1:29–30). If Adam was already standing on a graveyard of fossils from animals that had died from bloodshed, suffering, disease, and cancer, what would have been the significance of God's warning "… of the tree of the knowledge of good and evil you shall not eat, for in the day that you eat of it you shall surely die" (Genesis 2:17)? Adam could have replied, "Of course I'm going to die, just like all of these creatures have already died all around me already—it's the circle of life."

Adam and Eve standing on a graveyard of fossils would hardly be "very good." Indeed, Adam and Eve's fall resulted in everything under their dominion falling too:

- Sin brought **death**; Jesus raised the dead, and raised Himself from the grave.
- Sin brought **corruption** of God's original perfect design; Jesus healed the sick and cured diseases.
- The curse of sin brought **thorns and thistles** to plant life; Jesus triumphed over the curse of sin while wearing a crown of thorns on the Cross.
- Sin brought the first **bloodshed** (with God killing an animal to make a covering for Adam and Eve); Jesus was the last blood sacrifice necessary for our sins.
- All of **Creation groans** under the weight of sin (Romans 8); Jesus will redeem all of creation unto Himself (Colossians 1).

The Bible is clear that there was no sin or death until man brought them into the world: "by one man sin entered into the world, and death by sin" (Romans 5:12). First Corinthians 15:22 is also clear that there was no death in the world until man brought sin into it.

Also, the buried creatures from the devil's bygone world should share no similarities with today's living forms, and yet most basic fossil forms (which are marine invertebrates) look like living forms, and many specific fossils exactly resemble specific living creatures, called living fossils.

Finally, from a Scriptural and theological standpoint, the Gap Theory contradicts the very clear statement written by God with his own hand (in the 4th Commandment no less) that he "created the heavens, earth, the sea and everything in them" in six ordinary days (Exodus 20:8–11).

Genesis 1 and 2: Do They Provide Two Different Accounts of Creation?

Suggested Videos:

Myth 3: https://genesisapologetics.com/myth-3/

Did God Really Create in Six Ordinary Days?
https://youtu.be/pjx88K8JTY8

Young Earth v. Old Earth: What Does the Bible Say?
https://youtu.be/QzEzkrMdgIs

Many professors today promote the idea that Genesis 1 and 2 provide two different, even contradictory, accounts of Creation. At first blush, this may seem to be the case. But taking a careful look reveals something different. Let's find out why. Before we start, first consider that both chapters are inspired *and* historical—at least Jesus believed so when He quoted from both Genesis 1 and 2 in Matthew 19.

Looking at the big picture helps us understand how Genesis is laid out. While our Bibles today break Genesis into 50 chapters, the original text is actually broken into 11 sections, called *toledotes* (pronounced: "Toll-Dotes") which means "to bear" or "to generate" in Hebrew.

Genesis 1 provides the introduction—the overview of the creation of the entire universe in six days, which precedes the first toledote that begins in Genesis 2 verse 4: "These are the generations of the heavens and of the earth..." Genesis 1:1 through 2:3 provides a complete overview of the six days of Creation in a step-wise way, with each creation day starting out with "God said," followed by His creative works on that day, then concluded by "there was evening and morning" and a mention of the numerical day.

Genesis 2 is not concerned with the *steps* of the overall Creation account, but rather focuses on the events of Day 6, including the creation of Adam, the Garden of Eden and its river systems, Adam's instructions for the Garden, naming the animals, the creation of Eve, and the institution of marriage. *None* of these details are in the first Chapter of Genesis; they are saved for the second chapter that sets the stage for the third, which is the fall of man and the curse of sin, both of which happened in the Garden. The second chapter also does not mention important Creation events from the first chapter, such as the creation of earth, atmosphere, oceans, sea creatures, land, and the sun and stars—*showing that it was not attempting to be a second account of creation*. These two chapters actually tie into each other, with each chapter providing important details not in the other.

Some say that it appears that plants were created *after* people in Genesis 2, apparently conflicting with the Genesis 1 account of plants being made on Day 3 and man on Day 6. Genesis 2:5–7 says: "Before any plant of the field was in the earth and before any herb of the field had grown. For the Lord God had not caused it to rain on the earth, and there was no man to till the ground; but a mist went up from the earth and watered the whole face of the ground. And the Lord God formed man of the dust of the ground..."

In this passage, these verses call the plants: "plants *of the field*" and "herbs *of the field*." These terms are more specific than the "grass, herbs, and trees" described in Day 3 of Genesis 1 because none of these are accompanied with the "of the field" description. Hebrew scholar Dr. Mark Futato defines "plants of the field" as "wild shrubs of the steppe or grassland" and "herbs of the field" as "cultivated grain."[116] Both make sense, especially given the context that describes there being "no man to till the field" and no rain yet.

Then, in the very next chapter we see it is these very "herbs of the field" that are cursed with "thorns and thistles" that Adam would have to till and farm "by the sweat of his brow" as a consequence of the Fall (Genesis 3:17–18). Indeed,

82

because of Adam's sin, he would no longer have it easy. Instead of eating from abundant fruit trees in the garden, he would need to till the ground, contend with thorns and thistles, and grow crops for food.

The next contention that some people bring up with the Genesis 2 account is that verse 19 states, "Out of the ground the Lord God formed every beast of the field and every bird of the air, and brought them to Adam to see what he would call them." It's the word "formed" which gets people thinking the animal kinds were created right then and there—after man, and before woman—unlike the sequence in Chapter 1 where humans were created last. So, were the animals created *after* Adam? Actually, they weren't. The verse is simply stating the source and origin of the animal kinds, which were formed from dust and spoken into existence by God.

Also notice that God put Adam in charge over all the animals, taking dominion over all Creation. In Hebrew, the precise tense of a verb is determined by the *context*. Genesis 1 makes it clear that the animals were created *before* Adam, so Hebrew scholars would have understood the verb "formed" to mean "had formed" or "having formed," which is how many Bible translations state this passage (including Tyndale's translation, which predates the King James).

Moreover, Hebrew verbs focus on *completeness of action*, not past/present/future temporality. So, they do not have "tense" like English verbs. Instead, the past/present/future of an action verb is determined by context. Thus, in context with Genesis 1, Genesis 2:19, which uses a verb that denotes *completion of actions*, can be translated as "Now the Lord God <u>had formed</u> out of the ground all the beasts of the field and all the birds of the air."[117] Given this, the apparent disagreement with Genesis 1 disappears completely.

The extra details in the Genesis 2 account demonstrate several things. First, the account affirms Genesis 1 in *every way*, without contradiction. Second, we find that Genesis 1 and 2 are *complementary* rather than *contradictory*. Chapter 1 may be understood as Creation from God's perspective; it is the "big picture," an overview of the whole and the sequence of God's created works: light, atmosphere, vegetation, sun and stars, birds and fish, land animals and man. Chapter 2 views the more important aspects from man's perspective and expounds upon Day 6 events with details like the names of the first man and woman, their relationship with Creation, where they were first placed (in the Garden of Eden), naming the animals, and setting the stage for the events that would later occur in the garden.

Looking at it this way, the first two chapters of Genesis provide a cohesive and detailed account of Creation. They certainly don't represent two different accounts of Creation. They were produced by Moses, cited by Jesus, and referred to as authoritative by New Testament writers.

Genetics Part 1: Recent Variations Match Recent Creation[118]

A substantial amount of scientific evidence supports the recent creation described in the Bible. Little-known natural timeclocks from geology, paleontology, physics, and astronomy agree.[119] However, what does the field of genetics and modern genomics, one of the most rapidly advancing areas of science have to offer in this regard? As it turns out, new discoveries using the tools of modern biotechnology also showcase recent creation and events associated with the global flood.

Genetics allow us to test the *predictions* of creation science versus evolution. Creation science predicts that the genomes of all the different kinds of living creatures were created perfect *in the beginning*. However, due to the curse on creation—related to man's sin and rebellion—combined with the damaging effects of time, we should see degradation, corruption, and the *loss* of genetic information. While evolutionists do recognize that information loss occurs in short scales, the long-term, grand Darwinian scheme model predicts just the opposite of creationists. They believe that over vast amounts of time, genomes evolved and became more complex—gaining new information through random mutational processes. New results support biblical creation in unforeseen ways.

Cellular machinery that copies DNA during the standard process of cell division makes errors. These errors are called mutations. Sometimes they can lead to serious diseases such as cancer. However, when a mutation occurs in cell division that leads to making sperm or egg cells, these mutations can be inherited and passed on to the next generation. Scientists have measured this rate among humans and found it to be about 75 to 175 mutations per generation.[120] Using this known information about mutation rates, a research group led by Cornell University geneticist Dr. John Sanford modeled the accumulation of mutations in the human genome over generations using computer simulations that account for more real-life factors than any prior attempts. The algorithms incorporate the standard observations and theories behind population genetics. They found that the buildup of mutations would eventually reach a critical level and become so severe that humans would eventually go extinct. This process of genome degradation over time and successive generations is called *genetic entropy.* Remarkably, the timeframe of human genome degradation coincides closely with a recent creation of six to ten thousand years ago as predicted by the documented genealogies found in the Bible.[121]

After those results were published, two different large groups of scientists unwittingly vindicated the idea of genetic entropy and a recent creation.[122] In each study, they sequenced the protein coding regions of the human genome. One study examined 2,440 individuals and the other 6,515. From the DNA sequence data, they discovered many single nucleotide differences (variants) between people in their protein coding genes, with most of these being very rare types of variants. In addition, they found that over 80% of these variants were either deleterious or harmful mutations. They attributed the unexpected presence of these harmful mutations to "weak purifying selection." This essentially means that the alleged ability of natural selection to remove these harmful variants from human populations did nothing. Sanford's model predicted that natural selection could not remove these slightly harmful mutations, and these studies confirmed exactly that in the real world of human genetics.

Not only were these studies bad news for the evolutionary idea of mutation and natural selection as the supposed drivers of evolutionary change, but they also overwhelmingly illustrated genetic entropy. Most of the mutations resulted in heritable diseases afflicting important protein-coding genes. Protein-coding regions are less tolerant of mutations than other parts of the genome. Evolution-believing scientists usually pin their models of DNA change over time, referred to as molecular clocks, to millions of years before they even approach the data. In other words, they assume millions of years of human evolution and literally incorporate these deep time numbers into their models. The millions of years conclusion does not come from biology experiments.

Data revealed a very recent, massive burst of human genetic diversification. Most of it links with genetic entropy. One of the research papers stated, "The maximum likelihood time for accelerated growth was 5,115 years ago."[123] This places the beginning of the period of genetic diversification of humans close to the Genesis Flood and subsequent dispersion at the Tower of Babel, a point in time that the earth began to be repopulated through Noah's descendants. This recent explosion of human genetic variability through accumulated mutations follows the same pattern of decay that the Genesis 11 rapidly declining human life expectancy represents.[124]

Genetics Part 2: DNA Clocks Exactly Confirm Recent Creation

One more important realm of research demonstrating a recent creation comes from Harvard trained scientist Dr. Nathaniel Jeanson. He has been examining the mutation rates of

DNA in mitochondrial genomes.[125] Mitochondria are located outside the cell's nucleus. They provide energy for cells and contain their own DNA molecule that encodes a variety of proteins it uses for energy processing. The mitochondrial DNA molecule is typically inherited from the egg cell of a creature's mother. Its mutation rates can be accurately measured to produce a molecular-genetic clock. These genetic clocks are not calibrated by (theoretical) evolutionary timescales, but by the organism's *observed* mutation rate. They give a more realistic and unbiased estimate of that creature's genetic life history. By comparing the molecular clock rates in a few very different animals (fruit flies, round worms, water fleas, and humans), Dr. Jeanson demonstrated that a creation event for these organisms (including humans) occurred not more than 10,000 years ago! Each species holds today the number of mutations that creation history predicts, using that species' measured mitochondrial DNA mutation rate. It would blow old-earth biology out of the water if secularists were willing to learn about these results.

Buried deep within a secular research paper in 1997, the same thing regarding human mitochondrial DNA (mtDNA) mutation rate was reported, but it received little attention in the media. The authors of this paper wrote, "Using our empirical rate to calibrate the mtDNA molecular clock would result in an age of the mtDNA MRCA [the first human woman] of only ~6,500 years..."[126] One year later, another author wrote in the leading magazine *Science*, "Regardless of the cause, evolutionists are most concerned about the effect of a faster mutation rate. For example, researchers have calculated that "mitochondrial Eve"—the woman whose mtDNA was ancestral to that in all living people—lived 100,000 to 200,000 years ago in Africa. Using the new clock, she would be a mere 6,000 years old." The article also noted that the new findings of faster mutation rates pointing to mitochondrial Eve about 6,000 years ago have even contributed to the development of new mtDNA research guidelines used in the forensic investigations "adopted by the FBI."[127] Now, over 17 years later, and using even more mtDNA data, Dr. Jeanson is spectacularly confirming this previously unheralded discovery.

In addition, evolution predicts a net gain of information over time, accompanied by natural selection removing harmful genetic variants. But instead, we see a human (nuclear, not mitochondrial) genome filling up with about 100 harmful genetic variants in every generation. Information loss via genetic entropy rules over all genomes. Clearly, the predictions based on Scripture align with genetics discoveries.

The human genome has essentially been on a steep downhill slide ever since man's sin. This means that you and I have Adam, not apes, in our past. It also means we can trust the Bible's history and other teachings.

Gilgamesh (Epic): Which Came First–Noah's Flood or the Gilgamesh Epic?

Let's compare the Biblical Flood to the leading flood myth, the Epic of Gilgamesh. In 1853, archaeologists found a series of 12 tablets dated to around 650 BC, although parts of the story existed in earlier, fragmentary versions.[128] Because the story had many of the same elements as the Genesis account, skeptics believed that Gilgamesh preceded the Biblical account, negating the Genesis account as just a spin-off. Fortunately for Christians, however, there are major clues that point to the Biblical account as the accurate one, and Gilgamesh as a later work of fiction that incorporated legendary elements of a flood within a cultural fantasy. Here are the reasons why.

First, we have the feasibility of the Gilgamesh version of the Ark, described as a massive, unstable cube that was about 200 feet on each side with six decks that divided it into seven parts. Along with help from the community and craftsmen, he supposedly built this vessel—which was over three times the size of the Biblical Ark, in just a week.

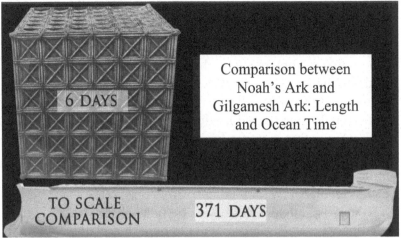

Figure 16. Noah's Ark vs. Gilgamesh Ark.[129]

How would something like this fare during a catastrophic, worldwide Flood? It would obviously tumble, killing or maiming its passengers. That's obviously quite different than the biblical Ark which had a 7-to-1 length-to-width ratio which is very similar to many of today's ocean barges, making it a feasible design for staying afloat during the Flood. Scripture provides clues that Noah and helpers likely had between 55 and 75 years to build the Ark.[130]

The second key for determining which of these Flood accounts is the original is the *duration* of the Flood provided by each. The Gilgamesh flood lasted a mere six days, whereas the Genesis Flood lasted 371 days. Both accounts claim the Flood was worldwide, but how could water cover earth in just six days? A floating, 200 X 200 X 200-foot cube and six days for worldwide inundation certainly stretch credulity.

The next consideration is the reasons for the Flood given by each of the two accounts. In the Genesis account, God's judgment is *just*—he was patient with utterly wicked mankind for 120 years before sending the Flood and showed mercy to the last righteous family. In the Gilgamesh account, the Flood was ordered by multiple, self-centered squabbling 'gods' that were 'starving' without humans to feed them sacrifices. These two are quite different!

Finally, there are several other parts of the Gilgamesh account that are obviously mythical, such as Gilgamesh being 2/3rds divine and 1/3rd mortal. After oppressing his people, Gilgamesh and others call upon the 'gods' and the sky-god Anu creates a wild man named Enkidu to fight Gilgamesh. The battle is a draw, and they become friends. Gilgamesh apparently also encounters talking monsters and a "Scorpion man" in his journeys.

Scholars rely on their anti-Bible bias, not science, to assert that the Gilgamesh story came first. These stark differences between Genesis and Gilgamesh accounts highlight the feasibility and priority of the biblical one. The Gilgamesh account was written 800 years[131] *after* Genesis and describes a cube-shaped Ark 200 feet on each side tumbling around in the ocean in a 6-day flood put on by the "angry, fighting gods" that sent it. The Bible's Flood was recorded earlier, has an Ark sealed on the inside and out with dimensions that are on par with today's ocean liners, lasted a full year, and was sent to judge an Earth that deserved it.

In fact, it's the similarities between these two accounts that shows the Bible's account to be the historical one. Many myths are based on historical accounts, but they get embellished over time, becoming more and more mythical as the story is repeated over generations. This is exactly what we see with flood myths like Gilgamesh—they take the original, historical account (the Biblical Flood) and grow it into a mythical, interesting story over time.

Human and Chimp DNA: Is It Really 98% Similar?[132]

Suggested Video:

Human Chimp DNA Similarity
https://youtu.be/Rav8sfuJFYc

One of the great trophies that evolutionists parade to prove human evolution from some common ape ancestor is the assertion that human and chimp DNA are 98 to 99% similar.[133] People quote this statistic in hundreds of textbooks, blogs, videos, and even scientific journals. Yet any high school student can debunk the "Human and Chimp DNA is 98% similar" mantra that this chapter covers.

Why does this matter? We know that genes determine body features from gender to hair color. If we are genetically related to chimps, some may conclude that humans should behave like animals, with no fear of divine justice. But if we all descended from Adam, not from animals, then common animal behavior such as sexual promiscuity cannot be justified on these grounds.[134] This has been a primary foundation for the mistreatment of humans worldwide by genocidal political leaders and governments over the past 150 or so years. One highly reputable study showed that the leading cause of death in the 20th century was "Democide"—or "murder by government," which has claimed well over 260 million lives.[135] All of the totalitarian murderous tyrannies the world over, despite their different political variations, maintained the same Darwinian evolutionary philosophy that humans are higher animals to be herded and culled in wars, death-camps, abortions, mass starvations, and outright slaughter.[136] Does this issue matter? Well, it's a matter of life and death. It needs to be refuted if it's not true.

We should evaluate the major evidences that exposes the 98% myth and supports the current conclusion that the actual similarity is 84.4%, or a difference of 15%, which translates to over 360 million base pairs' difference.[137] That is an enormous difference that produces an unbridgeable chasm between humans and chimpanzees. The chimp genome is much longer than the human genome. Humans have forty-six chromosomes, while chimps have forty-eight. According to the latest data, there are 3,096,649,726 base pairs in the human genome and 3,309,577,922 base pairs in the chimpanzee genome. This amounts to a 6.4% difference.[138] The 98% similarity claim fails on this basis alone.

If human and chimp DNA is nearly identical, why can't humans interbreed with chimps?[139] Furthermore, such an apparently minor difference in DNA (only 1%) does not account for the many obvious major differences between humans and chimps.

If humans and chimps are so similar, then why can't we interchange body parts with chimps? Over 30,000 organ transplants are made every year in the U.S. alone, and currently there are over 120,000 candidates on organ transplant lists—but *zero* of those transplants will be made using chimp organs.

Table 3. Organ Transplants[140]

Organ Transplants (2016)			
Organs	**# Currently Waiting**	**% of Transplants Made Using**	
		Human Organs	**Chimp Organs**
All Organs	121,520	100%	0%
Kidney	100,623	100%	0%
Liver	14,792	100%	0%
Pancreas	1,048	100%	0%
Kid./Panc.	1,953	100%	0%
Heart	4,167	100%	0%
Lung	1,495	100%	0%
Heart/Lung	47	100%	0%
Intestine	280	100%	0%

A Basic Overview

The living populations of the chimp kind include four species that can interbreed. From the beginning, they were *spirit-less* animals created on Day 6 of creation. Later that Day, God made a single man in His own image, and He gave him an everlasting *spirit* or *soul* (Genesis 2:7). Then God commanded man to "rule over the fish in the sea and the birds in the sky, over the livestock and all the animals," including chimps (Genesis 1:26).

If the creation narrative from the Bible is true, we would expect *exactly* what we see in today's ape-kinds. First, all varieties of chimps have no concept of eternity. For example, they do not bury their dead nor do they conduct funeral rituals. Secondly, apes use very limited verbal communication—they cannot write articles or even sentences. Thirdly, they do not display *spiritual or religious practices* as humans do. In other words, they show no capacity for knowing their creator through worship or prayer. This fits the Biblical creation account that God created humans as spiritual beings with an everlasting *spirit* or *soul* (Genesis 2:7).

It stands to reason that God, in His desire to create diverse life forms on Earth, would begin with the same building materials, such as DNA, carbohydrates, fats, and protein, when making various animal kinds. Research has revealed that He used similar building blocks for all the various physical life forms that He created. Genetic information in all living creatures is encoded as a sequence of principally 4 nucleotides (guanine, adenine, thymine, and cytosine, shown by the letters G, A, T, and C). We also see this principle in nature—such as many plants and animals sharing Fibonacci or similar spirals with clear algorithms and sequences as building patterns.

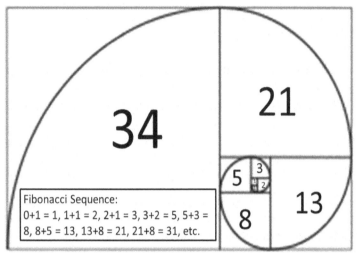

Figure 17. Fibonacci Number Sequence. A Fibonacci spiral approximates the golden spiral using quarter-circle arcs inscribed in squares of integer Fibonacci-number side, shown for square sizes 1, 1, 2, 3, 5, 8, 13, 21, 34 etc.

Figure 18. Examples of the Fibonacci Sequence in Nature.[141]

Chimp and human DNA use the same chemicals and share many sequence similarities. However, these likenesses do not prove that those similarities came from shared ancestors, since similar design can also explain them. After all, design constraints require an engineer to use many of the same raw materials and building plans to produce different types of biological machines—especially if those machines need to interact with the same building blocks for growth and life. For example, an automotive engineer could make a Volkswagen bug and a Porsche Carrera framework out of steel, glass, and plastic but not oxygen, carbon dioxide, and sulfuric acid. When experts talk about DNA similarity, they refer to a variety of different features. Sometimes they talk about humans and chimpanzees having the same genes. At other times, they talk about certain DNA sequences being 98 to 99% similar. First, let's consider why human and chimpanzee DNA sequences are actually closer to 84.4% than 98% similar.[142] Then, describing the concepts of genes and gene similarity will reveal much insight into human and chimp DNA dissimilarity.

Comparisons of Chimps and Humans

Once you understand that the new DNA evidence debunks the alleged human evolution paradigm, you will appreciate that you are a unique creation whom the Creator made in His own image. You are special and unique compared to all of creation.

A child that sees a chimpanzee can immediately tell that it is radically different from a human. Compared to chimps, humans are about 38% taller, are 80% heavier, live 50% longer, and have brains that are about 400% larger (1330 ccs compared to 330 ccs).[143] Look at someone next to you and roll your eyes at them. Chimps can't do that because their sclera, like most other animals, is hidden behind their eyelids. Now tap your fingertips with your thumb. Chimps can't do that either—their fingers are curved, their thumbs are both tiny and set further back on their wrists than humans, and they are missing the flexor pollicis longus—the major muscle that controls thumb dexterity in humans. Additionally, their knees point out, whereas ours point forward. Humans can build space shuttles and write songs. Chimps don't do anything close.

Scientists now know that chimpanzees are radically different than humans in many different ways besides their outward appearance. Humans and chimpanzees have differences in bone structures, in brain types, and in other major parts of their physiology. Humans also have the ability to express their thoughts abstractly in speech, writing, and music, as well as develop other complicated systems of expression and communication. This is why humans stand above all other types of creatures.

The claimed small genetic differences between human and chimp DNA (1 to 2%) must account for these and many other major differences! The difference between humans and chimpanzees is major and includes about 350 million different DNA bases. In fact, it is hard to compare the two genomes because of radical differences in arrangement.

Telomeres in Chimps and other apes are about 23 kilobases (a kilobase is 1,000 base pairs of DNA) long. Humans stand out from primates with much shorter telomeres only 10 kilobases long.[144] The human Y chromosome almost completely misaligns with chimpanzees.[145] Even if human and chimpanzee DNA sequences are as similar as some evolutionists claim, the DNA coding makes two entirely different creatures!

The chromosome fusion theory claims that two smaller chimpanzee chromosomes fused to form human chromosome 2. Geneticists have refuted the claim. Sadly, this false claim has been used as proof of human evolution, even in textbooks.

Research by Dr. David A. DeWitt has revealed new stunning insights regarding the major differences between human and chimp DNA: There exist 40–45 million bases [DNA "letters"] in humans missing from chimps and about the same number present in chimps that are absent from man. These extra DNA nucleotides are termed "insertions" and "deletions" because they are assumed to have been added or lost from the original common ancestor sequence. These differences alone put the total number of DNA differences at about 125 million. However, since the insertions can be more than one nucleotide long, about 40 million total separate mutation events would be required to separate the two species. To put this number into perspective, a typical 8½ x 11-inch page of text has about 4,000 letters and spaces. It would require 10,000 such pages of text equaling 40 million letters or 20 full-sized novels.

The difference between humans and chimpanzees includes about 45 million human base pairs that chimps don't have and about 45 million base pairs in the chimp absent from the human.[146] More research has left no doubt that a specific set of genetic programming exists for humans and another specific set exists for chimps. If chimps run on Microsoft, then humans run on Apple software. Both use binary code, and they have overlapping functions, but each has unique features.

Biology textbooks typically explain that humans descended from some common ancestor related to the great apes. This animal group consists of orangutans, gorillas, and chimpanzees. Of these apes, evolutionists claim that humans are most closely related to chimpanzees based on comparisons of human DNA to chimp DNA. The real-world consequences of this ideology involve concluding that humans are not special creations, but that they are evolved animals.

Reality of DNA and Genome Similarity

Let's review some basics to get a more accurate picture of genomes. Human, plant, and animal DNA is packaged into separate packages called chromosomes. Each one contains millions of the four different DNA bases (T, A, C, G), stacked like rungs on a ladder. Their specific order forms a complex set of instructions called the "genetic code." Humans have two copies of each chromosome: one set of 23 from the mother and one set of 23 from the father. Each chromosome set contains over 3 billion base pairs. The information they encode builds whole organisms from single egg cells and maintains each creature throughout its life. Our 46 chromosomes have a total of 6 billion DNA bases. Nearly every cell in our body has all of them. When scientists talk about a creature's genome, they refer to one set of chromosomes. Thus, the reference genome in humans is the sum total of one complete set of 23 chromosomes.

The "initial draft" of DNA sequences in the human genome was published in 2001. In 2004, scientists published a more complete version, but there were still small parts that remained to be sequenced, so researchers kept updating the human genome as DNA sequencing technologies improved and more data were acquired. The human genome is now one of the most complete of all known genome sequences–mostly because considerably more research money has been spent on it compared to other life forms.

To organize 3 billion bases, researchers use unique DNA sequences as reference markers. Then they determine where these short sequences are located on each chromosome. They assumed that comparing sequences between related creatures would help locate them. Scientists initially chose chimpanzees as the closest creature to humans because they knew that their proteins and DNA fragments had similar biochemical properties.[147] However, some curious researchers chose gorillas and orangutans for comparison. A recent research paper made the claim that orangutans' DNAs were more similar to humans' DNA in structure and appearance than chimpanzee, and thus orangutans should be considered our closest ancestor. Evolutionary scientists disregard this to maintain a consensus that chimpanzees are closest to humans on the hypothetical evolutionary tree. For this reason, most genetics studies assume this relationship before they even begin analyzing DNA.

In the early days of DNA sequencing, in the 1970s, scientists could sequence only very short segments of DNA. For this reason, they focused on DNA segments that they knew would be highly similar between animals, such as blood globin proteins and mitochondrial DNA (DNA which is inherited from the mother). They selected similar regions for comparison, because you cannot glean any meaningful comparisons between two DNA sequences that exist only in one and not the other. Researchers discovered that many of the short stretches of DNA genetic sequences that code for common proteins were not only highly similar in many types of animals, but that they were nearly identical between certain creatures including humans and apes.[148]

A basic understanding of what DNA sequencing actually entails helps us understand human and chimp genome accuracy. While the basic DNA sequencing techniques have not changed much since they were developed, the use of small-scale robotics and automation now enable researchers to sequence massive amounts of small DNA fragments. The DNA of an entire organism is too long to sequence all at once, thus they sequence millions of pieces, each hundreds of bases long. Workers then use computers to digitally assemble the small individual pieces into larger fragments based on overlapping sections.[149] DNA regions that have hundreds of repeating sequences are, for this reason, very difficult to reconstruct, yet we now know that they are important for cell function.

Enter New Technology

Despite the early, crude indications of apparently high DNA similarity between humans and chimps, precise DNA sequences began to present a very different picture. In 2002, a DNA sequencing lab produced over 3 million bases of chimp DNA sequence in small 50 to 900 base fragments that it obtained randomly across the entire chimp genome.[150] They then assembled the short sequences—get this—onto the human genomic framework.[151] Talk about circular reasoning. This turned out to be only one of many problems. When the chimp DNA sequences were matched with the human genome by computers, only two-thirds of the DNA sequences could be lined up with human DNA. While many short stretches of DNA existed that were very similar to human DNA, more than 30% of the chimp DNA sequence was not even close enough to attempt an alignment.

In 2005, a collaboration of different labs completed the first rough draft of the chimpanzee genome.[152] As a rough draft, even after the computational assembly based on the human genome, it still consisted of thousands of small chunks of DNA sequences. The researchers then assembled all the small sequences of chimp DNA together to estimate the complete genome. By assuming that humans evolved from a chimp-like ancestor, they used the human genome as the framework to assemble the chimp DNA sequences.[153] At least one lab that helped to assemble the chimp sequence admitted that they inserted chimp DNA sequences into the human genome layout based on evolution. They assumed that many human-like sequences were missing from the chimp DNA, so they added them electronically. That published chimp genome is thus partly based on the human genome. Because it contains human sequences, it appears more human than the chimp genome in fact is. The newest chimp genome, published in 2018, did not use human digital scaffolds and confirms a 15% dissimilarity between humans and chimps. How long will it take this correction to reach museums and textbooks that need bad science to prop up human evolution?

A large 2013 research project sequenced the genomes of chimpanzees, gorillas, and orangutans to determine their genetic variation. They again assembled all these genomes using the human genome as a framework![154]

Unfortunately, the research paper describing the 2005 chimp draft genome avoided the problem of overall average genome similarity with humans by analyzing the regions of the genomes that were already known to be highly similar. This cherry-picking deceptively reinforced the mythical 98% similarity notion. However, enough data were in the 2005 report to allow several independent researchers to calculate overall human-chimp genome similarities. They came up with estimates of 70 to 80% DNA sequence similarity.[155]

This result is important because evolutionary theory has a difficult enough time explaining how only 2% of 3 billion bases could have evolved in the 3–6 million years since they believe chimps and humans shared a common ancestor. They want to avoid the task of explaining how 15 or 20% of three billion bases evolved in such a short time! Natural processes cannot create 369 million letters of precisely coded information in a billion years, let alone a few million years.[156] Instead, as shown in the above section on genetics, more time produces more mutations, which lead to more extinctions.

Thus, the ever so popular high levels of human-chimp DNA similarity rely on highly similar, selected regions and exclude vastly different regions of these separately created genomes. Cherry-picking of data is bad science. Other published research studies completed between 2002 and 2006 compared certain isolated regions of the chimp genome to human DNA. These also seemed to add support to the evolutionary paradigm, but reinserted dissimilar DNA sequence data where it could be determined that evolutionists had omitted it from their analyses. This significantly changed the results, which showed that the actual DNA similarities for the analyzed regions varied between about 66% to 86%.[157] Again, this showed at least a 14% difference—not the fake 1%.

One of the main problems with comparing DNA segments between different organisms that contain regions of strong dissimilarity is that the computer program commonly used (called BLASTN) stops matching DNA when it hits regions that are markedly different. These unmatched sections consequently are not included in the final results, raising significantly the overall similarity between human and chimp DNA. In other words, the human-coded software automatically cherry picks the data. The computer settings can be changed to reject DNA sequences that are not similar enough for the research needs. The common default setting used by most evolutionary researchers kicks out anything less than 95% to 98% in similarity. In 2011, Dr. Tompkins compared 40,000 chimp DNA sequences (after removing them from the human-genome scaffold bias) that were about 740 bases long and already known to be highly similar to human.[158] The longest matches showed a DNA similarity of only 86%. A secular report independently found the same level of dissimilarity, again nailing the coffin on top of the false 98% claims.[159]

If chimp DNA is so dissimilar to human, and the computer software stops matching after only a few hundred bases, how can we find the actual similarity of the human and chimp genomes? A 2013 study resolved this problem by digitally slicing up chimp DNA into the small fragments that the software's algorithm could optimally match.[160] Using a powerful computer dedicated to this massive computation, all 24 chimp chromosomes were compared to humans' 23 chromosomes. The results showed that, depending on the chromosome, the chimp chromosomes were between 43% and 78% similar to humans. Overall, the chimp genome was only about 70%[161] similar to human. These data confirmed results published in secular evolutionary journals, but not popularized by the media or evolutionists.

Although textbooks still contain the 98% DNA similarity claim, many scientists in the human-chimp research community now recognize the 96% to 98% similarity was derived from isolated areas and biased assemblies. However, while the 98% similarity is crumbling, geneticists rarely make public statements about overall estimates because they know it would debunk human evolution. Although the human and chimpanzee genomes overall are only about 84.4% similar, some regions have high similarity, mostly due to protein-coding genes. Even these high similarity areas actually have only about 86% of matching sequences overall when the algorithm used to analyze them is set to produce a very long sequence match.[162]

The regions of high similarity can be explained by the fact that common genetic code elements are often found between different organisms because they code for genes that produce proteins with similar functions. For the same reason that different kinds of craftworkers all use hammers to drive or pry nails, different kinds of creatures use many of the same biochemical tools to perform common cellular functions. The genome is a very complex system of genetic codes, many of which are repeated in organisms with similar functions. This concept is easier to explain to computer programmers and engineers than biologists who are steeped in the evolutionary worldview.

102

Gene Similarities—the Big Picture

If two different kinds of creatures have the same basic gene sequence, they usually share only a certain part of that sequence. The entire gene could be only 88% similar, while a small part of it may be 98% similar. Protein-coding gene regions called "exons" in humans are on average only about 86% to 87% similar to chimps. Often, a matching chimp gene completely misses the exon sequences inside the human version of that gene.

The original definition of a gene describes it as a DNA section that produces a messenger RNA which in turn codes for a protein. Early estimates projected that humans contained about 22,000 of these protein-coding genes, and the most recent estimates suggest 28,000 to 30,000.[163] We now know that each of these protein-coding genes can produce many different individual messenger RNA variants due to gene regulation strategies. Cellular machinery cuts and splices gene sections to generate sometimes dozens of useful products from just one of those 28,000 or so traditional genes. Consequently, over a million RNA varieties can be made from 30,000 or fewer genes! Nevertheless, less than 5% of the human genome contains actual "exon" protein-coding sequences.

Humans have a high level of DNA/gene similarity with creatures other than chimps

The human body has many molecular similarities with other living things. After all, they all use the same basic molecules. They share the same water, oxygen, and food sources. Their metabolism and therefore their genetic makeup resemble one another in order to occupy the same world. However, these similarities do not mean they evolved from a common ancestor any more than all buildings constructed using brick, iron, cement, glass, etc. means that they share origins.

DNA contains much of the information necessary for an organism to develop. If two organisms look similar, we would expect DNA similarity between them. The DNA of a cow and a whale should be more alike than the DNA of a cow and a bacterium. Likewise, humans and apes have many body similarities like bones, hair, and the ability to produce milk, so we would expect DNA sequences to match that. Of all known animals, the great apes are most like humans, so we would expect that their DNA would be most like human DNA.[164]

This is not always the case, though. Some comparisons between human DNA/genes and other animals in the literature including cats have 90% of homologous genes with humans, dogs 82%, cows 80%,[165] chimpanzees 79%, rats 69%, and mice 67%.[166] Other comparisons found include fruit fly (Drosophila) with about 60%[167] and chickens with about 60% of genes corresponding to a similar human gene.[168] These estimates suffer from the same problems that humans-chimp comparisons do, but they illustrate the patterns of similarity that one would expect from a single divine designer.

The Myth of "Junk" DNA

The 30,000 or so genes of the human genome occupy less than 5% of the 3 billion total base pairs in the human genome. When researchers first made this estimate in the early 1990's, nobody knew what the other 95% of the genome did. Because evolution theorists needed raw genetic material for nature to tinker with over millions of years, they decided that it had no function. They labeled it "junk DNA." Oh, how wrong they were. After junk DNA became entrenched in textbooks, scientists began testing the 95% to see if cells use it for something other than protein codes. Beginning at around 2005, research from different labs all over the world has documented that cells transcribe and use over 90% of the entire human genome. The DNA codes for a dizzying array of RNA molecules. It performs many important jobs in the cell.[169] This phenomenon, called "pervasive transcription," was discovered in an offshoot of the human genome project called ENCODE, which stands for ENCyclopedia of DNA Elements.[170]

They discovered that most DNAs regulate the timing and amount of proteins produced. Imagine that the smart phone industry has no clue how many consumers want to buy smart phones. It could turn the world's petroleum into phones, leaving none to make dash board, refrigerators, or medicines. Chaos would reign. Or it could make only 10 phones a year. That would derail commerce worldwide. Chaos either way. Regulating the number, rate, and placement of bricks is even more important than just having bricks. In a similar way, every cell must regulate its proteins to avoid chaos. No wonder junk DNA advocates grow quiet.

While refuting "junk" DNA, the ENCODE project has also redefined our concept of a gene. At the time of this writing, experts estimate that non-protein-coding RNA genes called *long noncoding RNAs* or "lncRNAs" outnumber protein coding genes at least 2 to 1.[171] They have similar DNA structures and control features as protein-coding genes, but instead they produce useful RNA molecules.

Some RNAs remain in the cell nucleus with the DNA to regulate newborn RNA sequences. Other RNAs exit the nucleus to help regulate with the quality and speed of production, or the final shape and placement of other RNAs or proteins. The cell exports special RNAs called *lncRNAs* outside of the cell. It stands for "Long, Non-Coding RNA's." Whoever named them didn't bother to actually check whether or not they coded for any useful product. Later research found that lncRNAs communicate with other cells. But now we are stuck with the evolution-friendly name. Many of these lncRNA genes play important roles in a process called epigenetics. This records information on top of DNA, telling up to around six generations to keep certain gene regions closed.

Many evolutionary studies compared only highly similar protein-coding regions, the lncRNA regions are only about 67 to 76% similar—about 10 to 20% less identical than the protein-coding regions. Chimp and human lncRNAs are very different from each other, but they are critical to each life form.

Possibly the *entire genome* is a storehouse of important information. Using the construction project analogy, the protein-coding genes are like building blocks, and the noncoding regions regulate and determine how and where the building blocks get used. This is why the protein-coding regions tend to show more similarities between organisms and the noncoding regions show fewer similarities. Protein-coding regions specify skin, hair, hearts, and brains, but "noncoding" regions actually do code information that helps organize these components into useful arrangements. Given their millions of DNA differences, no wonder humans and chimps look and act so different!

Chromosome Fusion Debunked

One key argument that evolutionists use to support the human-chimp story is the supposed fusion of two ape-like chromosomes to form human chromosome number two. The great apes actually contain two more (diploid) chromosomes than humans. Humans have 46 and apes have 48. Portions of two small ape chromosomes look somewhat similar to human chromosome 2 when observed under a microscope after special staining. Evolutionists argue that they look so similar because they descended from one ancestral population with 2 chromosomes. At some point, those two supposedly joined into one chromosome and evolved into humans while another segment kept the 2 chromosome and evolved into chimps.[172] How do they know this happened? Does evidence inside human chromosomes fail to fit this story?

Taking their cues from evolutionary assumptions, secular researchers called these two chimp chromosomes 2A and 2B. Gorillas and orangutans also have chromosomes numbered 2A and 2B.

In 1991, scientists found a short segment of DNA on human chromosome 2 that they claimed was evidence for fusion. It looked to them like a genetic scar left over from two chromosome ends that were supposedly stitched together, even though it was not what they should have expected based on the analysis of known fusions in living mammals.[173] The alleged fusion sequence consisted of what looked like a degraded head-to-head fusion of chromosome ends called "telomeres." Could the similarities between these two ape chromosomes and human chromosome 2 come from some cause other than common ancestry? What detailed features would we expect to see if these chromosomes fused to become one in humans?

Telomeres contain repeats of the DNA sequence TTAGGG over and over. Geneticists first found them on the ends of each chromosome, like protective caps. T represents the chemical Tyrosine; A, Adenine; and G, Guanine. The organization of these chemicals encodes information, just like letters of the alphabet. Telomeres on human chromosomes are typically 5,000 to 15,000 bases long. If these fused, then they should have 10,000 to 30,000 TTAGGG repeats at the fusion site, plus or minus some from many generations of mutations.[174] The alleged fusion site, however, has only about 800 bases. Plus, these bases look only 70% similar to the expected. Plus, telomeres are specifically designed to prevent chromosomal fusion, and this is why a telomere-telomere fusion never has been observed in nature!

This fusion idea has for many years been masquerading as proof of human evolution, but genetic research has completely refuted the story. Not only is the site some orders of magnitude smaller than expected, but it has *functional* DNA. Cells access the "site" daily for its important *RNA gene*.[175] In 2002, researchers sequenced over 614,000 DNA bases surrounding the supposed fusion site and found that it was in a gene-rich region. The fusion site lies inside what they originally labeled a *pseudogene*. These describe supposedly damaged remnants of formerly useful protein-coding genes.[176] They supposedly represent more genetic junk from a messy evolutionary past. However, continual discoveries of important cellular roles for "pseudogenes" keep surprising evolutionists, who expect junk but keep finding functional genetic design. Why do college biochemistry and high school biology textbooks fail to explain these new results or to admit that science has refuted the chromosome fusion model?

Even more clear evidence for creation is the finding that not one of the other genes within 614,000 bases surrounding the alleged fusion site exists in chimpanzees. Although many evolutionists, perhaps unaware of the recent research, still promote it, the facts fail to fit fusion. They instead reveal how sensible is the idea that God created human chromosome 2.

Beta-globin Pseudogene Debunked

Another story that evolutionists use to promote human-ape ancestry holds that humans and chimps shared the same genetic mistakes. This supposedly explains why both of them have the same supposedly broken genes, called pseudogenes. Their story sounds sensible at first. Our common ancestor had a gene that mutated. After its descendants diverged, the chimp and human family trees both retained those old mutations. After all, they argue, how else could two different but similar species have the same mutations in the same genes unless they evolved from the same ancestor?

If this story was true, then we were obviously not created in God's image. Fortunately, exciting new research shows why science supports Scripture's documentation of creation. As noted, cells actually use many so-called "pseudogenes." They produce important noncoding RNAs discussed previously.[177] This means that the shared DNA sequence "mistakes" were purposefully created DNA sequences all along. They simply perform the same task in the two different organisms. Thus, common function, not common ancestry, gives the reason for their similar (and quite useful) sequence.

The beta-globin pseudogene exemplifies this. It turns out, of course, that this gene serves a helpful function in cells. Too bad evolutionists failed to look for function before they declared it had no function. The beta-globin sequence fits right in the middle of a cluster of five other genes. The other five

108

genes help produce useful proteins. Evolutionists originally claimed that the beta-globin gene was broken because it did not produce a protein. Now multiple studies have shown that it produces lncRNAs (see above) and is the most genetically networked gene in the entire beta-globin gene cluster. This means the cell accesses it more often than the others.[178] The supposed pseudo (or "false") gene regulates the production rates of the other genes. Over 250 different types of human cells actively use the gene! Why do chimps and humans share this very similar sequence? Not because they both inherited it from a common ancestor, but because they both use it for very similar purposes, like lungs for breathing.

GULO Pseudogene Debunked

Another case of textbook evidence for human evolution is the GULO pseudogene. This actually looks like a broken gene. It looks like the real GULO gene, which codes for an enzyme to help make vitamin C, but it has differences. It seems like mutations have garbled its once-useful code. Evolutionists claim that humans, chimps, and other apes share GULO genes that mutated in the same places because the mutations occurred in an ancestor that all three supposedly share. However, broken GULO pseudogenes are also found in mice, rats, bats, birds, pigs, and famously, guinea pigs. Did we evolve from guinea pigs?

When researchers recently analyzed the GULO gene in its entirety, they found no pattern of common ancestry.[179] Instead, it looks like this gene is predisposed to being mutated no matter what creature has it. Since humans and other animals can get vitamin C from their diet, they can survive without the gene. Also, the other genes in the GULO biochemical pathway produce proteins that aid other important cellular processes. Losing those could spell disaster for the organism. So, many creatures and humans can tolerate a damaged GULO gene by consuming plenty of vegetables with vitamin C.

The GULO gene region and the mutations that likely damaged it link to a system that use transposable elements. These are commonly called "jumping genes," and they can cut themselves out of one location in the genome and splice themselves into another location. The many different types of transposable elements in the human genome serve very important tasks. Sometimes, though, they splice themselves into the wrong location and disrupt genes.

In the case of GULO, the transposable element patterns between humans and each of the ape kinds that were evaluated show differences. Therefore, GULO shows no pattern of common ancestry for humans and apes—negating this evolutionary argument. Like the claims of 99% similarity, chromosome fusion, and Beta-globin, evolutionists built the GULO argument based on belief in evolution plus an ignorance of biology.

In reality, the GULO pseudogene data defy evolution and vindicate creation. According to the Genesis account of the fall that caused the curse on creation, we would expect genes to mutate. This one did. No known creature avoids this process of genetic decay, called genetic entropy (see above section on genetics). Cornell University Geneticist John Sanford has shown in several studies that the human genome shows no signs of evolving or getting better. Instead it irreversibly crumbles.[180] Perhaps our early ancestors had a working GULO gene that could manufacture vitamin C. Today, low vitamin C in our diets causes an illness called scurvy.

The Human-Chimp Evolution Magic Act

Stage magicians, otherwise known as illusionists, practice their trade by getting you to focus on some aspect of the magician's act to divert your focus from what the other hand is doing. This way, they get you to believe something that isn't true—a fake reality. The human-chimp DNA similarity "research" works almost the same way.

The evolutionist who promotes the human-chimp fake paradigm of DNA similarity accomplishes the magic act by getting you to focus on a small set of data representing bits and pieces of hand-picked evidence. In this way, you don't see the mountains of hard data that utterly defy evolution. While some parts of the human and chimpanzee genomes are very similar— those that the evolutionists focus on—the genomes overall are vastly different, and the hard scientific evidence now proves it. The magic act isn't working any longer, and more and more open-minded scientists are beginning to realize it.

Confronting Human-Chimp Propaganda

To close this section, let's discuss a hypothetical exchange. How can you use the information in this section in conversation? First, the person makes the claim that "human and chimp DNA are genetically 98–99% identical or similar." When such a person does not wish to listen, starting with a question, not a counter, almost always helps. If you have memorized the genome lengths, you can ask, "Do you know roughly how many bases are in the chimp and human genomes?" If they do, great. If not, then offer the fact that the chimp genome has 3.3 billion, and the human genome 3.1 billion bases. Then ask, "Do you think the percent difference between these numbers is 1, 2, or more?" You can then calculate it together. Use $((3.1/3.3) - 1) \times 100$. Ignore the negative sign (take the absolute value). When you both see that it equals about a 6% difference, then just ask, "How can the two be only 1% different if their total lengths are already 6% different?"

At this point in the conversation, you will rapidly find out if the person is really interested in learning more about the issue of human origins, or if they are so zealous about evolutionary beliefs that they refuse to listen to challenging evidence. If at that point they begin making up an answer, rest assured that they have no desire to learn anything from you. If, on the other hand, their confidence in the 1% assertion fades, then you may have just earned the right to offer more information.

When the other person shows interest in what you might have to say, you could mention, "The 99% similarity only applies to the highly similar regions. It ignores the many differences in the already dissimilar regions." You can then clarify this response by noting that "2018 research has shown that, overall, the entire genome is no more than 85% similar on average when you include all the DNA that researchers decoupled from the human genome in 2018. This equal to 15 percent difference demands hundreds of millions of precise base pair changes in just 3–6 million years. Can you help me explain how mutations could accomplish that?"

You can also add, "Several thousand genes unique to humans are completely missing in chimps, and scientists have found many genes that are unique to chimps are missing in humans." Then ask, "How can evolutionary processes explain these massive differences?" Take care to ask open-ended and genuine questions. Avoid using "you." We don't want to accuse anybody, just lead them to convince themselves that their own ideas have problems. Another useful question asks, "How could only 1–2% DNA difference account for such major body differences between humans and chimps, like thousands of new genes, different hand, muscle and brain architecture, and the 40 facial muscles that humans use to communicate, compared with the dozen or so in chimp faces?"

In reality, the whole modern research field of genetics and genomics is the worst enemy of evolution. As new genomes of different kinds of organisms are being sequenced, they consistently show unique sets of DNA containing many genes and other sequences that specify that type of creature. Evolutionists call these new creature-specific genes "orphan genes" because they are not found in any other type of known creature.[181] Orphan genes appear suddenly in the pattern of life as unique sections of genetic code with no hint of evolutionary history. Of course, believers in an omnipotent Creator know that each different genome, such as that for humans and that of

112

chimpanzees, was separately, uniquely, and masterfully engineered at the beginning of creation. God created and embedded each creature's orphan genes to network with all the rest of that creature's genetic coding instructions. The scientific data overwhelmingly show that God deserves the credit and evolution deserves none.

Conclusion

With so much at stake, like the answer to life's largest question, "Where did I come from?" do we want to trust in extremely biased answers? Every high school student can refute 98% similarity dogma by tracking the main points above as outlined below.

1. Overall, the entire genome is only about 84.4% similar on average when you include all the DNA. This is equal to a 15% difference, or 360 million+ base pair differences. (Slight differences exist between using the 2004 assembly, which made the data look more human than the unbiased 2018 assembly). Either assembly reveals a genetic chasm between our supposed closest evolutionary relative.
2. The "Junk" DNA claim has long been refuted and most of it has been found to have clear functions which are regulatory in nature.
3. The Chromosome Fusion claim is false for four reasons. First, telomeres are designed not to fuse. Telomere to telomere fusion is unknown in the natural world. This makes the evolutionary assertion hard for them to defend. Second, telomeres contain repeats of the DNA sequence TTAGGG over and over for thousands of bases. Human telomeres are from 5,000 to 15,000 bases long. If these actually fused, then they should have over ten thousand TTAGGG bases, but the alleged fusion site actually has about 800 bases. Third, the "fusion site" sequence shares only 70% similarity to what

113

expectations would dictate. Last, the claimed fusion site contains a gene, proof that it is not a genetic scar at all.

4. The Beta-globin Pseudogene is not a pseudogene! Without this status, its use to argue for human-chimp common ancestry crumbles. It is actually a functional gene in the middle of a cluster of five other genes.

5. The GULO Pseudogene does not show common decent, but simply shows an area of both genomes that is prone to mutate.

Human Fossils: Why Don't We Find Humans Buried with Dinosaurs?

Our ministry receives this question frequently, but few seem to see that inherent assumption upon which the question is based: the *assumption that we should in fact find human fossils with dinosaur fossils because they were living in proximity at the time of the Flood.* Once that's exposed, possible answers become clearer. Science writer Brian Thomas explains:

> Many assume that dinosaur layers should also contain human fossils. Not at all. Dinosaur fossil layers contain sea, swamp, and lake plants and animals, and mostly water birds. They have virtually no remains of land-dwellers like dogs, deer, bears, or bunnies. Humans live on solid ground, not in swamps [wetlands]—and definitely not in pre-Flood swamps where dinosaurs might treat them as light snacks. The best places to look for fossils of pre-Flood humans would be in deposits that contain land-dwellers like pre-Flood dogs and deer.[182]

As a case in point, one of the largest mass dinosaur bonebeds in the world is at Dinosaur Provincial Park in Canada. This massive Flood deposit has 49 different species of dinosaurs buried along with turtles, crocodiles, fish, flying reptiles, birds, and small mammals.[183] This is not exactly a place where humans would want to live—not then; not today. Four other important factors help answer this question:

1. While we don't know the pre-flood human population, most researchers would say that it was much smaller than the 7+ billion people on earth today. Also consider that humans had also not likely spread outside of the area that it currently called Mesopotamia yet.

2. Consider God's promise to wipe humans off the face of the earth: "I will destroy man whom I have created from the face of the earth, both man and beast, creeping thing and birds of the air…" (Genesis 6:7). The Flood mechanisms that He used (see **Noah's Flood: Catastrophic Plate Tectonics**) were the best possible way to scrub humans from existence. Rapidly spreading sea floor sunk beneath the continents. This produced cycles of tsunamis that catastrophically wiped out vast populations of life. This caused, for example, the Morrison Formation, filled with dead dinosaurs mixed with marine life, to cover a 13-state region in the middle of the U.S. This process resulted in an average sediment thickness of about one mile around the globe and 75% of earth being covered with sedimentary layers.

3. When looking at the fossil record as a whole, humans (and even apes) are extremely rare. In fact, the entire primate order represents a mere **0.3%** of the fossil occurrences in the currently known fossil population on record.[184] This is because about 95% of all fossils are marine invertebrates, mostly shellfish like clams. Of the remaining 5%, 95% are algae and plant fossils (5% x 95% or 4.75% of the total) and 5% (5% X 5%, or 0.25% of the total) are insects and other non-marine invertebrates and vertebrates. Of the remaining 0.25% of the total, 95% are insects and other non-marine invertebrates and only 5% (5% x 0.25%, or 1.25% of the

total) are vertebrate fossils (mostly fish, and finally, amphibians, reptiles, birds, and mammals).[185]

4. Fossilization requires quick and complete burial. During the onset of the Flood, humans may have tried to save themselves any way possible. It is probable that during the months of rising Flood waters, humans moved to higher ground. Then, as the humans and other animals died, many might have been washed away at the end of the Flood when the mountains rose and the waters rushed off of the earth (Psalm 104:8).[186] Geologist Dr. Tim Clarey's new research on continent-wide rock layers (based on drill core and seismic data) reveals that many Cenozoic deposits lie offshore since Flood waters washed off of continents and into today's oceans.[187] If many of the fossils are in layers trapped beneath the sea, they would of course be difficult to find.

Human Hearing System

> **Suggested Video:**
>
> The Amazing Hearing System
> https://youtu.be/3Lsegdfj2TE

Evolution is supposed to be a mindless, random process that takes place over millions of years. If this is the case, how did the human hearing system arise, with its five separate components that *don't function without the others*? Five separate parts to our hearing system all work in unison to enable us to hear, and *none* of the five make *any* sense by themselves. What good is an outer ear (engineered for capturing sound waves) if there's not an ear drum to capture the sound wave pulses? What good is a pulsing ear drum without the three tiny bones behind it that use leverage to amplify the sound signal by a factor of 1.7 and connect to a water-charged cochlea filled with fluid? The cochlea converts the mechanical leverage to a hydraulic system that amplifies the signal another 22 times. And what good is all of this without the 20,000 tiny hair cells (stereocilia) inside the cochlea that convert the fluid movement into an electrochemical signal that we can immediately comprehend as speech?

Creationists see this as an intentional design by a Divine Creator. Evolutionists see this as the result of time + chance + mutations + natural selection. Which explanation makes more sense? What creature would have devoted its genes and energies to crafting non-functional ear parts for generations while it waited for the fifth precision part to spontaneously appear?

Ice Age

There was a single Ice Age after the Flood. Hot oceans formed after the Genesis 7:11 "fountains of the great deep" burst open. Sea surface evaporation lifted water high. It cooled and fell as snow or rain. Volcanoes were much more active during and after the Flood. They added aerosols that blocked sunlight. This cooled the summers enough that winter's ice did not melt. Evolutionists who disdain the Flood deny that a worldwide catastrophe could have heated the oceans that much. They insert thousands of imaginary years between volcanic eruptions. No wonder they can't explain an ice age. The Flood created optimal conditions for the Ice Age to happen. It lasted for several hundred years. See the **Ice Cores** section for more detail.

Ice Cores

Suggested Videos:

Are Ice Cores Evidence for an Old Earth?
https://youtu.be/vYZ-RWbYUqs

Greenland is covered by ice sheets that span more than 700,000 square miles with an average depth of 5,300 feet. The deepest known section is estimated at around 11,300 feet.[188] Since the 1960s, scientists have drilled and extracted cylindrical cores from the ice sheets (called ice cores) from depths of over 10,000 feet.

According to some scientists, the age of these ice sheets can be estimated by counting the number of what they call "annual layers" in the cores. In the GISP2 Ice Core, which was taken from the Greenland ice sheet, scientists counted 110,000 layers. They insist 110,000 years must have made them. Is the dating process really that straightforward? Not at all. For example, they forget that one storm can deposit several layers. As we have seen with the fossil record, geologic rock layers, and other remnants from the past, the worldview and assumptions of the scientists analyzing the data play a big role in their conclusions. Let's take a closer look.

In the upper latitudes, snow accumulates on top of the ice sheet and eventually turns into ice. The weight of the top layer exerts pressure on the layers below and causes them to spread out and become thinner (Figure 19).

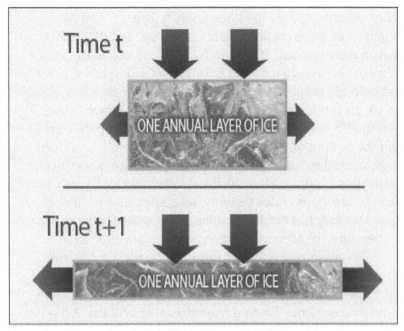

Figure 19: The weight of the top layers of ice exerts pressure on the layers below and causes them to spread and thin.[189]

Consequently, the layers near the bottom of the ice sheet are much thinner than the layers near the top. Some of the bottom layers are one millimeter thin.[190] There are too many layers to count and they are too thin to identify consistently. They therefore use flow models to estimate time for ice thicknesses. Guess what variable their models include: deep time. No wonder they think the ice is so old—they assumed it in the first place. Scientists have to use a variety of techniques (i.e. lasers, isotope readings, etc.) to identify the layers. Do they represent annual layers or something else? Secular scientists believe the "present is the key to the past" (uniformitarianism) and assume millions of years. Scientists who believe the Bible's timeline need to explain these many thin layers. The Flood explains it well, although indirectly. Here's how.

Warm ocean temperatures and volcanic activity following the Global Flood caused the Ice Age (see **Ice Age**).

When describing the Flood, the Bible tells us: "…all the fountains of the great deep were broken up, and the windows of heaven were opened" (Genesis 7:11). Many creation scientists believe this passage refers to tremendous earthquakes, tsunamis and volcanic eruptions and flooding occurring on a global scale. Ice sheets formed rapidly during the Ice Age, which lasted around 700 years.[191] Therefore, many of the compressed rings near the bottom of the ice sheets may not actually be annual rings, but rather formed during the frequent and powerful snow storms that occurred after the flood. Michael Oard's post flood Ice Age theory provides the only adequate cause for the Ice Age. This task has baffled secular scientists for half a century. Bottom line, the layers do not represent years after all.

Want more evidence? Fortunately, it exists! During World War II (July 1942), two B-17 bombers and six P-38 fighters encountered a severe snowstorm and were forced to make an emergency landing in southeast Greenland. All pilots were rescued, but the planes were abandoned, left to be covered by ice over the ensuing years.[192] In August 1992, a privately-funded team went back to recover one of the planes—thinking it would be easy to do so given uniformitarian assumptions of the slow, gradual accumulation of ice layers. They were surprised to find the planes covered with more than 260 feet of ice. It had accumulated in just fifty years.[193] The team recovered one of the P-38s and named it "Glacier Girl."

The fact that over 260 feet of ice had accumulated in just fifty years demonstrated that ice sheets can accumulate very quickly. At that rate of accumulation, it is reasonable to expect that Greenland's three-kilometer-thick ice sheet can form in much less than the ~4,400 years since the Flood.[194]

Kangaroos: How Did They Make It All the Way to Australia from Where the Ark Landed?

Surprisingly, one of the most frequently asked questions from skeptics goes something like this: "If the Ark landed on the Mountains of Ararat, how did kangaroos make it all the way to Australia (an island without present land bridges), a distance of about 7,000 miles?" Sometimes "without leaving any fossils" will be added to the question as an apparent "zinger." While many skeptics believe this is the "unanswerable" question for biblical creationists, the answer highlights evidence that supports biblical creation (the Babel dispersion and the Ice Age that followed the Flood).

To get the kangaroos—and humans for that matter—from where the Ark landed (the mountains of Ararat, Genesis 8:4) to Australia (a present island), two things need to happen: (1) they need to travel over 7,000 miles, and (2) they need to cross an area that is *currently* under water. Answering the first part is easy. Kangaroos are made for traveling long distances. Kangaroos can travel about 15 miles-per-hour over long distances.[195] Assuming they traveled at only one-half of this pace (7–8 miles-per-hour) and only traveled for 8–10 hours per day, they could migrate from the Middle East to Australia in just four months. However, given the unknown terrain and because it's unlikely they traveled straight to Australia after exiting the Ark, it probably took them several years and multiple generations (same with humans after Babel).

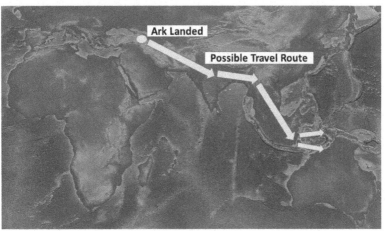

Figure 20. Map showing Lowered Sea Levels During the Ice Age and Possible Travel Route for Kangaroos.[196]

Next there's the challenge of crossing the southern-most part of what's currently Indonesia (Sunda) to Northern Australia (Sahul) (see Figure 21). Two possible answers explain this, and the second may have more legs than the first. The first possibility is that the lower sea levels during the Ice Age (Glacial Maximum) exposed a land bridge all the way from the southern parts of Indonesia to Northern Australia. With the present location of the land masses, this is unlikely because lower sea levels alone would still leave some sections uncrossable. Even though the sea levels during the Glacial Maximum were 100+ meters lower than current levels (with some estimates even much lower[197]), some deeper channel areas would have prevented crossing on dry land.

Looking at Figure 21, New Guinea, Australia, and Tasmania were in fact connected during the Ice Age (as a giant island known as Sahul).[198] However, Sahul was probably not completely connected to the Sunda region of Southeastern Asia. After all, the two regions also have different fauna and flora.[199] While much of the now submerged area between Sunda and Sahul would have been exposed and walkable during the Ice Age, sections that are separated by water channels are *currently* deeper than the lowest sea levels during the Glacial Maximum (see Figure 20 and 21).

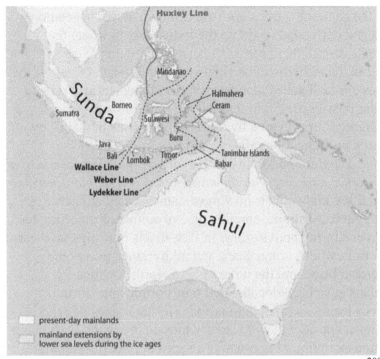

Figure 21. Australia and Indonesia During the Ice Age.[200]

This leaves three viable possibilities for kangaroos getting to Australia. The first possibility is that Sunda and Sahul were *closer together* during the Glacial Maximum stage of the Ice Age when the sea levels were lower. The challenge with this theory is, while some continental spreading after the Flood is likely (e.g., Australia has shifted about five feet since 1994[201]), moving these land masses close enough to create a land bridge when animals were living on both land masses is not likely, given the amount of energy involved in moving landmasses.[202] However, it is still possible that there could have been shifts in the ocean floor's elevations between the Indonesian islands and Australia due to earth movements, so the land bridge connection could have been more complete than otherwise portrayed.

The second possibility is that they floated across the Indian Ocean from Africa on a vegetation raft. In other words, they first migrated down to Africa, then when a river basin flooded some kangaroos got stranded on massive vegetation mats and got washed out into the Indian Ocean where the currents carried them across to Australia. There are currents that move in the right direction right across the Indian Ocean. If this seems too far-fetched, consider that evolutionists also rely on similar possibilities[203] for explaining how animals got to Madagascar from Africa by the same mechanism, that is, by floating on vegetation rafts.[204]

The third possibility is that *humans took kangaroos (and likely other animals) with them when they traveled to Australia by sea*. We know this is how most domesticated animals (e.g., dogs) got to Australia, and this type of animal introduction has happened throughout history. In fact, this is how pigs, soybeans, kiwi fruit, wheat, honey bees, and all livestock except the American bison and the turkey got to North America.[205] Humans have been documented transporting animals into various locations (including islands) for thousands of years. For example, consider the 4th Century mosaic in Figure 22 showing the transportation of non-native species in Italy (for hunting purposes).

Figure 22. Villa Romana del Casale: Big Game Hunt Mosaic (Rhino) (Italy, early 4th century AD).[206]

Secular scientists do not agree about *how* or *when* humans traveled to Australia. While the "by sea" theory has become widely supported in the secular literature,[207] this theory contradicts the secular worldview because scientists are troubled by the fact that Aborigines traveled so far by sea before such seafaring technology "developed." The *National Geographic's* Genographic Project[208] states, "About 50,000 years ago, a small band of humans landed in northern Australia, arriving on a primitive boat or raft. It is likely that the journey was planned because enough men and women arrived to found a new population there." They continue, "Another mystery is what kind of water vessels early humans used to reach Australia. None of the boats used by Aboriginal people in ancient times are suitable for major voyages, and some have suggested early humans reached the continent on rafts made of bamboo, a material common in Asia." From a Biblical perspective, however, people were "smart from the start." They had the same aptitudes for building seafaring vessels that Noah had. Of course, the cumulative technology for ship-building advances faster with non-nomadic people groups. Ironically, there is growing academic support for the validity of the oral history of the Aborigines regarding traveling across land bridges that are now currently covered with water.[209]

Lastly, let's address the alleged challenge of the absence of a "kangaroo fossil trail" from where the Ark landed to Australia. This is not a legitimate challenge for two reasons. First, consider the conditions necessary for fossilization. Fossilization needs rapid burial and lots of sediment like Noah's Flood provided. These mechanisms were not likely widespread areas across Indonesia after the Flood.[210] Consider that there used to be lions in Israel (based on historical records) and millions of bison in America. Where are all the fossils? There certainly aren't many!

Languages from Babel

After the Flood, God commanded humanity to "increase in number and fill the earth" (Genesis 9:1). Out of rebellion, we did the exact opposite: "Then they said, 'Come, let us build ourselves a city, with a tower that reaches to the heavens, so that we may make a name for ourselves and not be scattered over the face of the whole earth'" (Genesis 11:4). Rather than dispersing and multiplying as God asked, we congregated and started building a gigantic tower as a symbol of our power, known as the Tower of Babel.

God's response to this disobedience was to confuse our language and disperse humans around the globe. This resulted in the groups who shared the same (new) language to band together during the dispersal as we moved and settled in various parts of the world (Genesis 11:8–9). Genesis 10:5, 20 and 31 describes Noah's descendants spreading out over the earth "by their clans and languages, in their territories and nations." This dispersal included between 70 and 100 families that came out of Babel with new languages because Genesis 10 gives a listing of most of these families.[211]

How does this tally when considering all the languages we have today? Quite well. Today there are 7,097 languages and 136 language families. While 7,097 may seem like a high number (given the initial start of 70–100), 80% of the people in the entire world speak just 93 languages, with the remaining 20% speaking the other 7,004. In other words, 1.3% of the known languages in the world are spoken by 80% of the people in the world![212]

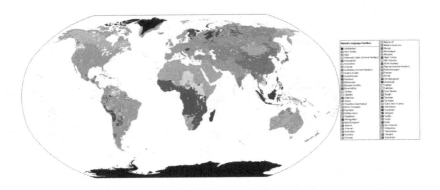

Figure 23. Distribution of Human Language Families.[213]

For more about this topic, we recommend Bill Cooper's book, *After the Flood: The Early Post-flood History of Europe Traced Back to Noah*.[214] This book does an exceptional job of tracing back modern languages to their roots at Babel and is free online at Lambert Dolphin's personal website. The Institute for Creation Research (ICR) also provides several informative articles on this topic.[215]

Leviathan

Job chapter 41 provides the longest description of any animal in the Bible—but Leviathan was not just any creature. It was a ferocious (Job 41:8–10), fiercely-toothed (Job 41:14), scale-armored (Job 41:15–17), immensely powerful (Job 41: 26–29), semi-aquatic (Job 41:30–33), fire-breathing (Job 41: 19–21) creature than invoked fear into anyone who saw it!

The description in Job 41 rules out a mythical creature. The passage describes where Leviathan lived (in the sea but sometimes on shore). It had armor scaling that was so tightly-knit that no air could pass between (capable of deflecting spears). It left luminescent wakes and had a mouth that was ringed with terrorizing teeth. We know from Psalm 104 that Leviathan "played around in ancient shipping lanes." Few doubt the reality of the horse, ostrich, eagle, goat, and other animals that God described for Job along with Leviathan. The Bible places Leviathan in a realistic context.

But wait a minute—Leviathan *breathed fire*? This single characteristic is enough for most people to move Leviathan from the "real" to "mythical" category—but not so fast. Brian Thomas (science writer with ICR) points out:

> These historical hints from the Bible refute the idea that Leviathan was a mythical creature that was being used as a literary metaphor. Metaphors don't deflect spears or scare the daylights out of onlookers. In fact, Leviathan must have really done these things for God to meaningfully compare it to His own might. Identifying Leviathan as a myth smuggles in the destructive idea that anything in Scripture could be interpreted as a myth. But since the Bible has proven itself true over centuries of scrutiny, the Leviathan must have really lived."[216]

Thomas also point out that, "Some Bible translation notes and even conservative commentaries identify Leviathan as a crocodile. While crocodiles do match several of Leviathan's attributes, they fall short of disrupting shipping lanes, breathing fire, generating luminescent wakes, being utterly unapproachable, and having impenetrable hides."

Many simply refuse to believe that God actually created a fire-breathing sea creature called Leviathan. However, consider three animals that are alive today that are, quite frankly, just as amazing as a fire-breathing dragon.

First, consider bombardier beetles. These beetles have a pair of glands that each contains two chambers. At the beetle's demand, the chambers combine their contents to make a scalding hot spray. They control the 212°F, 22 mph jet with tiny nozzles.[217] The chambers and nozzles are "specially coated so they can withstand the toxic chemicals, high temperatures, and elevated pressures that characterize the beetle's explosive discharge."[218]

Figure 24. Bombardier Beetle

What about fireflies? Fireflies "produce light in a similar way to how a glowstick works. The light results from a chemical reaction, or chemiluminescence…In fireflies, the chemical reaction that causes them to glow depends on an enzyme called luciferase."[219]

Let's not forget electric eels, which can generate 600 volts of electricity in short, intense bursts. They come from thousands of muscle cells that each create a tiny current. Being blasted by 600 volts (which is quintuple the voltage contained within of a standard wall socket in the United States) is enough to paralyze alligators. If God can create animals that steam, glow, and zap, then He can make animals that breathe fire.

So just what exactly was Leviathan? While many extinct fossil candidates have been proposed over the years, *Sarcosuchus* or *Spinosaurus* known from fossils may fit. *Sarcosuchus* was a massive crocodile (36–39 ft) that may have weighed up to nine tons. *Spinosaurus* was a massive dinosaur with a sail-like fin on its back. Its length surpassed even the *Tyrannosaurus*. One possibility pointed out by Brian Thomas is a giant creature that was on display in ancient Rome.[220] He wrote:

In his book *The Authenticity of the Book of Jonah*, historian Bill Cooper relayed a passage from Pliny the Elder's *Natural History*: 'The bones of this monster, to which Andromeda was said to have been exposed, were brought by Marcus Scaurus from Joppa in Judaea during his aedileship and shown at Rome among the rest of the amazing items displayed. The monster was over 40 feet long, and the height of its ribs was greater than that of Indian elephants, while its spine was 1-1/2 feet thick.'

Marcus Scaurus transported and displayed the bones in Rome's largest theatre around 64 BC. Cooper also relates Pliny's note of a washed-up carcass with 120 teeth, each between 9 and 6 inches long, and Pausanius' mention of 'an enormous sea monster's skull which was kept at a sanctuary in Asklepios.'

Many other accounts, plus paintings and carvings, convey encounters with monstrous marine reptiles.

Lifespans Before the Flood: How Did People Live to Be 900 Years Old Before the Flood?

> *Suggested Video:*
>
> John Sanford on Genomic Entropy
> https://youtu.be/_edD5HOx6Q0

Dr. Jon Sanford of Cornell University became famous for inventing the "gene gun." Dr. Sanford has extensively studied the long lifespans (~912 years on average) of the patriarchs who lived before the Flood. It turns out their lifespan data follows a very biological *logarithmic curve*. It shows biological decay consistent with restricting the human population to just eight at the time of the Flood.

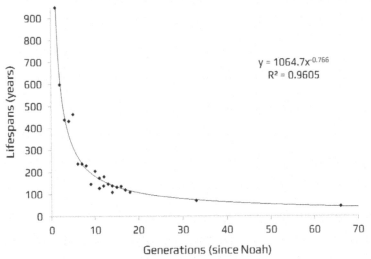

Figure 25. Lifespans of the Patriarchs Systematically Plummet after the Flood.[221]

Figure 25 shows that the lifespans of the patriarchs (listed in Genesis 5 and 10) *systematically* plummet after the Flood. The curve explains 96% of the data points! This would have been impossible for ancient writers to dream up—especially given that the authors and compilers of Genesis lived across *multiple lifespans.*

Either these dates are historically accurate (and explained by the science of mutation accumulation), or they were fabricated by multiple authors/compilers over several generations to accidentally but accurately mimic a biological trendline.[222] We recommend *www.geneticentropy.org* for further study.

Moses: Did He Really Produce the Torah (the first five books of the Bible)?

Professors in many colleges today assert that Moses did not produce the Torah, the first five books of the Bible. They allege that "Moses did not have the ability to write..." or, that "the Hebrew language doesn't date back far enough for the events recorded in the Bible." Let's find out why these claims couldn't be further from the truth.

To begin with, keep in mind that Jesus himself supported that Moses produced the Torah, stating in John 5, "For if you believed Moses, you would believe Me; for he wrote about Me. But if you do not believe his writings, how will you believe My words?" When praying to the Father in John 17, Jesus said this: "Sanctify them by Your truth. Your word is truth." Jesus had a high view of Scripture, and He clearly believed in the Mosaic authorship of the Torah.

New Testament authors mention Moses 80 times and always give him credit for producing the Torah. Paul even noted in Romans 3 that God committed His "oracles" and teachings to the Jewish people, and this came through Moses. But wait a minute—Moses wasn't *present* during the six days of creation recorded in the first chapter of Genesis—*no one was*, and Adam wasn't created until the *end* of creation week. Moses also didn't witness the Flood, or the events leading up to it. In fact, Moses didn't even show up until at least 700 years *after* the Flood. So just how did he write or compile the biblical history that came before him?

The answer is quite simple: they were transmitted orally or in writing, or both. Interestingly, the first set of writings referenced in the Bible is the "Book of the generations of Adam" in Genesis 5. This book is actually 1 of 11 *toledotes* (pronounced "Toll-Dotes") which means "histories" or "genealogies" that are included in the Book of Genesis, which is broken into 50 chapters in our Bibles today.

While we don't know for sure, it's likely that these 11 toledotes were memorized, compiled, or both by the generations that are relevant to them, and handed like historical batons between generations. For example, the toledote from Genesis 5:1 to 6:8 includes 13 people listed by name. The next one dealing with the Flood includes nine. The next toledote picks up in Chapter 10 and describes Noah's sons and grandchildren, with over 70 people listed by name. The events of the *toledot* for Terah, Ishmael, Isaac, Esau, and Jacob *even* occurred during the period for which we have evidence of Hebrew writing.

While we don't know for sure just how these histories were transmitted to Moses—whether by oral tradition, writing, or both—the Bible is clear and specific about the histories that pre-date Moses. It's hard to imagine how the birth, death, or lifespan years given for the 87 patriarchs in the first 11 chapters of Genesis were passed down through oral history alone. However, the ancients transmitted stories orally much more frequently than we do today, and they were often quite reliable when they did so. Also, remember that the Holy Spirit had no limitations for guiding Moses through the transmission process, as "men being borne along by the Holy Spirit spoke from God" (2 Peter 1:21).

Another major clue that the early chapters of Genesis were preserved and given to Moses is found in Genesis 2. This chapter describes river systems that encircled certain areas that were rich with precious minerals and gems. Moses was not around to see this landscape, as it was completely reworked by Noah's Flood which occurred long before his day. He knew about these things because they were passed down beforehand and given to him. So, if these accounts were preserved *through* the Flood and preserved *after* the Flood, it is conceivable that they were passed down from one generation to another by oral transmission or writing.

Liberal scholars today promote the "documentary hypothesis," which argues against the Mosaic authorship of the Torah and suggests instead that it was a compilation of four originally independent documents, abbreviated as the "J-E-P-D" sources. This idea originally was promoted by Julius Wellhausen in the 19th Century. Creation Ministries International provides a thorough rebuttal of this hypothesis, showing even how modern scholarship does not support it.[223]

Next we have the many instances in the Bible where Moses recorded the commands or words of God. For example, in Exodus 17:14, The Lord said to Moses, "Write this for a memorial in the book and recount it in the hearing of Joshua." Exodus 24:4 states that "Moses wrote all the words of the Lord," and verse 7 records that Moses "took the Book of the Covenant" and read it to the people. Deuteronomy 6 also indicates the Israelites were collectively using writing, being directed by God to write His commandments "on the doorposts of their houses and gates."

Then there are the 10 commandments, where God instructed Moses: "Come up to Me on the mountain and be there; and I will give you tablets of stone, and the law and commandments which I have written, that you may teach them." Exodus 32:15 even says that these "tablets were written on both sides."

So, it looks like God Himself was writing in a language that the Israelites would understand. Many Christians and Jews alike believe that this interchange occurred in ancient Hebrew. However, for one to compile a work like the Bible, the flexibility of an alphabet is necessary. While opinions vary, many secular scholars today hold that the Phoenicians developed the world's first alphabet around 1050 BC. How can this be when most biblical scholars hold the view that Moses wrote the Torah in the 15th Century BC?

In filmmaker Tim Mahoney's movie, "Patterns of Evidence: The Moses Controversy (2019)," he answers this question thoroughly. In this movie, Mahoney establishes Mosaic authorship by looking at evidence that answers four key questions: (1) Could Moses have written the Torah in a language by the time of the Exodus, (2) in the region of Egypt, (3) using the power of an alphabet, and (4) in a form of writing like Hebrew? This movie documents over two hours of

134

evidence that supports the Biblical case. We'll review some of the highlights here.

First, since at least the last third of the 19th century, we've known of alphabetic inscriptions that pre-date the alphabet-based writings from the Phoenicians that date to about 1,000 BC. Some of these discoveries were made in 1904 by Flinders Petrie, a man who has been called the father of Egyptian archaeology, in the turquoise mines that were controlled by the ancient Egyptians on the Sinai Peninsula. The inscriptions became known as "Proto-Sinaitic" and were dated to the middle of Egypt's 18th Dynasty, which equates to the 15th century BC.

A more recent discovery of two alphabetic inscriptions was made in 1999 at a place called Wadi el-Hol. These inscriptions, which use the same script as the ones from the turquoise mines, also are alphabetic letters that are based on 22 specific hieroglyphic signs from the Egyptian sign list, but they date back to 1834 BC.

An additional tablet, called "Sinai 375a" also dates to the 15th Century BC and has the name *Ahisamach* from Exodus 31:6 written on two horizontal lines. Dr. Doug Petrovich stated that there is no other instance of this name in any other Semitic language than Hebrew. In the Bible, Ahisamach was the father of Oholiab, who along with Bezalel was one of the chief craftsmen appointed for constructing the Tabernacle and its furnishings. Dr. Petrovich points out clear evidence that the Hebrew letters developed continuously, becoming less pictographic over time, until the Hebrew script eventually converted into block letters under the Persian administration (6th and 5th centuries BC).

Leading up to the 7th century BC an excavation of a burial tomb near Jerusalem in 1979 uncovered two small silver scrolls with the "priestly blessing" from the Book of Numbers chapter 6. Today this is regarded as the earliest known copy of the biblical text!

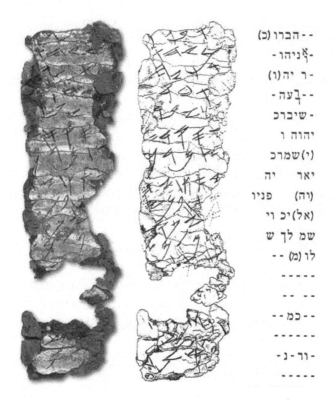

(כ) הברו - -

-Ăניה-

(ו)ר יה -

- בָּעה - -

- שיברכ

יהוה ו

(י)שמרכ

יאר   יה

(וה)   פניו

(אל)יכ וי

שמ לך ש

- - (מ) לו

- - - - -

- -   - -

- - כמ - -

- - - - - -

- נ - ור-

- - - - -

Figure 26. A photograph of the scroll KH2 and a transcription of the letters.[224]

Nephilim (Giants)

Yes—giants existed—and it wasn't just Goliath. Developing a well-rounded Biblical view about giants requires studying the entire set (and not just a few) of the following Biblical passages: Genesis 6:4, 14:5; Numbers 13:28–33; Deuteronomy 1:28–3:11, 9:2; Joshua 11:21, 13:12, 14:12–15, 15:8–14, 17:15, 18:16; 1 Samuel 17:4, 49–50; 2 Samuel 5:18–25, 21:15–22; Amos 2:9; 1 Chronicles 11:23, 20:4–8; Numbers 13:22; Judges 1:20; Isaiah 17:5; Psalm 82, and Job 4:13–18.

Scripture also includes passages that appear to highlight distinct characteristics about the giants/Nephilim, such as in

Numbers 13:23–25 where two men are required to carry a "cluster of grapes" (why does the writer need to point this out?) and certain unique characters and family lines that were pursued, engaged in battle, and conquered (such as Joshua 15:13–14: "Now to Caleb the son of Jephunneh he gave a share among the children of Judah, according to the commandment of the Lord to Joshua, namely, Kirjath Arba, which is Hebron (Arba was the father of Anak). Caleb drove out the three sons of Anak from there: Sheshai, Ahiman, and Talmai, the children of Anak").

We do not advocate the "reincursion" theory because the angels that "broke their domain" were punished and judged (Jude 1:6–8 and 2 Peter 2:4–11). The giants/Nephilim and their descendants that were pursued and annihilated after the Flood (e.g., by David and Joshua) were likely from the line of Ham's wife (see Genesis 9:18 and others).

Due to the crowded and controversial content so widely available online and in print on this subject, we advise being careful to stay within biblical boundaries. So many have taken this topic too far. We therefore recommend a single resource on this topic: "Fallen: The Sons of God and the Nephilim" by Tim Chaffey available on Amazon. Because of the New Testament connection (Jude 1:6–8 and 2 Peter 2:4–11) with the verses above, we agree with the conclusion in Chaffey's work.

Noah's Flood: Catastrophic Plate Tectonics

> **Suggested Videos:**
>
> Noah's Flood and Catastrophic Plate Tectonics
> https://youtu.be/i8SCjn1hubc

The Bible records that the Flood commenced by the "fountains of the great deep" *breaking open*. The Hebrew term used for this is bâqa' (pronounced "baw-kah") which means to "cleave, rend, or break and rip open; to make a breach." This "cleaving and breaking/ripping open" couldn't describe what we see on the planet today any better.

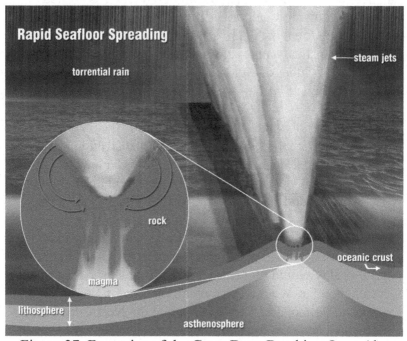

Figure 27. Fountains of the Great Deep Breaking Open (the Beginning of Noah's Flood).[225]

In 1994 six PhD scientists published a research paper titled, "Catastrophic Plate Tectonics: A Global Flood Model of Earth History,"[226] that substantiated this biblical aspect of the Flood. Their research revealed that fast-moving, subducting oceanic plates were responsible for the continents breaking apart and spreading to their current locations, in contrast to the evolutionary ideas of slow continental drift and equally slow seafloor spreading. Ongoing research in this area has shown that the model helps explain volcanoes, mountain ranges, the shapes and positions of continents, and the generation of global tsunamis that explain rock layers.

Genesis Apologetics worked with many of these leading Flood geologists to produce YouTube videos that visualize how CPT played such a large role in Noah's Flood.[227] Readers interested in a more technical explanation behind the catastrophic nature of the Flood are encouraged to view Dr. Steve Austin's presentation titled, "Continental Sprint: A Global Flood Model for Earth History."[228]

Much of the fundamental research on the topic of CPT has been undertaken by Dr. John Baumgardner over the past 40 years. As a professional scientist, Dr. Baumgardner is known for developing TERRA, a finite element code designed to study flow of rock within the Earth's mantle. In 1997, US News and World Report described him as "the world's pre-eminent expert in the design of computer models for geophysical convection."[229] Baumgardner has applied TERRA to demonstrate that the Earth's mantle is indeed vulnerable to runaway instability and that this instability is capable of resurfacing the planet in the time span of just a few months. We'll review many of Baumgardner's findings below.

Brief summary of plate tectonics concepts

Scientists of both creation and evolutionary persuasions conclude that new ocean crust forms at ocean rift zones where two tectonic plates are moving apart. The plates in the rift migrate apart, magma rises to fill the gap, is cooled by ocean water, and solidifies to make a strip of new ocean crust. The two plates are each like a conveyor belt that moves away from the rift zone along one edge and usually toward a subduction zone along the other edge. At the subduction zone, the moving plate plunges into the mantle beneath and thus disappears from the surface.

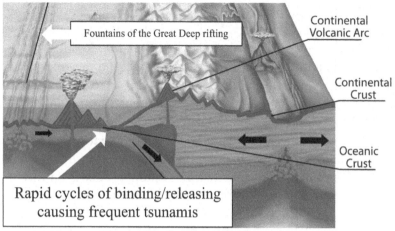

Figure 28. Subduction Overview.

The main difference between the creationist and secular understanding is that, in creationist understanding, during the Flood plate speeds were about five miles-per-hour instead of just a few inches per year, as they are measured to be today. The much higher speed is why the process during the Flood is referred to as *Catastrophic* Plate Tectonics.[230]

What evidence is there for plate tectonics?

The evidence supporting the concept of plate tectonics is overwhelming. Let's quickly tour some of the key evidences, starting first with the "big picture," then investigating some of the physical evidences in more detail.

Evidence 1: The continents fit together like puzzle pieces

One of the clearest evidences is that the continents fit together like puzzle pieces. While many school textbooks credit Alfred Wegener, a meteorologist, with the "discovery" that the continents "drifted" from an original super-continent (Pangea or similar configuration) to their current location, it was actually a creation scientist who brought this to light much earlier. His name was Antonio Snider-Pellegrini (1802–1885), a French geographer and scientist, who theorized about the possibility of continental drift. In 1858, Snider-Pellegrini published his book, La Création et ses mystères dévoilés ("The Creation and its Mysteries Unveiled") which included the image in Figure 29.

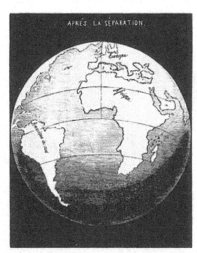

Figure 29. Snider-Pellegrini made these two maps in 1858, showing his interpretation of how the American and African continents once fit together before becoming separated.

Snider-Pellegrini based his theory on the Genesis Flood, the obvious shape and fitting of the continents, and the fact that plant fossils found in both Europe and the United States were identical.[231]

Modern mapping technologies and the help of bathymetric maps that reveal the shapes and contours of the continental shelf and the ocean floor allow us to clearly see that the continents were once connected and later torn apart. Figure 30 shows what earth looks like with all the ocean water removed. Without the oceans, the deep shelves on each side of the continents become visible and we can see how the continents fit together like puzzle pieces to shape an earth that used to be mostly a single land mass.

Interestingly, this perfectly fits the Genesis account: "Then God said, 'Let the waters under the heavens be gathered together into one place, and let the dry land appear'; and it was so. And God called the dry land Earth, and the gathering together of the waters He called Seas. And God saw that it was good" (Genesis 1:9–10). This is especially obvious when looking at the matching jagged edges of lower South America and Africa (see Figure 30).

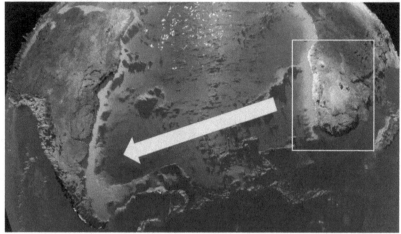

Figure 30. Lower South America Matching Africa.[232]

We can also see how a notch of submerged land off the grand banks of Newfoundland fits nearly perfectly into a slot north of Spain (see Figure 31).

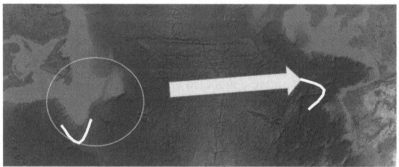

Figure 31. Submerged land off the Grand Banks of Newfoundland fitting into a Slot North of Spain (Google Earth).

142

From a Biblical standpoint, the continents fit together so well because of the catastrophic linear rifting that occurred when the fountains of the great deep were "cleaved" and pulled apart only a few thousand years ago.

Evidence 2: The Oceanic Ridge System

The oceanic ridge system covers more than 40,000 miles and circles the earth 1.6 times over.

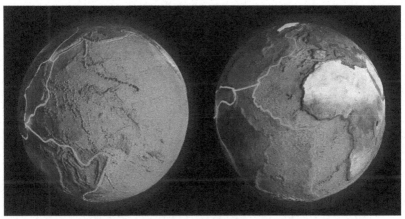

Figure 32. Oceanic Ridge System.

The Mid-Atlantic Ridge (MAR) represents one of the largest rifts left behind by the global seafloor spreading process. It looks like a giant baseball seam running around the face of the earth.

Figure 33. Mid-Atlantic Ridge (MAR).[233]

The MAR is part of the longest mountain range in the world and includes perpendicular faults along its entire length, known as transform faults, showing the formation of new seafloor involved a pulling apart of the ocean basin. The sharpness of the faults and the abrupt edges indicate that little time has expired since their formation. The raised and sloped features on each side of the rift also testify to the hot and buoyant rock that still lies beneath it. From a Biblical standpoint, the formation of the Atlantic basin occurred quickly during the Flood and then slowed down greatly to about an inch per year, as GPS measurements today indicate.

144

Evidence 3: Ring of Fire

The Ring of Fire is a 25,000-mile horseshoe-shaped string of oceanic trenches in the Pacific Ocean basin where about 90% of the world's earthquakes and a large fraction of the world's volcanoes occur.[234] It is also where most of the plate subduction is taking place today. From a Biblical perspective, this long belt of volcanoes and earthquakes marks the location where vast amounts of ocean plate was rapidly subducted into the earth's interior during the Flood. Today, by comparison, the speed of subduction is extremely slow, and the resulting earthquakes and tsunamis are dramatically less frequent.

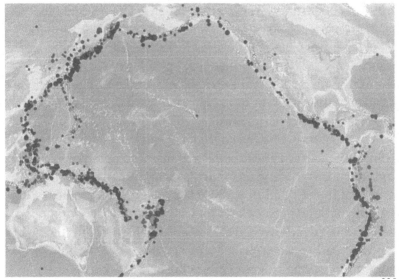

Figure 34. USGS 1900-2013 Earthquakes in the Ring of Fire.[235]

How is CPT different from the secular understanding of plate tectonics?

CPT is basically the expression at the earth's surface of a recent, massive, and rapid overturn of rock inside the region inside the Earth known as the mantle, which is the 1,800-mile thick layer of rock between the Earth's core and its crust. Regions of cooler rock in the upper part of the mantle have a natural tendency to sink downward toward the bottom, and regions of warmer rock at the bottom have a natural tendency to rise upward toward the surface. When conditions are right, this natural tendency for rising and sinking can "run away," such that both rising and sinking become faster and faster—up to a billion times faster. The force responsible for driving this behavior is simply gravity. From a Biblical perspective, the runaway episode responsible for CPT occurred during the Flood described in Genesis 6–8.

The possibility that runaway behavior might occur in the mantle was discovered decades ago in laboratory studies[236] that explored how mantle minerals deform at mantle temperature and stress conditions. These basic experiments revealed that mantle minerals weaken by factors of more than a billion for stress levels that can readily arise inside the earth. Computer experiments[237] later confirmed that episodes of runaway overturn in the mantle are inevitable under the right conditions because of this inherent weakening behavior demonstrated in these laboratory experiments.

What might be the consequences at the earth's surface of a runaway overturn event in the mantle? One notable consequence is that the tectonic plates at the earth's surface get caught up in the rapid flow of rock within the mantle beneath. In particular, the ocean plates that are currently diving into the mantle at the deep-ocean trenches during the overturn did so at a spectacularly accelerated pace. Likewise, in zones known today as spreading ridges (such as the Mid-Atlantic Ridge) where tectonic plates are moving apart from one another, the speed of separation during the overturn was dramatically higher.

Just how much faster would the plate motions during such an overturn event be compared with what is occurring today? This can be estimated based on the time frame provided in the Bible's account of the Flood and on the amount of plate motion associated with the part of the rock record that contains fossils of the plants and animals buried in the Flood. From these

146

numbers one obtains a plate speed on the order of five miles-per-hour. A typical plate speed today, as measured by GPS, is on the order of a couple inches per year. The ratio of these two speeds is about one billion to one.

What are other noteworthy consequences of such rapid plate motions? One is that water on the ocean bottom in the zones where plates were moving apart so rapidly was in direct contact with the molten rock which was rising from below to fill the gap between the plates. This molten rock at about 1300° C converted the ocean water to steam at extremely high pressure. This steam organized to form in a linear chain of intense supersonic jets along the entire midocean ridge system. As these jets pierced the layer of ocean water above where they were formed, they entrained massive amounts of liquid seawater, which was lofted high above the Earth. This liquid water then fell back to the surface as rain. Hence, a direct consequence of rapid plate motions was persisting rain over much if not most of the earth.

A second prominent consequence of rapid plate motion was a rising sea level that flooded the land surface with ocean water. The rising sea level resulted from a decrease in the volume of the ocean basins. Behind that decrease was the loss of original cold ocean plate as it plunged into the mantle at an ocean trench and its replacement with new and much warmer ocean plate produced by seafloor spreading at a mid-ocean ridge. The new plate was on average 500–1000° C warmer than the cold plate it replaced. Because warm rock of a given mass has more volume than cold rock of the same mass, the ocean floor above new ocean floor was 0.6–1.2 miles higher than was the old ocean floor. As more and more new ocean floor was generated at mid-ocean ridges, while more and more of the original ocean floor was removed by recycling into the mantle, the global sea level relative to the land surface rose by thousands of feet. Hence, a notable result of rapid plate motion was a rising sea level and a dramatic flooding of the continents by ocean water.

A third major consequence of the rapid plate motion is the generation of a huge number of giant tsunamis. In today's world, at an ocean trench where an oceanic plate is steadily slipping into the mantle, the adjacent overriding plate generally is locked against it and is bent downward as the other plate slides into the mantle (see Figure 35). As this motion proceeds, the overriding plate is deformed more and more in a spring-like manner until a stress limit is exceeded. At this point the two plates unlock, significant slip between the plates occurs, and the overriding plate returns to its original shape. Such an unlocking and slip event usually produces an earthquake. If the slip event is large enough it also can launch a tsunami. During the Flood, when plate speeds were a billion times higher than today, it is almost certain that this same locking and unlocking phenomenon also prevailed. The higher plate speeds and the huge amount of seafloor recycled into the mantle would have generated vast numbers of huge tsunamis. Conservative estimates are in the range of 50,000–100,000 or more tsunamis, with wave heights in the range of hundreds of feet or higher.

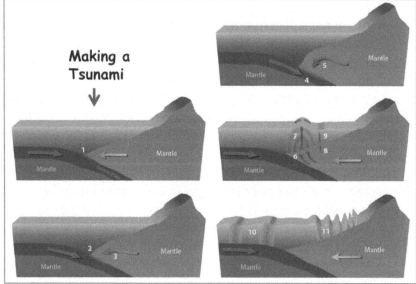

Figure 35. Making a Tsunami (Baumgardner, 2018).

Numerical experiments undertaken by Dr. Baumgardner to model the erosion and sediment deposition aspects of this sort of tsunami activity show that it is readily capable of producing the observed continent sediment record. This work is described in a recent paper titled, "Understanding how the Flood sediment record was formed: The role of large tsunamis."[238] Figure 36 shows a plot from this simulation that includes the plate motions.[239] Hence, a third major result of rapid plate motion is the formation of the observed layer-cake pattern of fossil-bearing sediments across the continents.

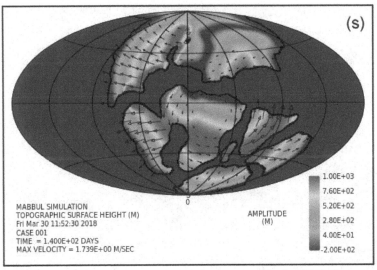

Figure 36. Plot from Dr. John Baumgardner's CPT Tsunami Simulation.[240]

Dr. Baumgardner's simulation allows us in a limited way to rewind time to gain some insight into what happened during the year-long Genesis Flood. Below we'll review some of the major physical evidences that support CPT.

Physical evidences that support the reality of CPT

Evidence 1: Catastrophic Subduction

The oceanic plates that rapidly subducted under the continents during the Flood are still visible! Seismic images of the mantle reveal a ring of unexpectedly cold rock at the bottom of the mantle, beneath the subduction zones that surround the Pacific Ocean. This structure is obtained using a technique known as seismic tomography that folds together data from 10,000 or more seismograms at once.

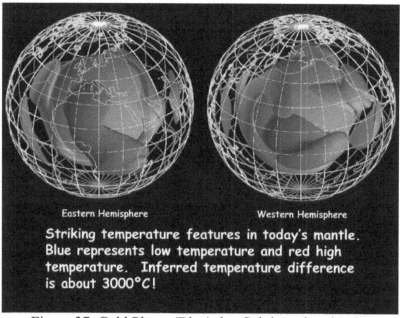

Figure 37. Cold Plates (Blue) that Subducted under the Continents During the Flood.[241]

Evidence 2: The Fossil Record

The action of CPT caused the oceanic plates to subduct rapidly under the land masses and generate cycles of tsunamis that brought staggering quantities of sediment onto land that

150

wiped out every living creature in their paths, burying them in the muddy layers we still see today. These types of tsunamis still occur, although much less frequently and on a smaller scale. The moving sea floor subducts, snags under the land masses, and then releases, creating mud-filled tsunamis that carry debris and sea life onto land, sorting them in layers.

Giant, high-frequency tsunamis that were occurring during the Flood explain why today we see dinosaur graveyards around the world, including 13 states in the middle of America, containing dead dinosaurs mixed with marine life (see Figure 38). What type of Flood could do this? Just how much water would it take to bury millions of land creatures under hundreds of feet of mud and sand in the Morrison Formation (a 13-state, 700,000 square mile area)?

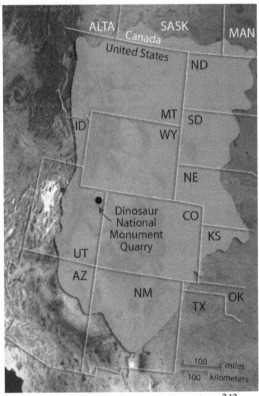

Figure 38. Morrison Formation.[242]

Just how did so many land creatures get buried together with marine life, with 97% of the dinosaurs found disarticulated,[243] and many of the remaining 3% that are found intact discovered in mud and sand layers with their necks arched back, suffocating as they died?[244]

A global inundation that covered most of North America is no secret to secular geologists, but they call it something different: the "widespread Late Cretaceous transgression"[245] (essentially technical jargon for "worldwide flood"). Studies have revealed that "a sea level rise of 310 meters is required to flood the Cretaceous layers based on their current elevation." The challenge for secular geologists, however, is that the maximum thickness of the fossil layers produced by a 310-meter sea level rise is only about 700 meters, but in North America, nearly 50 percent of the Cretaceous layers contain strata *thicker* than 700 meters.

Sediment transport via highly turbulent tsunami-driven flow described in Baumgardner's published work logically seems to be required to account for these thick layers. These layers also suggest that the continents also had to *downwarp* locally during this global inundation, as Baumgardner's modeling likewise suggests. This is what CPT predicts and what the Flood would have done. There's just no way that rising sea levels alone can explain the fossil record in North America— mechanisms much more powerful and catastrophic *had to be involved.*

Evidence 3: Fossil Correlation[246]

By comparing fossils of small organisms found on the ocean floor with fossils of the same organisms on different continents, it has been possible to determine when the ocean crust formed in terms of the fossil sequence found in the continental sediments. What has been discovered, both from a creationist as well as from a secular understanding, is that much of the continental fossil record was already in place before any of the present-day ocean crust had come into existence. For example, all the trilobite fossils had already been deposited, plus all the older coal deposits (Pennsylvanian System coals) had already been formed before any of the present-day ocean crust had formed.

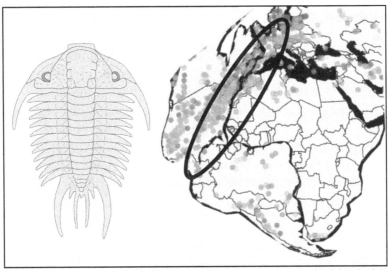

Figure 39. Reassembling the continents shows a trilobite habitat torn apart by the Flood.

The fossil record (e.g., certain trilobite species) that now straddles both sides of the MAR testify to the rapid nature of this catastrophe, with millions of the same kinds of animals that were once living together now found buried in mud and lime layers on either side.

In the creationist understanding, the presence of fossils is a trustworthy indicator of the action of Flood, meaning that a large part of the Flood cataclysm had already unfolded and had generated fossil-bearing sediments on the continental surface *before* any of the present-day ocean floor had appeared. It further implies that all of today's ocean floor formed *since the onset of the Flood*, during roughly the latter half of the cataclysm. It also means that all the pre-Flood ocean floor, plus any ocean floor formed during the earlier portion of the Flood, must have been recycled into the earth's interior during the cataclysm. These considerations indicate in a compelling way that rapid plate tectonics must have been a major aspect of the year-long Flood catastrophe.

Evidence 4: Buckled/Folded Sedimentary Layers

The Genesis Flood laid down tens of millions of cubic miles of sediment like sand and mud all over the globe. It soon hardened into rock. These layers contain most of the fossil record. Some of these massive layers are bent and even folded, proving they were laid down rapidly and then bent before hardening into rock. Otherwise they would have crumbled instead of bending. These folded and bent geological features are found all over the world and most occurred during the latter stages of the Flood when 80% of the world's mountains rapidly formed.

Figure 40. Example of Massive Geologic Folding.[247]

Evidence 5: River Fans

If the evolutionary view about the continents were true (that they moved apart slowly over millions of years), the large rivers on the continents that empty into the Atlantic Ocean would have left a connected trail of mud stretching from one side of the Atlantic to the other. But what the evidence actually shows is that most of the seafloor spreading that formed the Atlantic was *over* before continental runoff and major transport of sediment into the Atlantic basin *began*. Major rivers like the Congo, Mississippi, and Amazon run off the continents and have mud fans with only thousands of years' worth of mud deposits—not millions.

Figure 41. Amazon River Fan (Google Earth)

There are flat sand bottoms on each side of the continents showing they were split apart rapidly—they don't have millions of years' worth of runoff with considerable mud extending into the ocean. The continental shelves exhibit little erosion and still match nearly perfectly when put back together. Millions of years of erosion would have destroyed much of the sharp continental shelfs. These rivers began shaping and eroding only thousands of years ago, not millions.

Evidence 6: Sloss Megasequences

Dr. Tim Clarey has conducted extensive research on the Genesis Flood using over 2,000 stratigraphic columns (bore holes) from across North and South America, Africa, and Europe.[248] These data confirm the existence of six megasequences (called "Sloss-type megasequences"), large-scale sequences of sedimentary deposits that reveal six different stages of global depositions that occurred during the Flood.

The three earliest megasequences (Sauk, Tippecanoe and Kaskaskia) contained mostly marine fossils, indicating that only shallow marine areas were swamped and buried by CPT-caused tsunamis. The 4th megasequence (Absaroka) shows a dramatic rise in ocean level and overall global coverage and volume. This sequence also includes the first major plant (coal) and terrestrial animal fossils. The 5th megasequence (Zuni) was mostly responsible for the demise of the dinosaurs and appears to be the highest water point of the Flood (its zenith) because it shows the highest levels of sediment coverage and volume compared to earlier megasequences. The final megasequence (Tejas) contains fossils from the highest upland areas of the pre-Flood world. Together, these megasequences explain why over 75% of earth is covered by an average of about one mile of sedimentary deposits.

Figure 42. World Sediment Map (showing 75% of earth is covered by an average of about one mile of sedimentary deposits).

Evidence 7: Massive Coal Deposits

One of the highest and most severe stages of the Flood occurred during the 4th Sloss Megasequence, the Absaroka. Land creatures and plants start showing up in the fossil record laid down by this megasequence. This is also the time when the world's ocean floor began to be created anew. In other words, the oldest ocean crust today only goes back to the time of the deposition of the Absaroka Megasequence.

Notice the top bars in the first seven labeled rows in Figure 43. This shows the global animal fossil occurrences from the Paleodatabase.[249] The lower bars in each row represent aquatic animals and the top bars represent land animals. The megasequences are shown on the left. Note that few land animals appear until the end of the Kaskaskia, then land animals begin increasingly showing up in the fossil record as the Flood progressed.

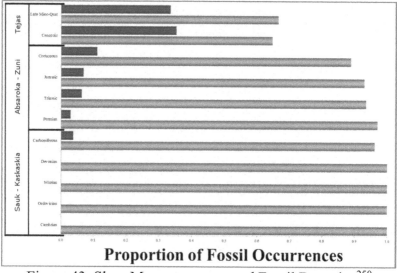

Proportion of Fossil Occurrences

Figure 43. Sloss Megasequences and Fossil Deposits.[250]

Entire ecosystems were buried during this megasequence in enormous deposits that later turned into coal, such as the extensive Appalachian coal beds. Even more coal was formed in the later Zuni and Tejas megasequences as the waters of the Flood rose yet higher. The U.S. has over seven trillion tons of coal reserves. Where did it all come from? While we know that coal is formed by dead plant material being sandwiched between sediment layers, we only have enough vegetation on the earth's surface today to produce just a fraction of the existing coal reserves.[251] This shows that the pre-Flood world was mostly covered by lush vegetation. The rising Flood waters and tsunamis that were necessary to sweep over the land and bury vast amounts of vegetation that turned into coal are best explained by a catastrophe of worldwide proportions.

158

Figure 44. United States Coal Beds.

In the later run-off stages of the Flood (called the Tejas sequence), plants swept off the pre-Flood lands formed massive coal beds such as in the Powder River Basin of Wyoming and Montana. The Powder River Basin layers are the largest coal deposits in North America, currently supplying over 40% of the coal in the U.S. Some of these stacked coal beds are up to 200 feet thick and cover areas that are 60 miles long by 60 miles wide. The sheer volume of plant material required to form such a massive layer of coal testifies to catastrophic circumstances.

Noah's Flood: How Could All the Animals Fit on the Ark?

One of the most frequently asked questions about the Ark is: "How could it fit all the animals?" Two factors help answer this question: (1) the size of the Ark, and (2) the number (and size) of the animals and supplies on board. First, the size. Given the size of the Ark (discussed above), the Ark had a total volume of at least 1,396,000 cubic feet.[252] The inside dimensions of a 40-foot school bus gives about 2,080 cubic feet of space. Therefore, at least 671 school buses without their wheels and axels could fit inside of Noah's Ark. If each bus carried 50 students, then 33,550 kids could easily fit in the Ark.

Next, we have the number of animals. The Genesis Flood account states that God brought two (male/female) of every *kind* of animal (and seven pairs of some) to Noah, who loaded them into the Ark. The Hebrew term for kind is *min*, which occurs only 31 times in the Old Testament. So just what is a biblical kind? Biblically and biologically speaking, a kind is a group of animals that were naturally interfertile at the time of the Flood. Some organisms have complex histories since then, so it's difficult to determine which of them belongs to which kind. Most often, however, plants and animals interbreed within their modern "Family" classification. Thus, each family—give or take—had at least two representatives on Noah's ark. Several creation scientists have spent considerable amount of time studying this very topic (it's called the field of *baraminology*, or the study of "created kinds").[253]

While there are various methods for determining "kinds," (e.g., cognitum and statistical baraminology), hybridization (whether two species can have offspring) is considered the most valuable evidence for inclusion within an Ark *kind*.

Take mammals for example. Some biologists list them in 28 orders that include 146 families and over 4,800 species.[254] Some place the species estimates higher, around 5,400.[255] So how many different mammal pairs would Noah have to take on the Ark to produce all the mammal species we have today? Take the dog (Canine) kind for starters. The World Canine Organization currently recognizes 339 different breeds of dogs—all are or were interfertile. There are 335 horse breeds that are all interfertile. There are eight bear species in the bear (Ursidae) family and all except for one are interfertile. Notice how the high number of species quickly collapses to a much smaller number?

Figure 45. Ursidae Family (Bears).

Some scientists have boiled down this list of mammal species to only 138 created kinds (using extant species, or animals still alive today). Including the extinct mammalian families known from the fossil record, the actual number on the Ark could have exceeded 300.[256] By collapsing the other animal categories in a similar manner, the total estimate of the number of kinds needed on the Ark is fewer than 2,000.[257] Dinosaurs were certainly included on the ark, since Scripture says any animal that walked and had nostrils went in, with many dinosaur count estimates at the species level less than 1,000 and fewer than 80 at the family level.[258] Probably only 160 individual dinosaurs survived the Flood on Noah's Ark. Noah's family could have loaded young behemoths, not the larger older ones. Dinosaur kinds, plus many other animals, went extinct after the Flood.

Noah's Flood: How Could the Ark Have Been Seaworthy?

Let's investigate whether the Ark was seaworthy. God gave certain dimensions to Noah for building the Ark: 300 cubits long, 50 cubits wide, and 30 cubits high. Using the Nippur Cubit[259] at 20.4 inches, this works out to a vessel about 510 feet long, 85 feet wide, and 51 feet high. Accounting for a 15% reduction in volume due to the hull curvature, the Ark had about 1.88 million cubic feet of space, the equivalent of 450 semi-trailers of cargo space.[260] Twice as long as a Boeing 747 and stretching over one-and-a-half football fields, this was a massive ship.

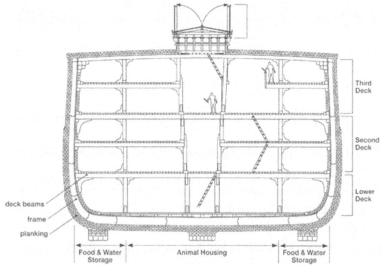

Figure 46. Cross-section view of a possible design of the interior of the ark.[261]

God knew *exactly what He was doing* when He gave Noah the specific dimensions of the Ark. In 1993 Dr. Seon Won Hong conducted a scientific study[262] to investigate the seaworthiness of the Ark at the renowned ship research center KRISO (now called MOERI) in South Korea.[263] After evaluating the seaworthiness of over 10 various ship dimensions, the study showed that the Ark dimensions given in the Bible were ideal for handling everything a highly turbulent sea could throw at it, while balancing the need for inhabitant safety. The study showed that the Ark could handle 100-foot waves.

An earlier study conducted in the 17th Century by Peter Jansen of Holland showed that the length-to-width ratio of the Ark (about 7-to-1) was ideal for such a massive, non-powered sea vessel. Some oil tankers have a 7-to-1 ratio as well. He also demonstrated using replica models of the Ark how tough it was to capsize.[264]

Noah was instructed by God to coat the inside and the outside of the Ark with pitch, a thick gooey substance secreted by trees as a means of protection against infection or insect attack. Isn't it interesting that one of the very first historical references to using pitch for ships is in the Bible? It's also interesting that pitch has been the most effective and widely-used ship waterproofing substance in history. For centuries, tar, which is made from pitch, was among Sweden's most important exports, peaking at over a quarter million barrels per year in the late 1800s. Many of the eastern states in the U.S. were also major tar exporters for ship building purposes until the 1900s.[265]

When heated into a liquid state and applied to ship planking, pitch hardens almost instantly into a protective, waterproof shell, very similar to how epoxy or fiberglass are used in shipbuilding today. The strong outer shell provided by hardened pitch adds both strength and waterproofing beyond the natural capability of the wood. These "divine shipbuilding instructions" given to Noah certainly seem to make realistic sense.

Noah's Flood: How Did People and Animals Disperse Around the World after the Flood?

After the Flood, God commanded humanity to "increase in number and fill the earth" (Genesis 9:1). As rebellious humans, we did the opposite: "Then they said, 'Come, let us build ourselves a city, with a tower that reaches to the heavens, so that we may make a name for ourselves and not be scattered over the face of the whole earth'" (Genesis 11:4). About 100 years after the Flood, God responded to this disobedience by confusing our language and dispersing us from the Tower of Babel around the globe. This dispersal included between 78 and 100 people groups (and languages).[266]

Assuming the Babel dispersion is a true account, how did people spread across the globe when much of it is presently covered by water? The answer is quite simple: during the (single) Ice Age (see **Ice Age**) that began after the Flood and lasted for a few hundred years after, the ocean levels were between 100 and 140 meters lower[267] than they are today. This made *land bridges* and *ice bridges* that melting ice has since submerged. Also, in many cases (e.g., Hawaii, North America, Tahiti, and other locations) both humans and animals arrived by boat. For more about this topic, we recommend Bill Cooper's book, *After the Flood: The Early Post-flood History of Europe Traced Back to Noah*[268] and other resources by Answers in Genesis.[269]

Noah's Flood: How Did Vegetation Spread Rapidly after the Flood?

How did vegetation spread rapidly after the Flood so that all the varieties of animals could have enough food to survive? Two considerations help answer this question: (1) How could the plants grow fast enough for the thousands of animals getting off the Ark, reproducing rapidly, and needing food sources? (2) How could the seeds and plants disperse around the world after the world-wide Flood? Let's answer each of these questions.

How could the plants grow fast enough?

The most important part to consider when answering this question is that plants had 220 days to grow after the Flood. The Flood account reports that the water rose for 150 days before beginning to recede. They didn't leave the ark until 370 days after the Flood began.

This left up to 220 days (over seven months) for plants to regrow.[270] Vegetation grows fast with the right conditions. Different varieties of grass take only 5–30 days to grow. Winter wheat takes about 7–8 months to reach maturity, and spring wheat is mature in only four months. Many vegetables grow to maturity in less than two months (including arugula, spinach, carrots, broccoli, radishes, onions, cucumbers, many types of beans and leafy vegetables, and even some root vegetables). Noah also took many seed varieties with him to plant in the new world. God told him, "You are to take every kind of food that is to be eaten and store it away as food for you and for them." (Genesis 6:21)

How could the seeds and plants disperse around the world after the Flood?

God has engineered a *wide variety* of ways for distributing plant life. In addition to intentional planting, there are five main ways that seeds are dispersed from the parent plant: gravity, wind, ballistic, animals, and by water.

Gravity is perhaps the most obvious way: plants drop their ripe fruit (containing seed) below the plant, the seeds nest into the soil and grow around the radius of the parent plant. Apples, citrus, coconuts, and passionfruit are examples of gravity dispersal.

Dandelions are a well-known example of wind dispersal. A 2003 study at the University of Regensburg in Germany found that 99.5% of dandelion seeds land within 10 meters of their parent. Each seed is designed with a "parachute" structure that lifts the seed for typically a one-second flight.[271]

A less common dispersal method is ballistic dispersal. This occurs where the seed is forcefully ejected by explosive dehiscence of the fruit. For example, the *Hura crepitans* plant is even called the dynamite tree due to the sound of the fruit exploding. The explosions are powerful enough to throw the seed up to 100 meters.[272]

Plants that rely on water dispersal have seeds that can travel for extremely long distances (especially those seeds that have hard shells and float). Water lilies and some palm trees do this.

Animal seed dispersion is perhaps the most fascinating and includes three primary methods. Some seeds have small hooks on the surface of a burr, so they attach themselves to animal fur for dispersion. The more obvious method that animals disperse seed is by eating the fruit and later excreting the undigestible seeds to form new plants—sometimes far away from the parent plant (e.g., blackberries, cherries, and apples). Many rodents (such as squirrels) and some birds disperse seeds by hoarding the seeds in hidden dens. This method alone is responsible for over 90% of seed dispersion in some tropical rain forests.[273]

When it comes to Noah's Flood specifically, Ginger Allen reminds us that seeds only had to endure water for a maximum of just over nine months. She wrote, "those that had hitched a ride on large mats of vegetation or on carcasses could be germinating while protected from the harsh conditions," and, "Most plants could have survived outside the Ark upon floating rafts of vegetation as seeds and as debris that could have gone a long way toward propagation of at least some plant life in the post-Flood world."[274] Finally, Noah did not open the ark until the dove brought back a leaf. This way he knew the world was ready to support the animals.

166

Noah's Flood: Where Did All the Water Come From?

Bible-believing geologists typically hold the view that most mountain ranges were "pushed up" during the final stages of the Flood (see Genesis 8-9 and Psalm 104). This means that the Flood did not need to cover today's tall peaks. Currently the total volume of water on the planet is estimated at 1.386 billion cubic kilometers. If we layer it on a smooth sphere it would be a layer with a radius of about 6,500 kilometers, subtracting from here and you get a depth of 2.61 km average. Without today's high mountain ranges that were created during the Flood, plenty of water (now in the oceans) could cover the world's land. That's why 75% of the continents are filled with sedimentary layers that average about 1 mile deep.

Noah's Flood: Worldwide or Local?

Some Christians believe the earth is 4.5 billion years old and that the Flood described in the book of Genesis (chapters 6–9) was a local event limited to the area where Noah lived, for example the Mesopotamian Valley region. Why? Primarily because of their perspectives on the fossil record and radiometric dating. They believe the fossil record was laid down over millions of years and know that a global flood would have disturbed those fossils. Yet, there is significant evidence that most of the fossil record was created by the Genesis Flood! By tracing genealogies in the Bible, we know the Flood occurred around ~4,400 years ago. Let's take a look at eight reasons for believing the Genesis Flood was a global, catastrophic event.

1. **Massive geologic layers**: The Genesis Flood laid down millions of cubic feet of sediment like sand and mud all over the globe. It soon hardened into rock. These layers contain most of the fossil record.

Some of these massive layers, such as the Kaibab Upwarp in the Grand Canyon, are bent and even folded, proving they were laid down rapidly and then bent before hardening into rock. Otherwise they would have crumbled instead of bending.

2.   **Fossil record**: The fossil record is world-wide and shows evidence of rapid burial. Specific examples include clam and oyster shells on mountain tops that were fossilized while still closed, fish buried in the process of eating other fish, and ichthyosaurs that were buried while giving birth. The Flood accounts for such widespread watery catastrophe.

3.   **The Flood covered the highest mountains**: Scripture says that the "waters rose and increased greatly on the earth, and the ark floated on the surface of the water. They rose greatly on the earth, and **all** the high mountains **under the entire heavens** were covered. The waters rose and covered the mountains to a depth of more than fifteen cubits [about 22 feet]" (Genesis 7:18–20, emphasis added). Of course, the writer refers to the mountains of the pre-Flood world, which were much shorter than today's tallest mountains. Since water seeks its own level, it would be impossible for the water to cover the highest mountains and still be only a local event.

4.   **Purpose of the Flood**: Due to widespread wickedness and violence, God decided to wipe out all of mankind, the land-dwelling animals and birds (except for those who were on the Ark). God said the earth "was corrupt and filled with violence" (Genesis 6:11–12), and that He was going to "bring floodwaters to destroy every creature on the face of the earth that has the breath of life in it" (Genesis 6:17). He also specifically mentioned people multiple times: "I will wipe from the face of the earth the human race I have created" (Genesis 6:7). Since it is highly improbable that all of the people on

earth lived in the Mesopotamian Valley region, a local flood would not have accomplished God's purpose.

5. **Use of the words "all" and "every" and "everything" in Genesis chapters 6–9**: The words "all," "every" and "everything" are used 66 times in the Genesis Flood account. Many of these verses describe the creatures and people that perished during the flood. It is very clear by the context of these passages that God meant He was going to destroy all living creatures that live on land (except for those on the Ark). For example: "**Every** living thing that moved on land perished—birds, livestock, wild animals, **all the creatures** that swarm over the earth, and **all mankind**. **Everything** on dry land that had the breath of life in its nostrils died. **Every** living thing on the face of the earth was **wiped out**; people and animals and the creatures that move along the ground and the birds were **wiped from the earth**. **Only Noah was left**, and those with him in the ark" (Genesis 7:21–23, emphasis added). If the text doesn't mean what it says, then it means nothing. Jesus and Peter also referred to the universality of Noah's Flood. Who are we (who were not even there) to say that they were wrong?

6. **The Ark: it took over 100 years to build the Ark**. If the Flood was just a local event, why would God tell Noah to build a ship over 400 feet long (Genesis 6:15) and then bring on board all the different kinds of animals including birds to be saved? (Genesis 6:19–21). If the flood was only a local event, there would be no need for an ark—Noah and the animals that God wanted to save would have had plenty of time to travel to a safer area.

7. **God's covenant**: in Genesis 9:11, God made a promise, "Never again will all life be destroyed by the waters of a flood; never again will there be a

flood to destroy the earth." If the flood was local, then every time a local flood happens, God would break his promise.

8.   **Jesus believed in a global flood**: "Just as it was in the days of Noah, so also will it be in the days of the Son of Man. People were eating, drinking, marrying and being given in marriage up to the day Noah entered the ark. Then the flood came and destroyed them all" (Luke 17:26–27). Peter also affirmed a worldwide Flood (2 Peter 3:6).

We recommend the following resources for more study:

- *Old Earth Creationism on Trial*, Tim Chaffey and Jason Lisle
- *The Global Flood; Unlocking Earth's Geologic History*, John D. Morris
- *The Fossil Record; Unearthing Nature's History of Life*, John D. Morris
- *The New Answers Book 3*, Andrew Snelling and Ken Ham. Available here: *https://answersingenesis.org/the-flood/global/was-the-flood-of-noah-global-or-local-in-extent/*

Pre-flood World—What Was It Like?

Biblical Creation holds that God created a perfect initial world with no death, no carnivory, and no "survival of the fittest."[275] Further, animals were created to reproduce—just as we observe today—after their "own kind." Creationists also believe that this perfect world held out until it was marred by the sin of Adam and Eve, which brought death, suffering, bloodshed, and disease.[276] Geographically, this pre-Flood world had only a single landmass (Rodinia[277]) until the Flood broke the continents apart. The Flood occurred 1,656 after Creation according to English Bible translations.

Biblical creationists have presented many pre-Flood climate models over the years, with many of them called "Canopy Models." While several variants exist, all canopy models interpret the "waters above" (firmament) in Genesis 1:7 as some type of water-based canopy encircling the Earth from the beginning of creation until the Flood. As models of history, these ideas held promise to explain the pre-Flood climate, but they produced problems. For example, meteorologist Dr. Larry Vardiman spent decades at the Institute for Creation Research modeling a pre-Flood vapor canopy. In the end, he found no way for the modeled steam to avoid making earth dangerously hot. While these models and others exist, we ultimately don't know what the pre-Flood world was like because we weren't there. Further, the Bible gives few insights. It does suggest the following features:

- Before the Fall, the atmosphere was *perfect* for sustaining life (Genesis 1:31) and there was no death (Genesis 2:17; Romans 5:12; 1 Corinthians 15:22). This soon ended.
- Earth's atmosphere likely had sunlight and temperature variations within the days and nights (Genesis 3:8).
- Given that Adam and Eve were told to be "fruitful and multiply and fill the earth" (Genesis 1:27; 3:21) and they were "naked and unashamed" before the Fall (Genesis 2:25), it appears they had no need of clothing before the Fall.
- The Flood ruptured earth's single land mass. It rearranged continents and pushed up today's mountains (Psalm 104:8).
- Genesis 2:5–6 states, "For the Lord God had not caused it to rain on the earth, and there was no man to till the ground; but a mist went up from the earth and watered the whole face of the ground." While this may mean that

there was no rain until the Flood, this passage is at least clear that God originally used an underground system to water plants. After the Flood, a new, above ground system we call the water cycle began.

- Because the rainbow was given to mark a new covenant between God and the Earth (to never again Flood the entire earth) (Genesis 9:13), there is the possibility that Earth's climate was changed after (and by) the Flood to allow rainbows.[278] However, God may have used an existing phenomenon as a sign of His covenant.

These insights point to the idea that the pre-Flood world was quite different than the post-Flood world of today. The New Testament also acknowledges this distinction. Second Peter 3:6 says, "by which the world that then existed perished, being flooded with water." The fossils also indicate differences in the pre-Flood.

- Giant land beasts, such as sauropod dinosaurs that grew as large as 115 feet and 200,000 pounds.
- Giant flying reptiles called pterosaurs had over 50-foot wingspans (e.g., *Quetzalcoatlus*).
- Giant dragonflies had 2-1/2 foot wingspans and 17-inch bodies (*Meganeura*).
- Mushrooms grew over 20-feet high (*Prototaxites*).[279]
- Giant millipedes grew over eight feet long (*Arthropleura*).
- Sea lilies (not plants, but Echinoderms) are measured in inches today, but reached over a dozen feet before the Flood.
- Millions or more fossils of shallow marine creatures show that the pre-Flood world had vast (continent-sized) stretches of shallow seas unlike today's deep oceans.

The above list could be much longer; these are just a few examples. Biblical creationists and evolutionists agree that these giant creatures, plants, and habitats existed. Indeed, they are in the fossil record for everyone to evaluate, regardless of the worldview lens through which they are viewed. We also agree that these ancient features existed in a *different version of the Earth*. Evolutionists place it millions of years ago, while Biblical creationists place it before the Flood, just thousands of years ago. Next, we'll look at some of these creatures more closely.

Giant Flying Reptiles (Pterosaurs)

One of the largest flying reptiles is *Quetzalcoatlus*, which was named after the Mesoamerican feathered serpent god, Quetzalcoatl. Many studies have attempted to estimate this creature's wingspan, with most estimates coming in over 36 feet.[280]

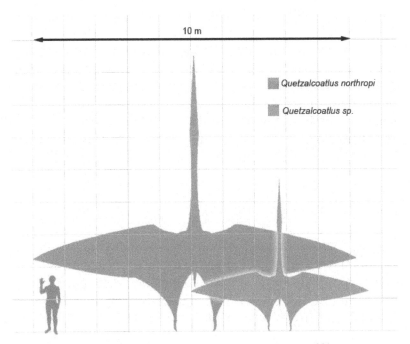

Figure 47. Quetzalcoatlus Wingspan[281]

The wingspan, however, is not what puzzles scientists about this giant—it's the *large wingspan given its weight.* While estimates vary, some studies estimate the weight of the larger specimens discovered to exceed 500 pounds.[282] That's likely too much weight for a flying creature to bear and still be able to fly. Several studies have investigated how these massive creatures could fly, with some reports even titled, *"This Pterodactyl was so big it couldn't fly"* and opening sentences such as *"Bad news dragon riders: Your dragon can't take off."*[283]

Scientists who have studied and published on this extensively have even admitted: "…it is now generally agreed that even the largest pterosaurs could not have flown in today's skies" and have offered explanations such as "warmer climate" or "higher levels of atmospheric oxygen" as reasons it could have flown only during the era in which it lived.[284]

Some secular studies that have investigated air bubbles trapped in amber that was dated to the "ancient world in which dinosaurs lived," have found *both* increased pressure as well as greater oxygen levels. The magazine *New Scientist* wrote, "One implication is that the atmospheric pressure of the Earth would have been much greater during the Cretaceous Era [rock system], when the bubbles formed in the resin. A dense atmosphere could also explain how the ungainly pterosaur, with its stubby body and wing span of up to 11 meters, could have stayed airborne."[285]

Giant Dragonflies (Meganeura)

The largest dragonfly species alive today (*Megaloprepus caerulatus*) has a wingspan of up to seven inches and a body up to five inches long. Based on the fossil record, the largest pre-Flood dragonflies (*Meganeura*) had wingspans up to 2-1/2 feet and a 17-inch body. See Figure 48.

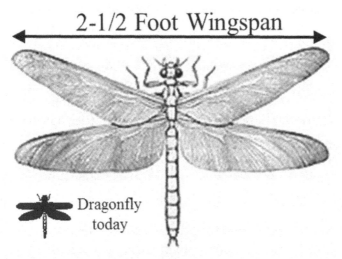

Fossilized Meganeura

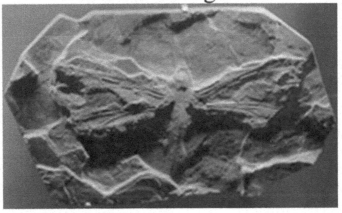

Figure 48. Giant Pre-Flood Dragonfly (*Meganeura*).[286]

In October 2006, *Science Daily* publicized a study led by Arizona State University staff titled "Giant Insects Might Reign if Only There Was More Oxygen in the Air."[287] The article claims:

> The delicate lady bug in your garden could be frighteningly large if only there was a greater concentration of oxygen in the air, a new study

concludes. The study adds support to the theory that some insects were much larger during the late Paleozoic period because they had a much richer oxygen supply, said the study's lead author Alexander Kaiser. The Paleozoic period…was a time of huge and abundant plant life and rather large insects—dragonflies had two-and-a-half-foot wing spans, for example. The air's oxygen content was 35% during this period, compared to the 21% we breathe now, Kaiser said.

This research lends evidence to the fact that the pre-Flood world was different than the one we live in today.

One study conducted in 2010 by researchers at Arizona State University tested this "more oxygen = bigger insects" theory directly by raising 12 different types of insects in simulated atmospheres with various oxygen levels. Their study included three sets of 75 dragonflies in atmospheres containing 12%, 21%, and 31% oxygen levels and their experiment confirmed that dragonflies grow bigger with more oxygen.[288] A host of reasons could explain why the pre-Flood dragonflies grew much larger than even those in the experiment. They probably had not yet lost the genetics for large size.

Giant Mushrooms (Prototaxites) and Plants

You don't need to read many secular-based books about the "ancient Earth" before learning about gigantic vegetation that existed supposedly millions of years ago. One example is the *Prototaxites* (see Figure 49). Some reports even state that these gigantic (now extinct) mushroom-like plants covered much of the Earth and "dotted the ancient landscape."[289]

Figure 49. *Prototaxites*

First discovered by a Canadian in 1859, no one seemed to know what they were. But after 130 years of debate whether this plant was a lichen, fungus, or some kind of tree, scientists have come to some level of agreement that it was essentially a "gigantic early mushroom."

Plants and fungi like these puzzle evolutionists, such as Kevin Boyce of Geophysical Sciences at University of Chicago, who stated, "A 20-foot tall fungus doesn't make any sense. Neither does a 20-foot tall algae make any sense, but here's the fossil."[290]

From a Biblical creation standpoint, this is simply a gigantic pre-Flood fungus that God created. It could thrive in the pre-Flood world, but not now. In a temperate, pre-Flood world where wearing clothing was (originally) "optional," it's no wonder that giant fungus and plants like this could have thrived.

Giant Millipedes (Arthropleura)

Giant millipedes (called *Arthropleura*) that grew to be over eight feet long[291] used to crawl around before the Flood in what became northeastern America and Scotland. The larger species of this group are the largest known land invertebrates of all time. Evolutionists attribute their grand size to different pressures and/or oxygen levels of Earth's ancient past.[292]

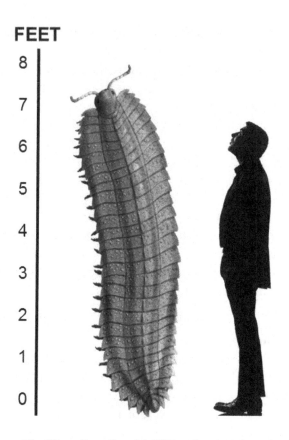

Figure 50. Giant Pre-flood Millipedes (*Arthropleura*)

Races: Where Did They Come From?[293]

Genesis teaches that God pronounced the first two created people *very good* when He created them at the very beginning. "Then God said, 'Let us make man in our image, in our likeness.' So God created man in His own image, in the image of God He created him; male and female He created them. God blessed them and said to them, 'Be fruitful and increase in number; fill the earth and subdue it.' God saw all that He had made, and it was very good" (Genesis 1:26–31 NIV).

Soon after, Adam and Eve openly violated God's command not to eat of the forbidden fruit. As a result, sin entered the human race. God had to curse all of creation, and on that day Adam and Eve began the process of aging that always ends in death. An originally perfect created mankind began accumulating genetic mutations both in body cells and in germ cells.

Every generation has suffered from these mutations ever since. They degenerate each person's body, sometimes causing death through cancer and other diseases. Mutations in the germ line over many generations have caused degeneration of the entire human race. This process has continued until today. Geneticists have identified the mutations that cause over five thousand specific diseases in humans. Although a rare few one of these DNA copying errors accidentally brings a benefit in very limited surroundings, 99.99% either cause harm or make virtually undetectable changes. But these small changes accumulate. After hundreds of generations, every person today inherits thousands of mutations that Adam and Eve and their immediate descendants never had.

As in body cells, near-neutral mutations cause miniscule damage. After enough of these accumulate, they cause a genetic meltdown leading to extinction of the species. The text *Principles of Medical Biochemistry*[294] under the subtitle "Mutations Are an Important Cause of Poor Health" states:

> At least one new mutation can be expected to occur in each round of cell division, even in cells with unimpaired DNA repair and in the absence of external mutagens [mutation-causing agents]. As a result, every child is born with an estimated 100 to 200 new mutations that were not present in the parents. Most of these mutations change only one or a few base pairs ... However, an estimated one or two new mutations are 'mildly

detrimental.' This means they are not bad enough to cause a disease on their own, but they can impair physiological functions to some extent, and they can contribute to multifactorial diseases [when many causes contribute to illness]. Finally, about 1 per 50 infants is born with a diagnosable genetic condition that can be attributed to a single major mutation (p. 153).

The authors concluded that, as a result:

Children are, on average, a little sicker than their parents because they have new mutations on top of those inherited from the parents. This mutational load is kept in check by natural selection. In most traditional societies, almost half of all children used to die before they had a chance to reproduce. Investigators can only guess that those who died had, on average, more "mildly detrimental" mutations than those who survived (p. 153).

If macro-evolution is true, it is *going the wrong way*! It does not cause the ascent of life by adding new and useful biological coding instructions, but rather the descent of life by eroding what remains of the originally created biological codes. Should we call it "devolution" instead?

What do mutations have to do with "races?" Geneticists have studied DNA sequences in all kinds of different people groups. These studies reveal that each people group—which is most easily identified on a cultural level by sharing a specific language—shares a set of mutations. They must have inherited these "race" mutations from their ancestors after the Tower of Babel, since their ancestors freely interbred for the several hundred years between the Flood and the Tower. Amazingly, however, all these mutations make up less than one percent of all human DNA in the human genome. This means that no matter how different from you someone looks, they are 99.9% genetically identical to you. For this reason, even evolutionary geneticists admit that the term "race" has virtually no biological backing. It comes from cultural and mostly language differences. Bottom line: all people have the same genetic basis to be considered fully human, while expressing interesting cultural and subtle physical variations.

Races: A DNA Bottleneck

According to the chronologies in Genesis 5 and 11, the Genesis Flood occurred about 1,656 years after Creation. From possibly millions of pre-Flood peoples, only three couples survived the Flood and had children afterward. This caused a severe DNA bottleneck. Genetic bottlenecks occur when circumstances suddenly squeeze populations down to small numbers. They concentrate mutations and thus accelerate diseases. This occurs, for example, when people or animals marry or mate with close relations. Children or offspring from these unions have a much higher chance of expressing inherited mutations in their bodies. The genetic bottleneck of the Flood accelerated the decay of the human genome from Adam and Eve's once perfect genome.

Then, not long after the Tower of Babel, a major dispersion of humans occurred. Diverse ethnicities tied to languages. The Bible records 70–100 families left the Tower. Many of them have gone extinct. Those few original languages have diversified into over 7,000+ languages and dialects today. For example, English descended from the same basic language as German, while Welsh and Mandarin descended from fundamentally different original languages. Details from genetics and linguistics confirm Paul's statement in Acts 17:26, "He has made from one blood every nation of men to dwell on all the face of the earth."

Charles Darwin grouped these "nations" into "races," then organized races into those he believed were less human—less evolved—than others. He was completely wrong.

Genetically, people in each ethnicity or nation share equal standing with other men. Biblically, they share equal standing before God, "For all have sinned and fallen short of the glory of God," according to Romans 3:23.

Physical Differences

As noted, all the differences between the human races are superficial, such as differences in skin, hair, and eye color. These traits account for less than 0.012% of human genetic differences, or 1 gene out of 12,000.[295] The two major traits that American society uses to label races are hair and skin color. About 350 years ago, primarily light-skinned people from Northern Europe and dark-skinned people from Africa immigrated to North America. However, when dark-skinned people marry those with light skin, their children usually show medium-tone skin. Adam and Eve must have had medium tone skin because they carried the necessary genetic variety for all humans to follow.

Sometime in history—probably at Babel—those with darker skin took their languages one direction, while those with lighter skin took theirs in another. Babel would have had a similar effect on many other traits. Different-looking peoples intermingled at Babel. But when God dispersed them from there, each family carried its language and traits away from the other families—at first. This way, many Asian groups carried their language and light skin and special eyes (with epicanthic folds). Middle-Easterners didn't go as far, but kept their languages and medium-tone skin.

Of course, these groups almost never remained in total isolation. Genetic tests reveal that probably everybody contains a mixture of ethnic-identifying genetic markers. Most people in the world have a skin tone between the extremes, having brown skin and brown hair. Others have a mixture of traits.

Hair

Subtle genetic differences develop different shaped hair follicles that produce straight, wavy, to curly human hairs. Round hair follicles manufacture tube-like, straight hair. Oval-shaped hair follicles produce flattened hair shafts, which curl. Flatter hairs make tighter curls.

SHAPE OF THE HAIR

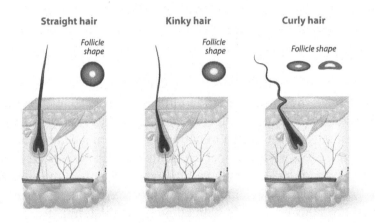

Figure 51. The Shape of the Hair.[296]

Human hair also shows a range of tones, from white to black, all depending on the amount and type of pigment they have. White hair, usually found in the elderly, almost totally lacks pigment. Brown hair contains a medium level, and black hair has the most pigment. A mutation in a gene that codes for a pigment receptor protein causes red hair. Some Neanderthal men had red hair, since their DNA shows this mutation on chromosome 16. Since the Neanderthal ethnic group went extinct long ago, this mutation must have happened early in human history.

Special cellular machinery manufactures melanin pigments. Many animals make and use it to darken their features, including insects. In humans, more melanin makes skin, hair, and eye irises darker.

Eye color

Melanin is responsible for much of our eye color. The color coats the iris diaphragm. The small black pupil of the eye is a hole that allows light to enter the inside of the eyeball, so it has no pigment. Variation in eye color from brown to green largely depends on the amount of melanin on the iris, which genetics determine. However, it involves dozens of genes, each with its own inheritance pattern, so it is difficult to pinpoint the exact color of a child's eyes by the genes alone. More melanin better block the sun's damaging ultraviolet rays. Blue eyes filter less ultraviolet light, which commonly damages retinas. Blue eyes actually result from a mutation that prevents adding the pigment necessary for proper eye protection. Persons with light blue, green, or hazel eyes have little protection from the sun, so they experience tissue damage if not protected by sunglasses. What does this have to do with ethnicities? First, mutations have clearly contributed to trait variations that we often associate with ethnicities, including eye color. Second, standard (but complicated) inheritance principles explain most color-based trait variations, including eye color. No wonder a child might seem to have "Aunt Linda's eyes." Third, the wide varieties and often stunning beauty in eye colors showcases God's creativity. Apes' and other animals' eyes are often simply dull in comparison.

Skin color

Like eye color, skin color depends on the level and type of melanin that special cells called melanocytes produce in the skin. In addition to showing variation, melanin protects the cell's nuclear DNA. It does not shield the entire cell, but it can cover the nucleus like a protective umbrella.

Figure 52. Skin Color tends to be a Major Factor in Determining Race.[297]

　　Melanin reduces ultraviolet type B (UVB) damage by absorbing or scattering the ultraviolet radiation that otherwise would have been absorbed by the DNA, causing mutations. This protects against skin cancer. The specific wavelengths of light that melanin absorbs match those of DNA, thus protecting DNA from the sun's damaging radiation. Skin color also depends upon the size, number, shape, and distribution of melanocytes, as well as the chemical nature of their melanin content.
　　Modern genetics reveals that Adam and Eve could have had within their created genes almost all the pigmentation

varieties seen today. If the trait of human skin color follows the "polygenic" inheritance pattern, then Adam and Eve's children could have appeared either very dark or very light, although most were probably medium brown, like their parents.

Vitamin D Triggered by Sunlight

A melanin balance is necessary to protect the skin's DNA from UV damage yet allow the light skin to "trigger" its benefits. Skin harvests UVB sunlight and uses it to process vitamin D, which the body requires. Vitamin D helps to promote proper bone density and growth by helping to regulate calcium and phosphorus in the body. Vitamin D deficiency leads to bones that lack the required calcium levels, causing rickets and even contributing to cancer, cardiovascular disease, mental impairment in older adults, and severe asthma in children.

What does all this have to do with the origin of people groups? As people migrated away from Babel in modern-day Iraq to northern latitudes, they had less exposure to sun. Others migrated to the tropics. Each person inherits their skin tone, and different skin tones interact differently with various climates.

Light-skinned people from the frozen north who visit lower latitude sunny locations have less melanin to block the sun's UVB rays. Without this protection, they may experience sunburn, which dramatically increases the odds of skin cancer. On the other hand, dark-skinned people visiting areas of dim sunlight may not produce enough vitamin D. They may need vitamin D supplements or obtain additional vitamin D from foods. For this reason, foods such as milk and bread are vitamin D fortified.

As global geographical distribution of various peoples shows, skin color variation is not determined by distance from the equator. Nevertheless, the skin tones we inherit can have different fits in different environments, and basic genetics reveal God could easily have programmed all human skin variation into the first created couple.

Eye Shape

Another example of superficial racial differences are the so-called almond eyes of many Asian people groups. The Asian eye has a fat layer in the upper eyelid that pushes the lid down, causing the eye to appear to be more closed. No Caucasian or Middle-Eastern ethnicities have this eye design, but two rare African tribes do. These tribes plus Asians must have inherited the trait from their ancestors at Babel. The information that codes for this trait was lost to Caucasians, Arabs, and others who migrated away from those who retained it.

All of these are normal variations and examples of the remarkable variety that exists in all life—even within each created kind. Genetics confirm that only two people, Adam and Eve, contained all the genes required to produce much of the basic variety seen across cultures today. In the end, as these people groups illustrate, race is not a biological but a sociological construct.

Darwin's Conclusions about Race and Sex

Charles Darwin, the founder of modern evolutionary theory, openly expressed racist and gender sentiments that make Bible believers cringe. As mentioned above, although the title of Darwin's most important book is often cited as *The Origin of Species*, the complete title is *The Origin of Species of Means of Natural Selection, or the Preservation of Favoured Races in the Struggle for Life*. The favored races, he argued in a later book titled *The Descent of Man* and *Selection in Relation to Sex*,[298] were supposedly Caucasians.

Darwin also taught that the "negro race" would become extinct, making the gap between whites and the lower apes wider. In his words:

> At some future period, not very distant as
> measured by centuries, the civilized races of man
> will almost certainly exterminate and replace

throughout the world the savage races ... The
break will then be rendered wider, for it will
intervene between man in a more civilized state
... than the Caucasian, and some ape as low as a
baboon, instead of as at present between the
negro or Australian and the gorilla.[299]

Darwin did not begin racism, but his ideas bolstered it
big time.[300] No science supports Darwin's main ideas, and the
Bible treats all people as equally human in God's sight.

Darwin also taught that women were biologically
inferior to men and that human sexual differences were due, in
part, to natural selection. As Darwin concluded in his *Descent
of Man* book: "the average mental power in man must be above
that of women." Darwin argued that the intellectual superiority
of males is proved by the fact that men attain:

a higher eminence, in whatever he takes up, than
can women—whether requiring deep thought,
reason, or imagination, or merely the use of the
senses and hands. If two lists were made of the
most eminent men and women in poetry,
painting, sculpture, music composition and
performance, history, science, and philosophy,
with half-a-dozen names under each subject, the
two lists would not bear comparison ...We may
also infer... that if men are capable of a decided
preeminence over women in many subjects, the
average of mental power in man must be above
that of women.[301]

Modern society has proved this naïve assumption to be
not only wrong but also irresponsible. Darwin used many
similar examples to illustrate the evolutionary forces that he
concluded produced men to be of superior physical and
intellectual strength and yet produce women to be more docile.
Thus, due to "...success in the general struggle for life; and as

in both cases the struggle will have been during maturity, the characters thus gained will have been transmitted more fully to the male than to the female offspring. Thus, man has ultimately become superior to woman."[302] All this imaginative drivel ignores God's Word entirely. Genesis 1 extols the equality of genders by telling us that God created both husband and wife together as a married couple to reflect His image. It takes both to reflect His image. As a divinity student, Darwin surely read this. Did he deliberately ignore it?

Radiometric Dating: Doesn't it Show that the Earth is 4.5 Billion Years Old?

Suggested Videos:

Radiometric Dating: https://youtu.be/fg6MfnmxPB4
Six Days: https://youtu.be/pjx88K8JTY8
Young/Old Earth: https://youtu.be/QzEzkrMdgIs
The Bible and History: https://youtu.be/6okZJlw84lo

Secular scientists date the Earth to about 4.5 billion years old by using selected radiometric dating results. Ultimately, what they call "deep time" serves as the very *foundation* of evolution theory. High school biology books openly acknowledge this necessary connection:

> Evolution takes a long time. If life has evolved, then Earth must be very old. Geologists now use radioactivity to establish the age of certain rocks and fossils. This kind of data could have shown that the Earth is young. If that had happened, Darwin's ideas would have been refuted and abandoned. Instead, radioactive dating indicates that Earth is about 4.5 billion years old—plenty of time for evolution and natural selection to take place.[303]

But as we show here, geologists do not use radioactivity to establish the age of certain rocks. They instead use selected radioactivity results to confirm what they need to see. As discussed in previous chapters, this viewpoint, being secular, contradicts God's stated Word in Genesis and even the Ten Commandments, where He wrote with His own hand that He created the heavens, Earth, sea, and all that is in them in six days (Exodus 20:11).

Belief in deep time rests upon evolution's required time. That's sure putting a lot of faith in something that can't be tested through direct observation. After all, plenty of assumptions go into the calculations, as we'll discuss in this chapter.

Keep in mind that while this chapter reviews the technical details behind radiometric dating, only two very basic but completely catastrophic "fatal flaws" undermine radiometric dating.

The **first fatal flaw** is that it relies upon *untestable assumptions*. The entire practice of radiometric dating stands or falls on the veracity of four *untestable* assumptions. The assumptions are untestable because we cannot go back millions of years to verify the findings done today in a laboratory, and we cannot go back in time to test the original conditions in which the rocks were formed. If these assumptions that underlie radiometric dating are not true, then the entire theory falls flat, like a chair without its four legs.

The **second fatal flaw** clearly reveals that at least one of those assumptions must actually be wrong because radiometric dating *fails to correctly date rocks of known ages*. For example, in the case of Mount St. Helens, we watched rocks being formed in the 1980s, but when sent to a laboratory 10 years later for dating, the 10-year-old rocks returned ages of hundreds of thousands to millions of years. Similarly, some rocks return radiometric "ages" twice as old as the accepted age for earth. Most rocks return conflicting radiometric "ages." In these cases, researchers select results that match what they already believe

190

about earth's age (see the section **Brand New Rocks Give Old "Ages"** for details of this study and several others like it).

Overview of Radiometric Dating[304]

Fossil remains are found in sedimentary rock layers. Layers of sediment form when various size particles (e.g., dirt, rocks, and vegetation) accumulate in places such as deserts, rivers, lakes, and the ocean. Most texts teach that it takes a long time for these sediments to build up, with older layers buried beneath younger layers. Fossils found in lower layers are deemed to be older than those in the upper layers, older on the bottom younger on the top. This is called relative age dating, the first step.

Next, evolutionary scientists then use *index fossils* to help establish the relative ages of rock layers that are not directly related to one another and their fossils. Index fossils are distinct fossils, usually of an extinct organism found in only one or a few layers, though that layer or layers outcrops in many places—at least that's the theory. They help establish and correlate the relative ages of rock layers. Index fossils typically have a short stratigraphic or vertical range. In reality, many index fossils occur above or below their expected ranges. In some cases, they turn up still alive today, but these can go unreported. Evolutionists assume that the creature evolved somehow, lived for a certain time period, and then died out. Textbooks are correct when they state that relative dating provides no information whatsoever about a fossil's absolute age. Nevertheless, most textbook writers and the scientists they rely on grew up with a belief in uniformitarian geologic processes. The principle of uniformity is a philosophy and an assumption that the slow geologic processes going on today must explain the deposits of the past. They teach the motto, "the present is the key to the past." It's not. As any judge in court will attest, eyewitness records record the past more accurately. Also, keen observations in the field testify that the sediments comprising the ancient rock layers were laid down *catastrophically,* not slowly over millions of years.

Today, the geologic time scale shows ages based on radiometric age dating. Many textbook authors consider radiometric ages as absolute ages. However, as you will soon learn, these techniques stray far from absolute dates, though they may reveal relative ages of some rocks.

The Age of the Earth

Today's evolutionists base their age of the Earth on their interpretation of radioactive elements. They assign 4.5 billion years to earth based on the belief that earth itself evolved, so to speak, from a molten mass. But they cannot directly date the earth using selected isotopes because they believe all rocks have cycled over imagined eons, leaving no original rocks to test. They assume meteorites formed when earth did. Researchers age-dated a meteorite to sometime around the age they would accept. Thus, the earth itself has no direct evidence for its vast evolutionary age assignment.

The various rock layers are given names with assigned ages (Figure 53). Those who believe these ever-changing but always unimaginably old age assignments call each rock System a "Period." The names help, but their age assignments derive from results chosen to agree with evolutionary time. To understand exactly why, we must first learn the basics of radioactive elements and of the techniques used when treating these systems of elements as clocks.

Many elements on the periodic table have radioactive forms. Stable atoms have a set number of protons, neutrons, and orbital electrons. Isotopes are atoms of the same elements with the same number of protons but different numbers of neutrons. Some isotopes are radioactive and others are stable. A radioactive nucleus is not stable. It changes into another element by emitting particles and/or radiation.

EON	ERA	PERIOD	EPOCH	Alleged Age Years	Young Earth Evidences
Phanerozoic This is where most fossils occur	Cenozoic	Quaternary	Holocene	10,000	
			Pleistocene	2,600,000	Soft Frog with bloody bone marrow
		Tertiary	Pliocene	5,300,000	Salamander muscle
			Miocene	23,000,000	
			Oligocene	30,900,000	Young coal, Penguin feathers, Lizard skin
			Eocene	55,800,000	
			Paleocene	65,500,000	
	Mesozoic	Cretaceous		145,500,000	Young Diamonds Young Coal
		Jurassic		201,600,000	Dinosaur DNA, blood, blood vessels and protein
		Triassic		251,000,000	
	Paleozoic	Permian		299,000,000	
		Pennsylvanian		318,000,000	Young Coal
		Mississippian		359,000,000	
		Devonian		416,000,000	
		Silurian		444,000,000	
		Ordovician		488,000,000	
		Cambrian		542,000,000	
Precambrian	Proterozoic Eon				Helium in zircon crystals
				2,500,000,000	
	Archean Eon				
				3,850,000,000	

Figure 53. Uniformitarian Geologic Time Scale with problems noted under "Young Earth Evidence." The time scale is placed vertically because older sedimentary deposits are buried beneath younger sedimentary deposits. The assumption of slow geologic processes and radiometric age dating has drastically inflated the age of the Earth and its strata.

A basic way to express the rate of radioactive decay is called the half-life. This equals the length of time needed for 50% of a quantity of radioactive material to decay. Unstable radioactive isotopes called parent elements become stable elements called daughter elements. Each radioactive element has its own specific half-life (see Table 4).

Table 4: Radiometric Isotopes and Half-Lives.

Examples of Radioactive Isotopes that Change into Stable Elements		
Radioactive Parent Element	**Stable Daughter Element**	**Half-Life**
Carbon-14 (^{14}C)	Nitrogen-14 (^{14}N)	5,730 Years
Potassium-40 (^{40}K)	Argon-40 (^{40}Ar)	1.3 Billion Years
Uranium-238 (^{238}U)	Lead-206 (^{206}Pb)	4.5 Billion Years
Rubidium-87 (^{87}Rb)	Strontium-87 (^{87}Sr)	48.6 Billion Years

Note: Carbon-14 is not used to date minerals or rocks, but is used for organic remains that contain carbon, such as wood, bone, or shells.

To estimate a radioisotope age of a crystalline rock, geologists measure the ratio between radioactive parent and stable daughter products in the rock. They can even isolate isotopes from specific, crystallized minerals within a rock. They then use a model to convert the measured ratio into an age estimate. The models incorporate key assumptions, like the ratio of parent to daughter isotopes in the originally formed rock. How can anyone know this information? We can't. We must assume some starting condition. Evolutionists assume that as soon as a crystalline rock cooled from melt, it inherited no daughter product from the melt. This way, they can have their clock start at zero. However, when they find isotope ratios that contradict other measurements or evolution, they often invoke inherited daughter product. This saves the desired age assignments.

Igneous (crystalline) rocks—those that have formed from molten magma or lava—are the primary rock types analyzed to determine radiometric ages. For example, let's assume that when an igneous rock solidified, a certain mineral in it contained 1,000 atoms of radioactive potassium (^{40}K) and zero atoms of argon (^{40}Ar). After one half-life of 1.3 billion years, the rock would contain 500 ^{40}K and 500 ^{40}Ar atoms, since 50% has decayed. This is a 500:500 or 500-parent:500-daughter ratio, which reduces to a 1:1 ratio. If the sample contained this ratio, then the rock would be declared 1.3 billion years old. If the ratio is greater than 1:1, then not even one half-life has expired, so the rock would be younger. However, if the ratio is less than 1:1, then the rock is considered older than the half-life for that system.

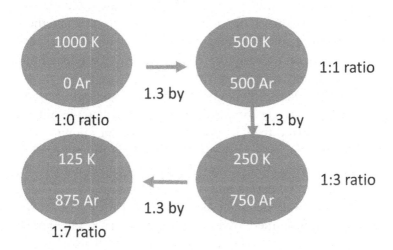

Figure 54. Decay of Radioactive potassium-40 to argon-40. "by" means "billions of years," K is potassium, Ar is argon. After three half-lives of this system, totaling 3.9 billion years, only 125 of the original 1000 radioactive potassium-40 atoms remain, assuming even decay for all that time.

Age-dating a rock requires at least these four basic assumptions:

1. Laboratory measurements that have no human error or misjudgments,
2. The rock began with zero daughter element isotopes,

3. The rock maintained a "closed system" (defined below), and
4. The decay rate remained constant.

Each of these deserves further description.

1. Measuring the radioactive parent and stable daughter elements to obtain the ratio between them must be accurate, and it usually is. Keep in mind that most laboratory technicians believe in deep time. This sets the time periods they expect. They all memorized the geologic time scale long before they approached their research, and thus may not even consider that processes other than radioisotope decay may have produced the accurately measured isotope ratios.
2. Next, this technician assumes that all the radioactive parent isotopes began decaying right when the mineral crystallized from a melt. He also assumes none of the stable daughter element was present at this time. How can anyone really know the mineral began with 100% radioactive parent and 0% daughter elements? What if some stable daughter element was already present when the rock formed? After all, these experts often explain away unexpected radioisotope age results using the excuse that daughter or parent isotopes must have been present when the rock formed. Without knowledge of the starting condition, the use of isotopes as clocks means nothing.
3. A closed system means that no extra parent or daughter elements have been added or removed throughout the history of the rock. Have you ever seen an atom? Of course not. It is too small, but we must think about this on an atomic level. Decay byproducts like argon and helium are both gases. Neither gas tends to attach to any other atom, meaning they rarely do chemistry. Instead of reacting with atoms in rock crystals, they build up in rock systems and can move in and out of the rocks. One

leading expert in isotope geology states that most minerals do not even form in closed systems. A closed system would retain all the argon that radioactive potassium produces. He emphasizes that for a radioactive-determined date to be true, the mineral must be in a closed system.[305] Is there any such thing as a closed system when speaking of rocks?

4. The constant-decay rate assumption assumes the decay rate remained the same throughout the history of the rock. Lab experiments have shown that most changes in temperature, pressure, and the chemical environment have very little effect on decay rates. These experiments have led researchers to have great confidence that this is a reasonable assumption, but it may not hold true. Is the following quote an overstatement of known science? "Radioactive transmutations must have gone on at the present rates under all the conditions that have existed on Earth in the geologic past."[306] Some scientists have found evidence that zircon crystals endured high levels of radioactive decay in the past, as discussed below. This evidence challenges assumption #4.

To illustrate how much radioisotope dating hinges on assumptions, imagine you encounter a burning candle sitting on a table. How long has that candle been burning? We can calculate the answer if we know the candle's *burn rate history* and *original length*. However, if the original length is not known, or if it cannot be verified that the burning rate has been constant, it is impossible to tell for sure how long the candle was burning. A similar problem occurs with radiometric dating of rocks. Since the initial physical state of the rock is unknowable, workers must assume it."[307]

Brand New Rocks Give Old "Ages"

Scientific literature omitted from public school textbooks reveal radioisotope age assignments much older than the known ages of many rocks. These results first arrived in the 1960s and 1970s, but most of the scientific community still pays no attention. Argon and helium isotopes were measured from recent basalt lava erupted on the deep ocean floor from the Kilauea volcano in Hawaii. Researchers calculated up to 22,000,000 years for brand new rocks![308] The problem is common. Table 5 gives six examples among many more.

Table 5: Young Volcanic Rocks with Really Old Whole-Rock K-Ar Model Ages.[309]

Lava Flow, Rock Type, and Location	Year Formed or Known Age	^{40}K-^{40}Ar "Age"
Kilauea Iki basalt, Hawaii	AD 1959	8,500,000 years
Volcanic bomb, Mt. Stromboli, Italy	AD 1963	2,400,000 years
Mt. Etna basalt, Sicily	AD 1964	700,000 years
Medicine Lake Highlands obsidian, Glass Mountains, California	<500 years	12,600,000 years
Hualalai basalt, Hawaii	AD 1800–1801	22,800,000 years
Mt. St. Helens dacite lava dome, Washington	AD 1986	350,000 years

The oldest real age of these recent volcanic rocks is less than 500 years. People witnessed and described the molten lava solidify into most of these rocks just decades ago. Many of these were only about 10 years old. And yet ^{40}K-^{40}Ar dating gives ages from 350,000 to >22,800,000 years.

Potassium-Argon (^{40}K-^{40}Ar) has been the most widespread method of radioactive age-dating for the Phanerozoic rocks, where most fossils occur. The misdated

198

rocks shown above violate the initial condition assumption of no radiogenic argon (^{40}Ar) present when the igneous rock formed. There is too much ^{40}Ar present in recent lava flows. Thus, the method gives excessively old ages for recent rocks. The amounts of argon in these rocks indicate they carry isotope "ages" much, much older than their known ages. Could the argon they measured have come from a source other than radioactive potassium decay? If so, then geologists have been trusting a faulty method. If they can't obtain correct values for rocks of known ages, then why should we trust the values they obtain for rocks of unknown ages?

These wrong radioisotope ages violate the initial condition assumption of zero (0%) parent argon present when the rock formed. Furthermore, the slow radioactive decay of ^{40}K shows that there was insufficient time since cooling for measurable amounts of ^{40}Ar to have accumulated in the rock. Therefore, radiogenic argon (^{40}Ar) was *already present* in the rocks as they formed.

Radiometric age dating should no longer be sold to the public as providing reliable, absolute ages. Excess argon invalidates the initial condition assumption for potassium dating, and excess helium invalidates the closed-system assumption for uranium dating. The ages shown on the uniformitarian geologic time scale should be removed.

"Young" Fossils in "Old" Mud

Researchers have scoured the Ono Formation near Redding in northern California. They described it in scientific publications for more than 140 years. Because the area has millions of fossils (including the valuable ammonites) and fossilized wood trapped in the same mudflow layers, it provides a unique opportunity for carbon dating. If the wood still has relatively short-lived radiocarbon inside it, then the age of the supposedly ancient fossils would need revision.

Geologist Andrew Snelling gathered four samples of ammonites and wood buried and fossilized together in this solidified mudstone and sent them to the IsoTrace Radiocarbon Laboratory at the University of Toronto, Canada for dating analysis.[310] Table 6 summarizes the results.

Table 6. Ono Formation Radiocarbon Dating Results.

Dating Results from Ammonites and Wood Fossils in the Ono Formation (Snelling, 2008)			
Specimen	Rock layers	Ammonites	Wood
Dating	112 to 120 Million (conventional age)	36,400 to 48,710 carbon years	32,780 to 42,390 carbon years

Because the ammonites and wood fossils came from a rock unit conventionally regarded as 112 to 120 million years old, the fossils should share that same age. Such an age far exceeds the limit of the radioactive carbon (^{14}C) method, which in theory extends to artifacts less than 100,000 carbon years old. In other words, if these fossils are really over 100 million years old, then there should have been absolutely no measurable ^{14}C in them—but there was—enough to produce easily measurable ages of 32,000 to 48,000 years!

Scientists who believe in long ages assert that the ammonites and wood samples were contaminated with modern carbon in the ground, during sampling, or even in the laboratory. But this study took extensive steps to guard against such contamination. So how can 36,000 carbon-year-old ammonites and 32,000 carbon-year-old wood be stuck in a mudflow of 112 million or more conventional years? Two logical options present themselves:

1. One of the three dates is correct and the other two are wrong.
2. All three of the dates are wrong.

If Biblical history is accurate as we believe it is, then the second option is the correct choice—*none of the dates are correct.* The fact that measurable ^{14}C existed in the ammonites and wood fossils shows that they are very young–certainly not 112–120 million years old. But how can they still outdate the Biblical age of Creation of about 6,000 years? A number of factors help explain this. First, the Earth's stronger magnetic field in the recent past would have reduced the atmospheric ^{14}C production rate. Second, "because the recent Genesis Flood removed so much carbon from the biosphere and buried it, the measured apparent radiocarbon ages are still much higher than the true ages of the fossil ammonites and wood."[311]

Therefore, the true ages of the ammonites and wood are consistent with their burial during the Genesis Flood about 4,400 years ago.[312] Back then, muddy waters washed sediments and ammonites onto land.

Figure 55. Fossil Ammonites in Rock Concretions in the Ono Formation, California.

Red in Tooth and Claw: If Animals Were First Created to Be Vegetarian, Why Do Many Look like They Were Designed to Be Carnivores?

If God created a perfect world at the beginning and animals were first designed as vegetarians, how did defense and attack structures like fangs and claws come about? There are two primary perspectives on this topic, so we'll briefly review each.

The first is that these features were not originally used for carnivory. In other words, the design was the same but the function was different. Take sharp teeth, for example. Panda bears have sharp teeth, but 99% of their diet is bamboo.[313] The same is true for numerous other creatures that appear to be vicious meat-eaters, but have a primarily vegetarian diet.

Figure 56. Pandas eat bamboo, but have teeth structures that appear to be designed as a "meat-eater."

Animals don't use their large canine teeth just to eat meat. They are also used in communication. For example, many apes, dogs, cats, and other animals expose their canines to express dominance, ownership of mates, and guard territory. The same teeth that are used by wolves for killing and eating are used by dogs today for eating domestic dog food. Even sharp claws that are used today for predation are used in many cases for climbing and defense. So, this first view avoids suggesting that God's initial design features were intended to be harmful to other creatures in His creation.

One of the limitations with this first viewpoint is that it excludes animals from changes that the Fall certainly introduced to the other parts of Creation, such as thorns and thistles being introduced to plants. Genesis 3:17–19 is clear that plants were cursed by man's Fall with thorns and thistles, and plants use thorns primarily as a defense mechanism. Were animals exempt from similar changes that were introduced by the Fall?

The second viewpoint is that defense and attack features were introduced by God as a result of the Fall. However, it is not a widely-held Biblical Creation position that animals quickly and recently developed all physical features used for predation. This is because physical change was not required to make plant-eaters into meat-eaters. It was merely a change in *behavior*. We see this happen today when captive plant eaters suddenly eat their cage-mates. Many of the features that animals use for predation also help them eat plants. Also, many predators must learn to kill, as many social predators like lions are not born with the knowledge of how to hunt and kill. Instead, other animals in their group must teach them.

Biblical Creationist and Biologist, Dr. Nathaniel Jeanson addresses this:

> How did these big cats acquire their sharp teeth? At the Curse, God probably didn't speak sharp teeth into existence out of nothing. His acts of global creation were finished by day seven of the creation week (Genesis 2:1–3; Exodus 20:11; Hebrews 4:3). So where did the lion's teeth come from? ... God may have created creatures with latent genetic information to be "switched on" only after Genesis 3, a concept similar to the

"mediated design" model. Alternatively, God may have created anatomical and physiological features capable of multiple purposes. Powerful jaws, now used to kill and tear flesh, may have initially been used to open fruits and plant seeds of the size and hardness of modern watermelons and coconuts. Could the lion's teeth have been used for tearing tough plants and roots in the beginning? Biblically, this latter hypothesis is compelling. Consider the effects of the reversal of the Curse in Isaiah 11:6–7: 'The wolf also shall dwell with the lamb, and the leopard shall lie down with the kid; and the calf and the young lion and the fatling together...*the lion shall eat straw like the ox.*' In reversing the Curse, God doesn't seem to change the lion's anatomy; He simply changes the lion's behavior. Furthermore, Scripture explicitly mentions God switching the mental states of animals after the Flood (Genesis 9:2). Might He also have done something much like this at the Curse?[314] (emphasis added)

Science: Does Evolution Theory Hold up to the Rigors of "True Science"?

Suggested Videos:

Observational Science: https://youtu.be/G1Z0PAqgjWo
Science & the Bible: https://youtu.be/CFYswvGoaPU
Seeing through Evolution: https://youtu.be/zr_NXmnC7hI

The real "scientific method" that establishes and underlies the tools that we use today for bringing about *knowledge* that is trustworthy, dependable, and verifiable employs the seven steps outlined in Figure 57. *Observational* science is much different than *historical* science. We cannot run *observable* experiments on the past. Experiments conducted today give clues about what was once possible or likely, but that's about all they can give. Often, vast inferences are made on *unobservable, untestable, non-replicable,* and therefore *unprovable* assumptions. True observational science typically involves six steps, and three of these are observation, repetition, and testing. None of these can be done for evolution or for any event that occurred in the *unrepeatable* past. We can't go back to test something that occurred 1 million supposed years ago. For example, in all recorded history (the last 4,000 to 5,000 years), no one has ever documented a case of *true vertical evolution*, for example where an almost-bird evolved a beak, or an almost-fish evolved fins. Yes, we see *change* and *adaptability* but always within the God-prescribed limits of the original animal "kinds."

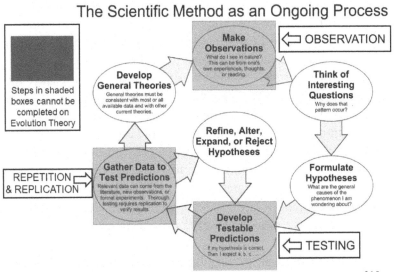

Figure 57. The Scientific Method as an Ongoing Process.[315]

Starlight: Doesn't Distant Starlight Prove Creation Is Billions of Years Old?

> *Suggested Video:*
>
> Distant Starlight: https://youtu.be/BGvds-t5Jy0

Distant starlight is very explainable, both biblically and technically. Let's start with the short answer based on the Bible. First, humans were not present when God created light, space, speed, time, gravity, and the stars. These were all formed during the first five days of creation, miraculously (Hebrews 11:3). This means that the natural confines, measurements, and relationships between these things were not the same as they are today. The way God spoke to Job about this still applies today. He said, "Do you know the ordinances of the heavens? Can you set their dominion over the earth?" God—almost sarcastically—asks Job if He knows how the rules and laws of the heavens work. Today, we still cannot answer this question.

God also asked Job if he knows the "way to the dwelling of light?" (Job 38:19). Today, we still cannot even measure the one-way speed of light. Therefore, the Biblical answer is that there will always be—this side of heaven—some mysteries surrounding His Creation that we will never be able to understand. The universe is one of the greatest displays of God's awesome power and creativity. As David wrote in Psalm 19:1, "The heavens declare the glory of God, and the sky above proclaims his handiwork." Indeed, the size and scope of the heavenly bodies reminds us of the infinite wisdom of our Creator.

When we use our very limited, finite reasoning to understand how a miraculous, infinite God created the expansive universe and stars, we sometimes run into challenges. One of these challenges is trying to understand how, based on our present understanding, it apparently takes billions of years for light to travel from distant galaxies to earth. Indeed, we can measure these distances today using operational science.

However, to properly understand this issue, there are some things we should first consider.

First, the Bible holds that Creation was a one-time event. We cannot repeat the events that occurred at creation—not with the stars, the earth, the heavens, or anything else. God's creative works are not subject to a laboratory experiment. They are not repeatable, testable, or observable. We cannot, therefore, understand the mechanisms and powers involved in the initial Creation process.

Second, Creation was a supernatural event; therefore, some aspects cannot be understood with our limited understanding (Isaiah 55:9). The natural laws in place today describe God's normal way of upholding the universe. They were not yet in place when He created the universe! For example, the law of conservation of mass, which says that mass can neither be created nor destroyed, was not in place during Creation week. God was "speaking" new matter and energy into existence (Psalm 33:9).

Because Creation was a one-time, supernatural event, our ability to understand how He Created things and how it fits into the world we see today is very limited. We only have one side of the Creation Equation—what we see today, and what laws are in place today. We cannot assume that we can understand the "Creation side" of this equation, which is the most important part!

It is important to remember that God is not bound by the same natural laws that govern His creation, because He was the One who put them in place. He is not constrained by distance or time—two laws that govern our world today. When God finished His creation, it all worked! It didn't need time to "get up to speed" to function. Adam was created as a mature man when he was only minutes old, as we might perceive him. We don't know how fast light was traveling during the Creation week.

We see examples of God intervening in our world's laws of distance and time in the Gospel accounts of Christ's miracles. When Christ healed the centurion's servant, the centurion

207

expressed his belief that Christ had power over distance. In Luke 7:6–7, he said, "Lord, do not trouble yourself, for I am not worthy to have you come under my roof... But say the word, and let my servant be healed." The servant was instantly healed, without having to wait for the normal process of healing to occur. There is also no indication in John 2:9 that Christ had to wait for the water to turn into wine. Both are examples of "miracles" because they were supernatural, not following the natural laws of nature.

Next, let's look at what the Bible says about Creation. A straightforward reading of Genesis and other passages seem to indicate that each creative act preceded by a "let there be" command was immediately followed. In Genesis 1, every time this phrase appears, it is directly followed by the statement, "and it was so," with no hint that any significant amount of time passed between God's command and its fulfillment. This same pattern appears in the description of the creation of heavenly bodies in Genesis 1:14-15, "And God said, 'Let there be lights in the expanse of the heavens to separate the day from the night. And let them be for signs and for seasons, and for days and years, and let them be lights in the expanse of the heavens to give light upon the earth. And it was so.'" This same phrase— and it was so—is repeated six times in Genesis 1, all describing how God's spoken Creation manifested right after it was spoken. The text knows nothing of evolutionary time. God said, and it was so; "He spoke, and it was done" (Genesis 1:9). There is no billions-of-years gap in between those two. If there was, then why doesn't the text just say so?

The Genesis 1 Creation text also fits other Scriptures, such as Hebrews 11:3, which states: "By faith we understand that the worlds were prepared by the word of God, so that what is seen was not made out of things which are visible." In Romans 4:17, Paul says that Abraham believed God, who "calls into being that which does not exist."

But just how was this done? What might it have looked like? Prominent astrophysicist Dr. Danny Faulkner has drawn insight from the Hebrew text in Genesis regarding the creation of the stars and related starlight.[316] He said, "It is instructive to examine God's activities on the other days of the Creation Week to perhaps gain insight into patterns that might be useful to explore on Day Four. Of particular interest is the creation of plants on Day Three (Gen. 1:11, KJV), which states, 'Then God said, 'Let the earth bring forth grass, the herb that yields seed, and the fruit tree that yields fruit according to its kind, whose seed is in itself, on the earth'; and it was so' and Verse 12 goes on to state: 'And the earth brought forth grass, the herb that yields seed according to its kind, and the tree that yields fruit, whose seed is in itself according to its kind. And God saw that it was good.'" Dr. Faulkner points out that God commands the earth to "bring forth" and then the earth, in obedience, "brought forth." He continues:

> Genesis 1:11 employs the hiphil stem of דשא (dš'), which is used to express causative action with an active voice. The KJV fittingly translates this as, "Let … bring forth." The New American Standard Bible renders it similarly, "Let … sprout." Lexically speaking, דשא does not indicate anything about how the earth brought forth plants; however, contextual clues indicate that the use of דשא in Genesis 1:11 involves a rapid-growth process. That is, on Day Three, plants did not instantly appear. Instead, plants grew up to become mature. It is clear from the blessing that God saw that it was good (v. 12b) and the immediate closure of the Third Day (v. 13) that this was not the usual, slow process that we see today in plants, but rather it was an abnormally very rapid growth and development of plants. At the very least, the plants (including trees with fruit) had to have mature fruit by Days Five and Six, for animals and people made then required them for food, which God ordained for them (vv. 29–30). It is very easy to imagine this very rapid Day Three sprouting and growing to maturity of plants as resembling a time-lapse movie of plant growth today.

Dr. Faulkner points out that this abnormally fast growth and development of plants on Day Three may be like the pattern of making the astronomical bodies on Day Four. He says this understanding is consistent with the concept of the stretching (נטה; ntḥ) or the spreading out (מתח; mtḥ) of the heavens found in the Old Testament (Isaiah 40:22, 42:5, 44:24, 45:12, and 51:13).

While many hold to the "big bang" theory (the universe was in a very high-density state and then expanded about 13.8 billion years ago), many scientists do not.[317] Distant starlight is a bigger dilemma for big-bang proponents than it is for those who hold to a straightforward reading of Scripture. For example, here are two problems that distant starlight poses to the big-bang model:[318]

Horizon Problem: Astronomers and physicists predicted, based on the big-bang model, that the Cosmic Microwave Background (CMB) radiation would display an uneven temperature due to temperature fluctuations in the early universe. But the physical data shows that the CMB is extremely uniform in temperature, thus confounding the predictions of big-bang theorists.[319] According to these scientists, not enough time has passed for energy to transfer from "hot" areas to "cold" areas in the form of electromagnetic radiation (light), even in the supposed 13.8 billion years since the big bang.

Distant Mature Galaxies Problem: According to big bang cosmology, "primitive" galaxies began to form within the first few billion years after the big bang. If this is true, then we should be able to see these galaxies the further we look out in space (since the light from these galaxies supposedly only reached us for the first time in the recent past). However, when astronomers scan the heavens, they find 'mature' galaxies up to 12 billion light-years away, existing supposedly less than 2 billion years after the big bang.[320]

Let's remember that we have a very limited understanding with zero ability to create anything like an all-powerful God. Let's also remember that God is not bound by

210

the same natural laws that govern His Creation, because He was the One who put them in place. He is not constrained by distance or time, as He demonstrated by the miracles He conducted on Earth.

Sun Day 4: How Can Light Exist During the First Three Days of Creation When the Sun Was Not Created until the Fourth Day?

Genesis 1:3–5 states, "Then God said, "Let there be light"; and there was light. And God saw the light, that it was good; and God divided the light from the darkness. God called the light Day, and the darkness He called Night. So the evening and the morning were the first day." A few verses later God created the "lights in the expanse of the sky to separate the day from the night… [and the] two great lights—the greater light to govern the day and the lesser light to govern the night… And there was evening, and there was morning—the fourth day" (Genesis 1:14–19). How can there be light, mornings, and evenings on the first, second, and third days if the sun, moon, and stars were not created until the fourth day?

The answer is found in Scripture and not inside of our limited minds with understanding based on how we see natural laws and relationships in play in the modern world. The Bible states that *God Himself is light*: "This is the message we have heard from him and declare to you: God is light; in Him there is no darkness at all" (1 John 1:5). Therefore, possibly God Himself was the light for the first three days of Creation. Something similar may also be in the case when God creates the new heavens and earth: "There will be no more night. They will not need the light of a lamp or the light of the sun, for the Lord God will give them light. And they will reign for ever and ever" (Revelation 22:5).

Theistic Evolution: What's Wrong with the Idea That God Used Evolution to Create Everything?

In a nutshell, theistic evolution is the belief that God used evolution to bring about the variety of life on Earth over millions of years. The Bible plainly disagrees with theistic evolution. More and more student-aged Christians are becoming theistic evolutionists—especially those raised in public school and don't receive much biblical training at home or in church.

One of the most common testimonies we hear from high schoolers goes something like this: They become Christians at a young age, but they don't get much training in doctrine, especially creation-evolution related topics. After being saturated in public school evolutionary teaching (and not hearing the Biblical Creation view from parents or church leaders), they start developing *cognitive dissonance*—the tension that develops when holding two contradictory beliefs. They begin questioning: "I know that God exists, but they seem to present so much credible evidence for evolution at school, and it seems like the 'smart scientists' tend to believe it." Many take the shortest route to resolving this mental tension by adopting a worldview that is somewhere between their Christian faith and evolution. Without even knowing it, they have just adopted the view of theistic evolution and compromised their trust and reliance on the Bible.

In one subtle play, the enemy replaces belief in an all-powerful God who spoke creation into existence with a "god" who creates life through a slow, random, murderous process of death and suffering. If true, the Bible wouldn't really mean what it says. Should we trust a god who lied to us about our beginnings? Those who pretend there's nothing wrong with this, downgrade the Bible and suspend reason. Exposing six fatal flaws with theistic evolution resolves the issue by leaving the Genesis record standing tall.

The Six Fatal Flaws of Theistic Evolution

We've distilled the major problems of theistic evolution into a list of the top six. As we'll see, the problems with theistic evolution are not just some abstract theological problems—they bring a serious impact in the daily lives of believers. After all, our beliefs form the roots of our actions and the sum of our actions make up our lives and our choices.

Adam Versus Apes: Theistic Evolution Denies the Biblical Creation of Adam and Makes Apes Our Ancestors

The Bible is clear that Adam was created spontaneously and supernaturally by God, in God's own image and likeness, out of the dust of the Earth (Genesis 1:26 and following). We are not made in the image of some lower ape-like creature, and the "image" of God and His "likeness" certainly does not match that of an ape.

Genesis also gives us a strong clue that we did not evolve from any type of "lower life form" or ape-like ancestor. Adam's first order from God was to study and name all the animal *kinds*. After doing this, Adam noticed that none of them represented a suitable "match" for his "kind" (humans) (Genesis 2:20). God's solution was to draw a helper/companion from Adam's own side and create Eve. Adam's response to this was: "This is now *bone of my bones, and flesh of my flesh*; she shall be called Woman, because she was *taken out of Man*" (Genesis 2:23) (emphasis added).

How is it possible that we evolved from ape-like creatures if Adam had single-handedly studied and named all the animal kinds on earth and determined there wasn't a single creature—chimps included—that resembled his *kind*? Christians who ascribe to theistic evolution simply cannot reconcile monkey-to-man evolution with the Bible.

Making this idea even worse, evolution holds that humans exist as they are today because our particular line of ape-like ancestors out-lasted and even out-killed other varieties.

This is a far cry from humans being specially created out of the dust of the Earth in the image of a loving and intentional God. Jesus Himself clearly disagreed with the ideas that millions of years of human evolution occurred by stating, "But *from the beginning* of the creation, God 'made them male and female'" (Mark 10:6) (emphasis added).

Biblical Order of Creation

The basic order of the Creation account in Genesis 1 disagrees with modern, man-made ideas of how evolution supposedly unfolded (see Table 7).

Table 7. Differences between the Bible and Evolution.

Bible	Evolution
Earth before the sun	**Sun** before the earth
Oceans before land	**Land** before oceans
Land plants first	**Oceanlife** first
Fish before insects	**Insects** before fish
Plants before sun	**Sun** before plants
Birds before reptiles	**Reptiles** before birds
God created man instantly after all other animals were created	The **process of death** created man, and evolution is still occuring, though invisible because it takes millions of years

Table 7 lays out how the Biblical order of Creation is opposite to how evolution supposedly happened.

Theistic Evolution Makes Death, and not God, Our Creator

No matter which "version" of evolution one holds to—whether naturalistic evolution without a God or theistic evolution with a process started by God and left to run its course, or progressive creation where God uses cosmological and geological evolution while occasionally wiping out and creating new life forms along the way—the core problem with all versions of evolution is its proposal that the process of *death is set up as the creator of life.* Each version of evolution has a bloody, competitive, "survival of the fittest" process as the creator of new life forms. Each starts from lower life forms and eventually leads to man over millions of years. There are some serious problems with this view, and it could not differ more from the biblical account! What kind of all-powerful God would need to use a cruel, experimental process to bring about the variety of life on earth?

The idea of *punctuated equilibrium* (a view even held, in some form, by many progressive creationists) holds that God advances evolutionary development by isolated episodes of rapid speciation between long periods of little or no change. In other words, God used "random, wasteful, inefficiencies" to create the world into which Adam was placed.[321] What kind of God couldn't get it right the first time, so He had to experiment with hapless life forms?

To the contrary, the Bible holds that God initially created everything perfect, and then our sin initiated the process of death, suffering, and bloodshed. How could God look upon all His Creation and call it "very good" (Genesis 1:31) if animals (and later humans) were tearing each other apart to survive...for millions of years before Adam? Why would an all-powerful, loving, merciful God need to use a blood-filled, clumsy, random process to populate the Earth with animal variety? God's initial Creation was perfect, but we messed it up! Theistic evolution violates clear Bible statements and clearly seen attributes of God.

If natural selection and survival of the fittest is going on in today's world, this process is a "mindless" one without creative agency. For example, consider a large field with a healthy population of grasshoppers in two color varieties, green and yellow. When the fields are green in the springtime, the green grasshoppers may thrive more than the yellow ones because they blend in to their surroundings, being less visible to their predators. Then, in the fall when the fields turn yellow, this process is reversed, and the yellow grasshoppers thrive. Would this natural selection produce new and useful genetic information? Certainly not! Rather, the pre-programmed gene variability that God installed into the grasshoppers interacts with their environment. The grasshoppers are all still grasshoppers! We see the same principle in oscillating bird beak shapes. Darwin's finches are proudly used to promote evolution in today's school textbooks. However, they show no net evolution—just a long cycle between skinny and stout beak shapes.

Theistic Evolution Places Death before Sin

Perhaps the most serious problem with theistic evolution is that it has man coming on the scene after billions of years of death-filled evolution has taken place. This makes the brutal "survival of the fittest" process God's idea instead of the consequence of sin. To the contrary, according to the Bible, when man appears in Creation, he is perfect and sinless and there's no such thing as death. Death does not come into the picture *until man sins* ("but of the tree of the knowledge of good and evil you shall not eat, for in the day that you eat of it you shall surely die," Genesis 2:17). So, you can't have death of mankind before the Fall of man and have a logical foundation for the Gospel (see also Romans 5:12 and 1 Corinthians 15:22). If death already existed all around Adam, God's warning of death as a consequence for eating the forbidden fruit would have been meaningless and idle.

In addition to God clearly warning Adam that "death will come" if he sins, two stark truths in Genesis address this important "death before sin" topic.

First, animals did not eat each other at the beginning of Creation, and thus there was no "survival of the fittest" or "natural selection" process available to drive evolution. Humans and animals originally ate vegetation:

> And God said, 'See, I have given you every herb
> that yields seed which is on the face of all the
> earth, and every tree whose fruit yields seed; to

216

you it shall be for food. Also, to every beast of the earth, to every bird of the air, and to everything that creeps on the earth, in which there is life, I have given every green herb for food' (Genesis 1:29–30).

God did not endorse humans using animals as food until *after* the Flood: "Everything that lives and moves about will be food for you. *Just as I gave you the green plants, I now give you everything*" (Genesis 9:3, emphasis added). Further, God put the fear of man into animals *after* the Flood because they would be a food source from that point forward: "And the fear of you and the dread of you shall be on every beast of the earth, on every bird of the air, on all that move on the earth, and on all the fish of the sea" (Genesis 9:2).

Second, how could God look over the billions of years of blood-filled "survival of the fittest" evolution until it finally reached man and then call Creation "very good" (Genesis 1:31)? This would make Adam's sin and the curse of death meaningless! If death was used to create Adam and Eve, what was the real consequence of sin?

Figure 58. Is this a "very good" creation? Carnivory entered the world after sin.

God's original creation was perfect. The first chapter of Genesis states six times that what God had made was "good" and the seventh time that "God saw everything that He had made, and indeed it was *very* good" (Genesis 1:31). Now, however, we can look at the world around us and see there has been an obvious change. Many animals live by predation. Lions eat their prey while still alive. Bears eat young deer shortly after they are born.

The Believer Loses the Power That Comes from Fully Believing in God's Word

Put simply, there is power that comes from fully believing in the Word of God. A straightforward reading of the Bible's account of origins as laid out in Genesis 1 and 5 and Exodus 20:11—without spin or interpreting it through man's lens of "science"—will lead an honest reader to six days of Creation just thousands of years ago. If God really used evolution to create everything, He could have simply told Moses to write it down that way! But He didn't, and the Creation account reads much differently than how it might read if evolution took place over millions of years. The Bible is clear in several places that God "spoke" creation into existence (every time before creative acts in Genesis as well as elsewhere in the Bible—e.g., Psalm 33:4–11).

Compromising on God's Word by agreeing with theistic evolution robs the Christian of the power that comes from standing fully on the Word of God and claiming its authority. When Dr. Charles Jackson with Creation Truth Foundation was asked, "Do you meet many Christians at college who are drifting away from the faith?" his response was eye-opening:

> They're more than being drifted away from the faith; there's a current that's created under them that pulls them away from the faith. When you put a question mark after any Bible verses that

218

don't have them there already (or verses that give a disclaimer like, 'this is a mystery'), like 'in six days the Lord God created heaven and earth and all that's in them' (Exodus 20:11), instantly you have a quantum drop in the joy and power of the Christian walk—all of the gifts of God in you—you can feel it. It's like someone pulled the plug and you are running on battery now, and a low battery at that. [322]

There is a close association between the Word of God and the Power of God (Hebrews 4:12, 6:5; Matthew 22:29). Can a Christian live a power-filled life and walk in God's will while denying the Word of God? Christians will live a more power-filled life when they strongly align what they believe and how they live to the Word of God. Every stanza of Psalm 119 mentions the Word in some way for this reason.

Denying God's special creation and not believing that He created the world by His Word (Hebrews 11:3; Psalm 33:6) creates a deep crack in the foundation of a Christian, even in ways that are sometimes not known by the person doubting. John Macarthur[323] adds to this discussing by stating:

Christians will get out there, saying "Boy, we're against abortion, and we're against homosexuality, and we're against Jack Kevorkian because he's murdering people, and we're against euthanasia, and we're against genocide and, you know, we're against the moral evils of our society, etc." Why are we against those things? Can you tell me why? Why are we against those things? Give me one reason. Here it is, because they're forbidden in Scripture. Is that not true? The only reason we're against abortion is because God's against it. How do we know that? Because it's in the Word of God. The reason we're against homosexuality, adultery, etc. is because of the Bible. You see, we stand on the Scripture. But the problem is we don't want to stand on the Scripture in Genesis. So we equivocate on whether the Bible is an authority at all. What do you think the watching world thinks about our commitment to Scripture? Pretty selective, isn't it?

Theistic Evolution Has Christ Dying for the Sins of a Mythical Adam

The genealogies in Genesis 5 and 10 and Luke 3 lead directly back to Adam, the first man created by God. But if these genealogies don't lead back to a real Adam who sinned, then who do they lead back to? Because the "sinner" Adam and the Savior Jesus are linked together in Romans 5:16–18, any theological view which mythologizes Adam undermines the biblical basis of Jesus' work of redemption.

Tiktaalik & Coelacanth

Tiktaalik is also a widely-used "transitional" fossil in textbooks—supposedly representing a missing link between fish and four-legged creatures that first walked on land.

Figure 59. *Tiktaalik* (Credit: Wikipedia)[324]

Tiktaalik is typically shown in textbooks as a 375-million-year-old fossil that was "on its way" to progressing into a land-dwelling creature. Sometimes the Coelacanth is also shown in this same line-up, supposedly living about the same timeframe.[325]

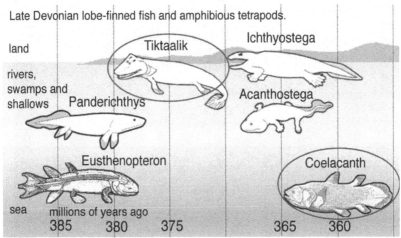

Figure 60. *Tiktaalik* and the Coelacanth: Supposed Evolutionary Transitions from Fish to Amphibians.[326]

Now, however, both fish have been ejected out of the evolutionary line-up. Until recently, evolutionists thought that *Tiktaalik*'s strong front fins did most of the work to pull this "transitional fish" up onto land, leaving the hind legs to evolve later. However, after more investigation of *Tiktaalik*'s pelvis and pelvic fins, the discoverers of *Tiktaalik* have developed updated illustrations showing how it used its strong pelvic structure for *paddling*. Now they believe that *Tiktaalik*'s hind-parts had so much power that it had "pelvic-propelled locomotion"[327] (see Figure 61).

Figure 61. Updated illustration of *Tiktaalik* in its natural environment.[328]

Even more amazing is the fact that scientists announced in 2010 in the journal *Nature* that they had found footprints of a four-legged land creature in Poland that they deemed ten million years older than *Tiktaalik*.[329] How could land creature fossils exist 10 million years before their ancestor?

The story behind the Coelacanth is even more amazing. Evolutionists believed that these creatures lived between about 400 million and 66 million years ago, but they were found *living* in 1938![330]

FOSSIL   LIVING

Figure 62. Coelacanths were thought to go extinct over 60 million years ago, but you can swim with one today![331]

Coelacanths were used in textbooks for decades to promote evolutionary teaching because their fins *looked to evolutionists like* they were in the primitive first stages of becoming arms and legs. This made coelacanths a perfect fit for the supposed transition from sea to land creatures.

But all of this changed on December 23, 1938, when Marjorie Courtenay Latimer, a curator in a museum in South Africa found one alive. She went to the docks to wish the crew of the fishing ship named "Nerine" a merry Christmas. After delivering her greetings, she noticed "a blue fin protruding beneath a pile of rays and sharks on the deck. Pushing the overlaying fish aside revealed, as she would later write, 'the most beautiful fish I had ever seen, five feet long, and a pale mauve blue with iridescent silver markings.'"[332] At first, she had no idea what the fish was, but after careful examination, it turned out to be a real, living Coelacanth. This discovery was such a shock among scientific circles that it was named the "zoological discovery of the century." In 1998, another Coelacanth population was found in northern Sulawesi, Indonesia, where the locals call it "rajalaut"—which means "king of the sea." How did this creature not evolve for over 300 million years? The fact is, it didn't. It's probably very close to the original design blueprint God used to create it!

Water: When was it Created?

Genesis 1:1–2 states, "In the beginning God created the heavens and the earth. The earth was without form, and void; and darkness was on the *face of the deep*. And the Spirit of God was hovering over the *face of the waters*." These verses say that at the beginning of Day 1, the whole world was watery.

The Scripture is clear that all things were created by God and through His power:

- "In the beginning was the Word, and the Word was with God, and the Word was God. He was in the beginning with God. All things were made through Him, and without Him nothing was made that was made." (John 1:1–3)
- "By faith we understand that the worlds were framed by the word of God, so that the things which are seen were not made of things which are visible." (Hebrews 11:3)

Further, in the only part of Scripture that God wrote with His own hand, God said "For in six days the Lord made the heavens and the earth, the sea, and all that is in them, and rested the seventh day" (Exodus 20:11, the 4th Commandment). Given these verses, it is clear that God created everything during the six days of Creation Week. The earth (with water), space (which was empty, except for the earth), time, and light were created on Day One. None of these things existed before Day One (Hebrews 11:3, Colossians 1:16).

Wisdom Teeth: Are they Leftovers from Evolution?

Most evolutionists believe that humans evolved from ape-like ancestors that had larger jaws and teeth than humans. The story holds that our jaws became smaller over millions of years as we "progressed," trading our crunching power for brain power. This supposedly resulted in the present challenge for wisdom teeth to grow in.[333] However, studies over the last few decades have shown that the "evolutionary process" is not the best explanation for why many people groups have challenges with their wisdom teeth growing in. Decades of research into this area has now identified a more complicated (and less "evolutionary") explanation:

> Our better understanding of the complex teeth-jaw relationship has revealed this explanation is far too simplistic. Research now indicates that the reasons for most third molar problems today are not due to evolutionary changes but other reasons. These reasons include a change from a course abrasive diet to a soft western diet, lack of proper dental care, and genetic factors possibly including mutations. Common past dental practice was a tendency to routinely remove wisdom teeth. Recent empirical research has concluded that this practice is unwise. Third molars in general should be left alone unless a problem develops and then they should be treated as any other teeth. At times removal is required, but appropriate efforts to deal with problem teeth should be implemented before resorting to their extraction.[334]

An Oxford Medical publication by A. J. MacGregor summarizes 20 years of research on this very topic in a work titled, "The Impacted Lower Wisdom Tooth."[335] MacGregor states:

> Evidence derived from paleontology, anthropology, and experiment indicates very convincingly that a reduction in jaw size has occurred due to **civilization**. The main associated factor appears to be the virtual absence of inter

proximal attrition, but initial tooth size may have some effect. Jaw size and dental attrition are related and they have both decreased with **modern diet**. Jaws were thought to be reduced in size in the course of evolution, but **close examination reveals that within the species *Homo sapiens*, this may not have occurred. What was thought to be a good example of evolution in progress has been shown to be better explained otherwise**.[336] [emphasis added]

These developments have led to a better understanding of wisdom teeth that have changed the practice of dentistry. In fact, in an article titled, "The Prophylactic Extraction of Third Molars: A Public Health Hazard,"[337] Dr. Jay W. Friedman points out that wisdom tooth extraction (a $3 billion-dollar enterprise) should not be the default practice for most individuals, but should be only done on a case-by-case basis. Dr. Friedman argues:

> More than 11 million patient days of 'standard discomfort or disability'—pain, swelling, bruising, and malaise—result postoperatively, and more than 11,000 people suffer permanent paresthesia—numbness of the lip, tongue, and cheek—as a consequence of nerve injury during the surgery. **At least two thirds of these extractions, associated costs, and injuries are unnecessary**, constituting a silent epidemic of iatrogenic injury that afflicts tens of thousands of people with lifelong discomfort and disability....Avoidance of prophylactic extraction of third molars can prevent this public health hazard.

For many of the same reasons, the UK even stopped routinely removing wisdom teeth (without solid evidence of required removal) in 1998, after a study at the University of York concluded that there was no scientific evidence to support it.[338]

People groups vary by several factors: skin color, hair color and type, eye shape, body size and shapes, and yes, even wisdom teeth. In fact, some people groups (e.g., Mexican Indians) don't even typically erupt wisdom teeth![339] On the other hand, nearly 100% of indigenous Tasmanians fully grow in their wisdom teeth. Other people groups are in-between these two extremes (see Figure 63).

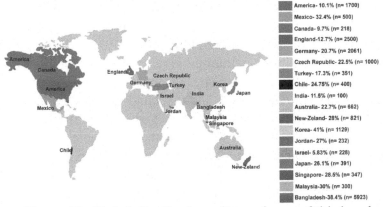

America- 10.1% (n= 1700)
Mexico- 32.4% (n= 500)
Canada- 9.7% (n= 218)
England-12.7% (n= 2500)
Germany- 20.7% (n= 2061)
Czech Republic- 22.5% (n= 1000)
Turkey- 17.3% (n= 351)
Chile- 24.75% (n= 400)
India- 11.5% (n= 100)
Australia- 22.7% (n= 662)
New-Zeland- 28% (n= 821)
Korea- 41% (n= 1129)
Jordan- 27% (n= 232)
Israel- 5.83% (n= 228)
Japan- 26.1% (n= 391)
Singapore- 28.5% (n= 347)
Malaysia-30% (n= 300)
Bangladesh-38.4% (n= 5923)

Figure 63. Global distribution of prevalence of third molar Agenesis (not growing wisdom teeth).

Figure 63 shows a wide variability between various people groups with respect to the percentage of people who don't grow in their wisdom teeth.[340] One study with 2,482 people also revealed that different people groups even grow in their wisdom teeth at different stages of maturity, with the German population in the middle in terms of the age of wisdom tooth eruption, South Africans the fastest, and Japanese the slowest.[341]

Are some of these people groups more or less "evolved" than others? From a Biblical Creation standpoint, certainly not! They do, however, vary on dietary history, industrialization, food types and production methods (especially in the past), and other characteristics by which people groups sometimes vary.

Orthodontist John Cuozzo has studied this topic extensively in both modern humans and Neanderthal fossils. Because Neanderthals had larger brains and jaws than modern humans (by 10% and 15%)[342] they had plenty of space for their wisdom teeth.[343] Because evolutionists place Neanderthals in the distant lineage of "modern" humans, have humans been "devolving" (by having smaller brains and less room for growing wisdom teeth) or just changing within the **pre-engineered adaptability** designed by God.

Dr. Cuozzo's studies have led to the discovery that children are maturing much faster today than in the past. He wrote, "Three or four hundred years ago a child took 13 years to reach the stage that our children today do in 9 1/2 to 10 years. This points to a rapid maturation today."[344] Dr. Cuozzo reasons that wisdom teeth need more space than can develop in our shortened jaw growth period, and that children are taller (and mature earlier) today because of improved early nutrition—not evolution. His research has led him to the reasonable conclusion: "This is not from a process of evolution, but devolution... The de-generation and reduction of complexity of the human body is what is really happening...This, of course, is due to the fact that Adam fell and we have been suffering and groaning under the curse resulting from this fall ever since."

Helpful Resources

Genesis Apologetics

Mobile App:
Search for "Genesis Apologetics" in the iTunes or Google Play stores or visit:
http://myapp.boundarytechnology.com/promo/#Genesis%20Apologetics

Free Books and Videos:
www.debunkevolution.com
https://genesisapologetics.com/store/

YouTube Channel:
Channel Name: Genesis Apologetics

Dinosaurs:
http://genesisapologetics.com/dinosaurs

Theistic Evolution
http://genesisapologetics.com/theistic

"Lucy" (leading human evolution icon):
http://genesisapologetics.com/lucy

Answers in Genesis
www.answersingenesis.org

Institute for Creation Research
www.ICR.org

Evolution Grand Experiment
www.thegrandexperiment.com

Creation Website Search Tool
www.searchcreation.org

Prayer of Salvation

You're not here by accident—God *loves* you and He *knows* who you are like no one else. His Word says:

Lord, You have searched me and known me. You know my sitting down and my rising up; you understand my thought afar off. You comprehend my path and my lying down, and are acquainted with all my ways. For there is not a word on my tongue, but behold, O Lord, You know it altogether. You have hedged me behind and before, and laid Your hand upon me. Such knowledge is too wonderful for me; It is high, I cannot attain it. (Psalm 139:1–6)

God loves you with an everlasting love, and with a love that can cover all of your transgressions—all that you have ever done wrong. But you have to repent of those sins and trust the Lord Jesus Christ for forgiveness. Your past is in the past. He wants to give you a new future and new hope.

But starting this new journey requires a step—a step of faith. God has already reached out to you as far as He can. By giving His Son to die for your sins on the Cross, He's done everything He can to reach out to you. The next step is yours to take, and this step requires faith to receive His son into your heart. It also requires repentance (turning away) from sin–a surrendered heart that is willing to reject a sinful lifestyle. Many believers have a much easier time leaving sinful lifestyles after they fully trust Jesus and nobody else and nothing else. Along with forgiveness, the Holy Spirit enters your life when you receive Jesus, and He will lead you into a different lifestyle and way—a way that will lead to blessing, joy, patient endurance under trials, and eternal life with Him.

If you are ready to receive Him, then consider four key Biblical truths.

1. Acknowledge that your sin separates you from God. Most simply, sin is our failure to measure up to God's holiness and His righteous standards. We sin by things we do, choices we make, attitudes we show, and thoughts we entertain. We also sin when we fail to do right things or even think right thoughts. The Bible also says that all people are sinners: "there is none righteous, not even one." No matter how good we try to be, none of us does right things all the time. The Bible is clear, "For all have sinned and come short of the glory of God" (Romans 3:23). Admit it. Agree with God on this one.

2. Our sins demand punishment—the punishment of death and separation from God. However, because of His great love, God sent His only Son Jesus to die for our sins: "God demonstrates His own love for us in this: While we were still sinners, Christ died for us" (Romans 5:8). For you to come to God you have to get rid of your sin problem. But, in our own strength, not one of us can do this! You can't make yourself right with God by being a better person. Only God can rescue us from our sins. He is willing to do this not because of anything you can offer Him, but **just because He loves you**! "He saved us, not because of righteous things we had done, but because of His mercy" (Titus 3:5).

3. It's only God's grace that allows you to come to Him— not your efforts to "clean up your life" or work your way to Heaven. You can't earn it. It's a free gift: "For it is by grace you have been saved, through faith—and this not from yourselves, it is the gift of God—not by works, so that no one can boast" (Ephesians 2:8–9). Will you accept this gift?

4. For you to come to God, the penalty for your sin must be paid. God's gift to you is His son, Jesus, who paid the debt for you when He died on the Cross. "For the wages of sin is death, but the gift of God is eternal life in Jesus

Christ our Lord" (Romans 6:23). God brought Jesus back from the dead. He provided the way for you to have a personal relationship with Him through Jesus. Trust Him. Pursue Him.

When we realize how deeply our sin grieves the heart of God and how desperately we need a Savior, we are ready to receive God's offer of salvation. To admit we are sinners means turning away from our sin and selfishness and turning to follow Jesus. The Bible word for this is "repentance"—to change our thinking to acknowledge how grievous sin is, so our thinking is in line with God's.

All that's left for you to do is to accept the gift that Jesus is holding out for you right now: "If you confess with your mouth, 'Jesus is Lord,' and believe in your heart that God raised him from the dead, you will be saved. For it is with your heart that you believe and are justified, and it is with your mouth that you confess and are saved" (Romans 10:9–10). God says that if you believe in His son, Jesus, you can live forever with Him in glory: "For God so loved the world that He gave his one and only Son, that whoever believes in him shall not perish, but have eternal life" (John 3:16).

Are you ready to accept the gift of eternal life that Jesus is offering you right now? Let's review what this commitment involves:

- I acknowledge I am a sinner in need of a Savior. I repent or turn away from my sin.
- I believe in my heart that God raised Jesus from the dead. I trust that Jesus paid the full penalty for my sins.
- I confess Jesus as my Lord and my God. I surrender control of my life to Jesus.
- I trust Jesus as my Savior forever. I accept that God has done for me what I could never do for myself when He forgives my sins.

If it is your sincere desire to receive Jesus into your heart as your personal Lord and Savior, then talk to God from your heart. Here's a suggested prayer:

Lord Jesus, I know that I am a sinner and I do not deserve eternal life. But, I believe You died and rose from the grave to make me a new creation and to prepare me to dwell in your presence forever. Jesus, come into my life, take control of my life, forgive my sins and save me. I am now placing my trust in You alone for my salvation and I accept your free gift of eternal life.

If you've prayed this prayer, it's important that you take these three next steps: First, go tell another Christian! Second, get plugged into a local church. Third, begin reading your Bible every day (we suggest starting with the book of John). Welcome to God's forever family!

Endnotes

[1] Dan Biddle & Jerry Bergman. "Strategically Dismantling the Evolutionary Idea Strongholds," *Journal of Creation,* 31 (1) (2017): 116–117.

[2] Linking from the present to Abraham's day is well established historically based on correlations between inscriptions and the biblical chronology of the Kings.

[3] The Biblical timelines that rely on the 17th-century chronology formulated by Bishop James Ussher place Creation at 4,004 BC and the Flood at 2,348 BC. Some recent research into the copyist differences in the early Masoretic and early Septuagint texts place the Flood around 2,518 BC based on the Masoretic text and between 3,168 BC and 3,298 BC based on the Septuagint (and other early texts), with Creation as early as 5,554 BC. These differences, however, can be settled by comparing multiple texts to reveal the perfect nature of the original writings which were "written through man by God" without error. These issues have been discussed in papers from three leading creation ministries. See, for example: Brian Thomas, "Two date range options for Noah's Flood," *Journal of Creation* 31(1) (2017); Henry B. Smith Jr., "Methuselah's Begetting Age in Genesis 5:25 and the Primeval Chronology of the Septuagint: A Closer Look at the Textual and Historical Evidence," *Answers Research Journal* 10 (2017): 169–179. Answers in Genesis: *www.answersingenesis.org/arj/v10/methuselah-primeval-chronology-septuagint.pdf* (November 5, 2018); and Lita Cosner and Robert Carter, "Textual Traditions and Biblical Chronology," *Journal of Creation* 29 (2) 2015. Journal of Creation: *https://creation.com/images/pdfs/tj/j29_2/j29_2_99-105.pdf* (November 5, 2018).

[4] See 2 Peter 1:31; 2 Timothy 3:16; Numbers 23:19; Titus 1:2; Matthew 24:35; Psalm 12:6–7; Proverbs 30:5; and Psalm 138:2.

[5] Ewald Plass. *What Martin Luther Says: A Practical In-Home Anthology for the Active Christian,* 1523.

[6] God Himself provided the light source on day one.

[7] Leading Progressive Creationist, Dr. Hugh Ross, places the emergence of the human race via Adam and Eve about 50,000 years ago: Fazale Rana with Hugh Ross, *Who Was Adam?* (Colorado Springs, CO: NavPress, 2005), p. 45. See also: *www.reasons.org/articles/new-date-for-first-aussies* (January 26, 2017).

[8] Alejandro Rojas, "New survey shows nearly half of Americans believe in aliens," (August 2, 2017). Huffington Post: *www.huffingtonpost.com/entry/new-survey-shows-nearly-half-of-americans-believe-in_us_59824c11e4b03d0624b0abe4*) (November 5, 2018).

[9] Brian Thomas. "Antibiotic Resistance in Bacteria Shows Adaptive Design," (June 30, 2011). Institute for Creation Research:

234

www.icr.org/article/6202 (November 5, 2018). See also: Brian Thomas, "Antibiotic Resistance in Bacteria Did Not Evolve." *ICR News* (May 10, 2011, accessed May 19, 2011).

[10] Credit: Wikipedia.

[11] Allan Feduccia, "*Archaeopteryx*: Early Bird Catches a Can of Worms," *Science*, Vol. 259, 5 February 1993, p. 764. See also: *Archaeopteryx*: Early Bird Catches a Can of Worms by V. Morell, *Science* 259 (5096):764–65, (February 1993): 5.

[12] T. Beardsley, "Fossil Bird Shakes Evolutionary Hypotheses," *Nature* 322 (6081): 1986, 677; X. Xu, et al., An *Archaeopteryx*-like theropod from China and the origin of Avialae, *Nature* 475 (7357) (2011): 465–470.

[13] See the following three resources:
https://answersingenesis.org/dinosaurs/extinction/do-data-support-large-meteorite-impact-chicxulub/;
https://answersingenesis.org/the-flood/did-meteors-trigger-noahs-flood/
http://www.icr.org/article/chicxulub-crater-theory-mostly-smoke

[14] J. A. Tennessen, et al., "Evolution and Functional Impact of Rare Coding Variation from Deep Sequencing of Human Exomes," *Science* 337 (6090) (2012): 64–69; W. Fu, et al., "Analysis of 6,515 Exomes Reveals the Recent Origin of Most Human Protein-coding Variants," *Nature* 493 (7431) (2013): 216–220.

[15] "Fast Facts about the Bible." Bible Resources:
http://bibleresources.org/bibleresources/bible-facts/ (January 26, 2017).

[16] M. P. Taylor and M. J. Wedel. "Why sauropods had long necks; and why giraffes have short necks." *PeerJ* 1: (2013), e36.

[17] Image Credit: Wikipedia (*https://en.wikipedia.org/wiki/Mamenchisaurus*) (January 26, 2017).

[18] M.J. Wedel, "Aligerando a los gigantes (Lightening the giants)." *¡Fundamental!* 2007, 12:1–84. [in Spanish, with English translation]

[19] See also: "Mechanical implications of pneumatic neck vertebrae in sauropod dinosaurs." Daniela Schwarz-Wings, Christian A. Meyer, Eberhard Frey, Hans-Rudolf Manz-Steiner, Ralf Schumacher *Proc. R. Soc. B* 2010 277 11–17.

[20] Wedel, 2007.

[21] Matt Wedel, "Hunting the Inflatable Dinosaur," University of California Museum of Paleontology:
www.ucmp.berkeley.edu/science/profiles/wedel_0609.php (January 26, 2017).

[22] Taylor & Wedel, 2013.

[23] While sauropods also may have lived post-flood (as indicated by Job 40), their design features provide clues that they likely thrived better in a pre-flood environment.

[24] David Catchpoole, "Grass-eating Dinos: A 'Time-travel' Problem for Evolution (*www.creation.com/grass-eating-dinos*) (August 22, 2017); Brian Thomas, "Dinosaurs Ate Rice," *www.icr.org/article/6428/* (August 22, 2017).

[25] Nicole Klein, Kristian Remes, Carole T. Gee, and P. Martin Sander, *Biology of the Sauropod Dinosaurs Understanding the Life of Giants* (Indiana University Press, 2011).

[26] M. Hallett & M. Wedel, *The Sauropod Dinosaurs: Life in the Age of Giants,* (Johns Hopkins University Press, 2016).

[27] Patrick Moser, Jordan River could die by 2011, *Phys Org. www.phys.org/news/2010-05-jordan-river-die.html* (May 2, 2010) (August 22, 2017).

[28] For example, see the English Standard Version or the Life Application Study Bible notes.

[29] J. Carballido, D. Pol, A. Otero, I. Cerda, L. Salgado, A. Garrido, J. Ramezani, N. Cúneo, M. Krause, "A New Giant Titanosaur Sheds Light on Body Mass Evolution Amongst Sauropod Dinosaurs," *Proceedings of the Royal Society B* (August 9, 2017).

[30] Nathan P. Myhrvold and Philip J. Currie, Supersonic Sauropods? Tail Dynamics in the Diplodocids, *Paleobiology* 23 (December, 1997): 393—409; Benjamin Meyers, W. Wayt Gibbs, Did a Dinosaur Break the Sound Barrier before We Did? (*www.scientificamerican.com/video/did-a-dinosaur-break-the-sound-barrier-before-we-did/*) (November 3, 2015) (August 22, 2017).

[31] Dattatreya Mandal, *Hexapolis*, Physical Model To Show How Dinosaurs May Have Whipped Their Tails In Supersonic Speed (October 16, 2015). (*www.hexapolis.com/2015/10/16/physical-model-to-show-how-dinosaurs-may-have-whipped-their-tails-in-supersonic-speed/*) (August 23, 2017).

[32] Don Stewart, "Where Did Cain Get His Wife?" Blue Letter Bible: *http://v3.blueletterbible.org/faq/don_stewart/don_stewart_717.cfm* (November 5, 2018).

[33] See Paul Giem, Carbon-14 Content of Fossil Carbon, *Origins* 51 (2001): 6-30; J. Baumgardner, Andrew Snelling, D.R. Humphreys, and Steve Austin, Measurable 14C in Fossilized Organic Materials: Confirming the Young Earth Creation-Flood Model. In Ivey, H (editor) *Proceedings of the Fifth International Conference on Creationism*, 2003, 127–142. Pittsburgh, PA: Creation Science Fellowship (see also: *www.icr.org/article/young-earth-creation-flood-14c/*); J. Baumgardner, 14C evidence for a recent global flood and a young earth. In Vardiman, L., Snelling, A.A. and Chaffin, E.F. (editors), Radioisotopes and the Age of the Earth: Results of a Young-Earth Creationist Research Initiative, 2005, pp. 587–630. (El Cajon, CA: Institute for Creation Research and Chino Valley, AZ: Creation Research Society). (See also: *www.icr.org/article/carbon-14-evidence-for-recent-global*).

[34] G. Faure, *Principles of Isotope Geology*, 2nd ed., (New York: John Wiley & Sons, 1986): 391.

[35] K. J. Heckman, H. Campbell, H. Powers, B. Law, C. Swanston. "The Influence of Fire on the Radiocarbon Signature and Character of Soil Organic Matter in the Siskiyou National Forest, Oregon, USA." *Fire Ecology* 9 (2) (2013): 40–56.

[36] Robert Krulwich, "How A-Bomb Testing Changed Our Trees." August 25, 2010 (*www.npr.org/templates/story/story.php?storyId=96750869*) (February 3, 2016).

[37] Image Credit: Wikipedia: *https://it.wikipedia.org/wiki/File:Radiocarbon_bomb_spike.svg* (January 26, 2017)

[38] Sheridan Bowman, *Radiocarbon Dating*. (London: British Museum Press, 1995), p. 24–27.

[39] Tree ring dating (dendrochronology) has been used in an attempt to extend the calibration of carbon-14 dating earlier than historical records allow, but this depends on *temporal placement of fragments of wood from trees that have been dead for ages* using carbon-14 dating. For example, the Bristlecone Pines in California were dated to be 4,700+ years old by counting the tree rings, which is within the age brackets of the Flood. However, research conducted on the *same type of tree* shows that seasonal effects can cause multiple rings (up to five) to grow in the same year. It is likely that the world following the Flood would have been much wetter with fewer contrasting seasons until after the Ice Age, which could explain the apparent date of the tree based on counting its rings. When scientists build calibration models for radiocarbon dating that extend back many thousands of years, they attempt to build tree ring chronologies by *"cross-matching" tree ring patterns of pieces of dead wood found near living trees*. This process relies on circular reasoning because it assumes that the "carbon clock" can be moved backwards in time in a straight line, and the Flood greatly disrupted carbon ratios in the earth, as well as the atmosphere that produces the ratios of radioactive and stable carbon. Carbon dating today assumes that the system has been in equilibrium for many thousands of years. However, the Flood buried large quantities of organic matter containing stable carbon (^{12}C) changing the $^{14}C/^{12}C$ ratios. Further, tree ring patterns are not unique (like fingerprints). Dr. Batten (Batten, Don. "Tree ring dating (dendrochronology)." Creation.com: *www.creation.com/tree-ring-dating-dendrochronology* (February 10, 2016): "There are many points in a given sequence where a sequence from a new piece of wood matches well (note that even two trees growing next to each other will not have identical growth ring patterns). D.K. Yamaguchi, "Interpretation of cross-correlation between tree-ring series." *Tree Ring Bulletin*, 46 (1986): 47–54: Yamaguchi recognized that ring pattern matches

are not unique. The best match (using statistical tests) is often rejected in favor of a less exact match because the best match is deemed to be 'incorrect' (particularly if it is too far away from the carbon-14 'age'). So the carbon 'date' is used to constrain just which match is acceptable. Consequently, the calibration is a circular process and the tree ring chronology extension is also a circular process that is dependent on assumptions about the carbon dating system (see: B. Newgrosh, "Living with radiocarbon dates: a response to Mike Baillie." *Journal of the Ancient Chronology Forum* 5:59–67, 1992.).

[40] G. Faure, *Principles of Isotope Geology*, 2nd ed. (New York: John Wiley & Sons, 1986), p. 391; Ken Ham, Andrew Snelling, and Carl Weiland, *The Answers Book*, (El Cajon, CA.: Master Books, 1992): 68.

[41] F. Miyake, K. Nagaya, K. Masuda, T. Nakamura, "A signature of cosmic-ray increase in AD 774–775 from tree rings in Japan," *Nature* 486 (7402) (2012): 240–242.

[42] I.G. Usoskin, "The AD 775 cosmic event revisited: The Sun is to blame," *Astronomy & Astrophysics* 552 (1) (2013): L3.

[43] Minze Stuiver, "Variations in Radiocarbon Concentration and Sunspot Activity," *J. Geophysical Research* 66 (1961): 273–76.

[44] R.E. Taylor and O. Bar-Yosef. *Radiocarbon Dating: An Archaeological Perspective*, 2nd Ed. (Left Coast Press, Walnut Creek, CA, 2014), pp. 31–32; 150–155.

[45] Ibid., 45–46.

[46] J. Baumgardner, "14C evidence for a recent global flood and a young earth." In L. Vardiman, Andrew Snelling, and E.F. Chaffin (editors), *Radioisotopes and the Age of the Earth: Results of a Young-Earth Creationist Research Initiative*. (El Cajon, CA: Institute for Creation Research and Chino Valley, AZ, 2005): 618. Creation Research Society. (*www.icr.org/article/carbon-14-evidence-for-recent-global*) (January 26, 2017).

[47] Heather D Graven, "Impact of fossil fuel emissions on radiocarbon," *Proceedings of the National Academy of Sciences* (August 2015), 112 (31): 9542–9545.

[48] Von Kaenel, Camille. "Fossil Fuel Burning Obscures Radiocarbon Dates Increasing atmospheric carbon from burned fossil fuels will make historic dating more difficult," ClimateWire: *www.scientificamerican.com/article/fossil-fuel-burning-obscures-radiocarbon-dates/* (July 21, 2015).

[49] W. Libby, *Radiocarbon Dating*, University of Chicago Press, Chicago, Illinois, 1952, 8.

[50] C. Sewell, "Carbon-14 and the Age of the Earth," 1999. *www.rae.org/essay-links/bits23/* (November 12, 2018).

[51] Charles Foley, "Dating the Shroud," *The Tablet: International Catholic News Weekly*, (July 7, 1990): 13.

[52] Brian Thomas and Vance Nelson, "Radiocarbon in Dinosaur and Other Fossils," *Creation Research Society Quarterly*, 51 (4) (2015): 299–311.

[53] T.L. Clarey and D.J. Werner, "Use of Sedimentary Megasequences to Recreate Pre-Flood Geography." In *Proceedings of the Eighth International Conference on Creationism*, ed. J.H. Whitmore, pp. 351–372. Pittsburgh, Pennsylvania: Creation Science Fellowship (2018).

[54] Another confirmation is the conjunction of the word work and day twice in Genesis 2:2 "on the seventh 'day' God ended his "work" which he had made; and he rested on the seventh "day" from all his "work" which he had made (confirming that Day 7 was a "work day" like in Exodus 20:11).

[55] See: Sequoia Research: *www.nps.gov/yose/learn/nature/sequoia-research.htm* (November 5, 2018).

[56] See: *https://answersingenesis.org/age-of-the-earth/do-varves-tree-rings-radiocarbon-measurements-prove-old-earth/* and *www.icr.org/article/8050* (November 5, 2018).

[57] *Creation Research Society Quarterly Journal* Spring 2015 (Volume 51, Number 4): *www.creationresearch.org/index.php/component/k2/item/118-2015-volume-51-number-4-spring* (January 27, 2017).

[58] Jeff Hecht, Daily News, "Blood vessels recovered from T. rex bone," New Scientist: *www.newscientist.com/article/dn7195-blood-vessels-recovered-from-t-rex-bone/* (March 24, 2005).

[59] Science via AP (*www.msnbc.msn.com/id/7285683/*) (January 27, 2017).

[60] For example, see: R. Pawlicki and M. Wowogrodzka-Zagorska. "Blood vessels and red blood cells preserved in dinosaur bones." Annals of Anatomy 180 (1998): 73–77; M. H. Schweitzer, J.L. Wittmeyer, J.R. Horner, and J.K Toporske. "Soft-tissue vessels and cellular preservation in Tyrannosaurus rex." *Science,* 307 (2005): 1952; M.H. Schweitzer, J.L. Wittmeyer, and J.R. Horner. "Soft tissue and cellular preservation in vertebrate skeletal elements from the Cretaceous to the present." *Proceedings of the Royal Society B* 274 (2007): 183–197; M.H. Schweitzer, W. Zheng, C.L. Organ, R. Avci, Z. Suo, L.M. Freimark, V.S. Lebleu, M.B. Duncan, M.G. Vander Heiden, J.M. Neveu, W.S. Lane, J.S. Cottrell, J.R. Horner, L.C. Cantley, R. Kalluri, and J.M. Asara. "Biomolecular characterization and protein sequences of the campanian Hadrosaur B. Canadensis." *Science,* 324 (2009): 626–631.

[61] M. Schweitzer and I. Staedter, *The Real Jurassic Park, Earth*, June 1997, pp. 55–57.

[62] R. Pawlicki and M. Wowogrodzka-Zagorska. "Blood vessels and red blood cells preserved in dinosaur bones." *Annals of Anatomy* 180 (1998): 73–77; M. H. Schweitzer, J.L. Wittmeyer, J.R. Horner, and J.K Toporske. "Soft-tissue vessels and cellular preservation in Tyrannosaurus rex." *Science,* 307 (2005): 1952; M.H. Schweitzer, J.L. Wittmeyer, and J.R. Horner. "Soft

tissue and cellular preservation in vertebrate skeletal elements from the Cretaceous to the present." *Proceedings of the Royal Society B* 274 (2007): 183–197; M.H. Schweitzer, W. Zheng, C.L. Organ, R. Avci, Z. Suo, L.M. Freimark, V.S. Lebleu, M.B. Duncan, M.G. Vander Heiden, J.M. Neveu, W.S. Lane, J.S. Cottrell, J.R. Horner, L.C. Cantley, R. Kalluri, and J.M. Asara. "Biomolecular characterization and protein sequences of the campanian Hadrosaur B. Canadensis." *Science* 324 (2009): 626–631; J. Lindgren, M.W. Caldwell, T. Konishi, L.M. Chiappe, "Convergent Evolution in Aquatic Tetrapods: Insights from an Exceptional Fossil Mosasaur." *PLoS ONE* 5(8) (2010): e11998.

[63] Barry Yeoman, "Schweitzer's Dangerous Discovery," Discovery Magazine: *www.discovermagazine.com/2006/apr/dinosaur-dna* (April 27, 2006) (January 27, 2017).

[64] M.H. Schweitzer, M. Marhsall, K. Carron, D.S. Bohle, S.C. Busse, E.V. Arnold, D. Barnard, J.R. Horner, and J.R. Starkey. "Heme compounds in dinosaur trabecular bone." *Proceedings of the National Academy of Sciences USA 94*, (1997), p. 6295.

[65] J.M. Asara, M.H. Schweitzer, L.M. Freimark, M. Phillips, and L.C. Cantley. "Protein sequences from mastodon and Tyrannosaurus rex revealed by mass spectrometry." *Science*, 316 (2007): 280–285.

[66] M. Armitage, "Soft bone material from a brow horn of a Triceratops horridus from Hell Creek Formation, MT." *Creation Research Society Quarterly,* 51 (2015): 248–258.

[67] M.H. Schweitzer, W. Zheng, T.P. Cleland, and M. Bern. "Molecular analyses of dinosaur osteocytes support the presence of endogenous molecules." *Bone,* 52 (2013): 414–423; M. Armitage, "Soft bone material from a brow horn of a Triceratops horridus from Hell Creek Formation, MT." *Creation Research Society Quarterly,* 51 (2015): 248–258; M. Armitage and K.L. Anderson. "Soft tissue of fibrillar bone from a fossil of the supraorbital horn of the dinosaur Triceratops horridus." *Acta Histochemica*, 115 (2013):603–608; R. Pawlicki, "Histochemical demonstration of DNA in osteocytes from dinosaur bones." *Folia Histochemica Et Cytobiologica*, 33 (1995): 183–186.

[68] M.H. Schweitzer, et al. 2005. "Molecular preservation in Late Cretaceous sauropod dinosaur eggshells." *Proceedings of the Royal Society B: Biological Sciences.* 272 (1565): 775–784.

[69] G.D. Cody, N.S. Gupta, D.E.G. Briggs, A.L.D. Kilcoyne, R.E. Summons, F. Kenig, R.E. Plotnick, and A. C. Scott. "Molecular signature of chitin-protein complex in Paleozoic arthropods." *Geology*, 39 (3) (2011): 255–258; H. Ehrlich, J.K. Rigby, J.P. Botting, M.V. Tsurkan, C. Werner, P. Schwille, Z. Petrášek, A. Pisera, P. Simon, V.N. Sivkov, D.V. Vyalikh, S.L. Molodtsov, D. Kurek, M. Kammer, S. Hunoldt, R. Born, D. Stawski, A. Steinhof, V.V. Bazhenov, and T. Geisler. "Discovery of 505-million-year

old chitin in the basal demosponge Vauxia gracilenta." *Scientific Reports*. 3 (2013): 3497.

[70] M. Helder, "Fresh dinosaur bones found," *Creation* 14(3) (1992): 16–17, *www.creation.com/fresh-dinosaur-bones-found* (January 27, 2017).

[71] "Fossils of new duck-billed, plant-eating dinosaur species found in Alaska, researchers say" (*www:accesswdun.com/article/2015/9/337248*) (September 22, 2015).

[72] Schweitzer, Wittmeyer, & Horner (2007), 183–197.

[73] Hirotsugu Mori, Patrick S. Druckenmiller, and Gregory M. Erickson, "A new Arctic hadrosaurid from the Prince Creek Formation (lower Maastrichtian) of northern Alaska." *Acta Palaeontologica Polonica* 61 (1), (2016): 15–32; A.R. Fiorillo, P.J. McCarthy, and P.P. Flaig "Taphonomic and sedimentologic interpretations of the dinosaur-bearing Upper Cretaceous Strata of the Prince Creek Formation, Northern Alaska: Insights from an ancient high-latitude terrestrial ecosystem." *Palaeogeography, Palaeoclimatology, Palaeoecology* 295 (2010): 376–388; R.A. Gangloff and A.R. Fiorillo, "Taphonomy and paleoecology of a bonebed from the Prince Creek Formation, North Slope, Alaska." *Palaios*, 25 (2010): 299–317; M.H. Schweitzer, C. Johnson, T.G. Zocco, J.R. Horner, and J.R. Starkey, "Preservation of biomolecules in cancellous bone of Tyrannosaurus rex," *J. Vertebrate paleontology* 17 (2) (1997): 349–359;

M.H. Schweitzer, M. Marshall, K. Carron, D.S. Bohle, S.C. Busse, E.V. Arnold, D. Barnard, J.R. Horner, and J.R. Starkey, "Heme compounds in dinosaur trabecular bone," *Proceedings of the National Academy of Science* 94 (1997): 6291–6296; As stated in Helder (above): "An initial announcement was printed in 1985 in Geological Society of America abstract programs Vol.17, p. 548. Already in press at that time was an article describing the site and the condition of the bones (Kyle L. Davies, 'Duck-bill Dinosaurs (Hadrosauridae, Ornithischia) from the North Slope of Alaska', Journal of Paleontology, Vol.61 No.1, pp.198–200); M.H. Schweitzer, J.L. Wittmeyer, and J.R. Horner. "Soft tissue and cellular preservation in vertebrate skeletal elements from the Cretaceous to the present." *Proceedings of the Royal Society B,* 274 (2007): 183–197.

[74] Barry Yeoman, "Schweitzer's Dangerous Discovery," Discovery Magazine: *www.discovermagazine.com/2006/apr/dinosaur-dna* (April 27, 2006) (January 27, 2017).

[75] Severo Avila, "Alan Stout is the Bone Collector," Northwest Georgia News: *www.northwestgeorgianews.com/rome/lifestyles/alan-stout-is-the-bone-collector/article_6b1268e7-3350-5dfd-a3dc-652dcf27d174.html* (April 11, 2010) (January 27, 2017).

[76] Alan Stout, Personal communication, January 16, 2017.

[77] Marshall Bern, Brett S. Phinney, and David Goldberg. "Reanalysis of Tyrannosaurus Rex Mass Spectra." *Journal of Proteome Research* 8.9 (2009): 4328–4332.

[78] Brian Thomas, "Original Biomaterials in Fossils." *Creation Research Society Quarterly*, 51 (2015): 234–347.

[79] Elena R. Schroeter, Caroline J. DeHart, Timothy P. Cleland, Wenxia Zheng, Paul M. Thomas, Neil L. Kelleher, Marshall Bern, and Mary H. Schweitzer, "Expansion for the Brachylophosaurus canadensis Collagen I Sequence and Additional Evidence of the Preservation of Cretaceous Protein." Journal of Proteome Research Article.

[80] See UPI News: *www.upi.com/Science_News/2017/01/23/Scientists-find-ancient-dinosaur-collagen/6091485202598/* (January 23, 2017).

[81] S. Bertazzo, et al. "Fibres and cellular structures preserved in 75-million-year-old dinosaur specimens," *Nature Communications*, 6, (2015).

[82] M. Buckley and M.J. Collins. "Collagen survival and its use for species identification in Holocene-Lower Pleistocene bone fragments from British archaeological and paleontological sites." *Antiqua*, 1 (2011): e1.

[83] Robert F. Service, "Scientists retrieve 80-million-year-old dinosaur protein in 'milestone' paper," Science.com: *www.sciencemag.org/news/2017/01/scientists-retrieve-80-million-year-old-dinosaur-protein-milestone-paper* (January 31, 2017) (February 5, 2017).

[84] M. H. Schweitzer, et al. "Molecular analyses of dinosaur osteocytes support the presence of endogenous molecules." *Bone*, 52 (1) (2013): 414–423. S. R. Woodward, N. J. Weyand, and M. Bunnell. "DNA Sequence from Cretaceous Period Bone Fragments." *Science*, 266 (5188) (1994): 1229–1232.

[85] T. Lingham-Soliar, "A unique cross section through the skin of the dinosaur Psittacosaurus from China showing a complex fibre architecture." *Proceedings of the Royal Society B: Biological Sciences* 275 (2008): 775–780. T. Lingham-Soliar and G. Plodowski. "The integument of Psittacosaurus from Liaoning Province, China: taphonomy, epidermal patterns and color of a ceratopsian dinosaur." *Naturwissenschaften* 97 (2010): 479–486.

[86] Schweitzer, Zheng, Cleland, & Bern (2013): 414–423.

[87] Ibid.

[88] N.P. Edwards, H.E. Barden, B.E. van Dongen, P.L. Manning, P.O. Larson, U. Bergmann, W.I. Sellers, and R.A. Wogelius. "Infrared mapping resolves soft tissue preservation in 50 million year-old reptile skin." *Proceedings of the Royal Society B,* 278 (2011): 3209–3218.

[89] U. Bergmann, et al., "Archaeopteryx feathers and bone chemistry fully revealed via synchrotron imaging." *Proceedings of the National Academy of Sciences.* 107 (20) (2010), 9060–9065.

[90] S. Hayashi, K. Carpenter, M. Watabe, and L.A. McWhinney, "Ontogenetic histology of Stegosaurus plates and spikes." *Palaeontology* 55 (2012), 145–161.

[91] M.H. Schweitzer, W. Zheng, C.L. Organ, R. Avci, Z. Suo, L.M. Freimark, V.S. Lebleu, M.B. Duncan, M.G. Vander Heiden, J.M. Neveu, W.S. Lane, J.S. Cottrell, J.R. Horner, L.C. Cantley, R. Kalluri, and J.M. Asara. "Biomolecular characterization and protein sequences of the campanian Hadrosaur B. Canadensis." *Science,* 324 (2009): 626–631.

[92] M. Buckley and M.J. Collins. "Collagen survival and its use for species identification in Holocene-Lower Pleistocene bone fragments from British archaeological and paleontological sites." *Antiqua,* 1 (2011): e1. Hypothetically, if dinosaurs include an unrealistically large mass of initial collagen, it may last as long as 1.7 million years (see Brian Thomas, "A Review of Original Tissue Fossils and their Age Implications," Proceedings of the Seventh International Conference on Creationism [Pittsburgh, PA: Creation Science Fellowship]). However, this upper estimate assumes that skin, muscles, and connective tissue collagen decays as slowly as bone collagen, which is not typically the case (Brian Thomas, personal communication, February 15, 2017).

[93] Charles Gould, *Mythical Monsters*, W.H. Allen & Co., London, 1886, pp. 382–383.

[94] Flavius Philostratus, "The Life of Apollonius of Tyana" (Vol. 1, Book III) (F. C. Conybeare, trans. New York: Macmillan Co., 243-247, 1912).

[95] Dr. Danny Faulkner, "Does the Bible Teach That the Earth Is Flat?" April 4, 2017 *https://answersingenesis.org/astronomy/earth/does-bible-teach-earth-flat/* (November 5, 2018).

[96] David V. Bassett, M.S. contributed the majority of this section. The complete work can be found in *Debunking Evolution* (Genesis Apologetics).

[97] Gon III, S. M. The Trilobite Eye, (*www.trilobites.info/eyes.htm*) (September 1, 2014); See also: Jerry Bergman, "The Trilobite Eye A Wonder of Complex Design," (December 2007) (*www.create.ab.ca/the-trilobite-eye-a-wonder-of-complex-design/*). Holochroal eyes are the ancestral eye of trilobites, and are by far the most common, found in all orders except the Agnostida, and through the entirety of the Trilobites' existence Clarkson, E. N. K. (1979), "The Visual System of Trilobites," *Palaeontology, Encyclopedia of Earth Science* 22: 1–22.

[98] The Coelacanth is supposedly an ancestor to amphibians that dates back 300 million years; however, the Coelacanth appears "suddenly" in the fossil record, and modern coelacanths "were also found to give birth to live young (like some sharks), unlike their supposed descendants, the amphibians." See: K.S. Thomson, *Living Fossil.* New York, NY: W.W. Norton & Company, 1991), 137–144.

[99] Creationwiki.com: *www.creationwiki.org/Archaeopteryx* (January 3, 2014).

[100] Percival Davis, Dean H. Kenyon, & Charles B. Thaxton (ed). *Of Pandas and People: The Central Question of Biological Origins,* 2d ed. (Dallas, TX: Haughton Publishing Company, 1989), 22–23.

[101] John D. Morris, *The Young Earth: The Real History of the Earth, Past, Present, and Future* (Colorado Springs, CO: Master Books, 1994).

[102] Jerry Adler & John Carey, "Is Man a Subtle Accident?" *Newsweek*, 8, no. 95 (Nov. 3, 1980): 96.

[103] Stephen J Gould & Niles Eldredge, "Punctuated Equilibria: The Tempo and Mode of Evolution Reconsidered," *Paleobiology*, 3, no. 2 (April 1977): 115–151.

[104] Brian Thomas, "150 Years Later, Fossils Still Don't Help Darwin," Institute for Creation Research Online: *www.icr.org/article/4546/* (December 20, 2013).

[105] Carl Werner, "Evolution the Grand Experiment," The Grand Experiment: *www.thegrandexperiment.com/index.html* (January 1, 2014).

[106] Carl Werner, *Living Fossils. Evolution: The Grand Experiment* (Vol. 2). Green Forest, AR: New Leaf Press, 2008, 242.

[107] Carl Werner, *Evolution: The Grand Experiment.* Green Forest, AR: New Leaf Press, 2007, 86.

[108] Chart adapted from: Michael Denton, *Evolution: A Theory in Crisis.* Bethesda: Adler & Adler, 1985.

[109] Charles Darwin, *The Origin of Species by Means of Natural Selection.* New York: The Modern Library, 1859, 124–125.

[110] Jonathan Wells, *Icons of Evolution: Science or Myth?—Why Much of What We Teach About Evolution Is Wrong*, (Regnery Publishing, 2000): 41–42.

[111] Robert F. DeHaan & John L. Wiester, "*The Cambrian Explosion: The Fossil Record & Intelligent Design," Touchstone (*July/August 1999), 65–69.

[112] Wells, 2000, 42.

[113] DeHaan & Wiester, 1999, p. 68.

[114] Raymond R. Rogers, David A. Eberth and Anthony R. Fiorillo Bonebeds: Genesis, Analysis, and Paleobiological Significance, University of Chicago Press, 2008, and related database.

[115] Randy Moore & Mark D. Decker, *More Than Darwin: An Encyclopedia of the People and Places of the Evolution-creationism Controversy* (Greenwood Press, 2008): 302.

[116] Tim Chaffey, "Planting Confusion: Were plants created on Day Three or Day Six? (April 10, 2012). Available: *https://answersingenesis.org/biology/plants/planting-confusion/*. See also: Mark Futato, "Because It Had Rained: A Study of Gen 2:5–7 With

Implications for Gen 2:4–25 and Gen 1:1–2:3." Westminster Theological Journal, 60:1–21, (Spring 1998), 4. It may not be the best practice to identify something as "wild" prior to the Fall, but the definition given here is based on how the term is commonly understood—not just before sin.

[117] Jason Lisle, "Two Creation Accounts?" (August 31, 2015). *https://www.icr.org/article/two-creation-accounts/*

[118] Jeffrey P. Tomkins, Ph.D. contributed the majority of this section. The complete work can be found in *Debunking Human Evolution Taught in our Public Schools* (Genesis Apologetics).

[119] Dan Biddle, *Creation v. Evolution: What They Won't Tell You in Biology Class* (Maitland, FL: Xulon Press); H. Morris, et al., *Creation Basics & Beyond: An In-Depth Look at Science, Origins, and Evolution* (Dallas, TX: Institute for Creation Research, 2013).

[120] J. C. Sanford, *Genetic Entropy and the Mystery of the Genome*, 3rd ed. (Waterloo, NY: FMS Publications, 2008).

[121] Ibid.

[122] J. A. Tennessen, et al., "Evolution and Functional Impact of Rare Coding Variation from Deep Sequencing of Human Exomes," *Science* 337 (6090) (2012): 64–69; W. Fu, et al., "Analysis of 6,515 Exomes Reveals the Recent Origin of Most Human Protein-coding Variants," *Nature* 493 (7431) (2013): 216–220.

[123] Tennessen, *Evolution and Functional Impact of Rare Coding Variation from Deep Sequencing of Human Exomes*, 64–69.

[124] J. Sanford, J. Pamplin, & C. Rupe, "Genetic Entropy Recorded in the Bible?" (FMS Foundation. Posted on kolbecenter.org July 2014, accessed July 25, 2014).

[125] N. T. Jeanson, "Recent, Functionally Diverse Origin for Mitochondrial Genes from ~2700 Metazoan Species," *Answers Research Journal* 6 (2013): 467–501.

[126] T.J. Parsons, et al., "A High Observed Substitution Rate in the Human Mitochondrial DNA Control Region," *Nature Genetics* 15 (1997): 363–368.

[127] A. Gibbons, "Calibrating the Mitochondrial Clock," *Science* 279 (1998): 28–29.

[128] Frank Lorey, The Flood of Noah and the Flood of Gilgamesh (March 1, 1997): *https://www.icr.org/article/noah-flood-gilgamesh/*

[129] Tim Lovett, "Comparing Gilgamesh," (October, 2004) (*http://worldwideflood.com/ark/gilgamesh/gilgamesh.htm#gilgamesh*).

[130] Gotquestions.org: *https://www.gotquestions.org/Noahs-ark-questions.html*; Ark Encounter, "How Long for Noah to Build the Ark?" (November 18, 2011): *https://arkencounter.com/blog/2011/11/18/how-long-for-noah-to-build-the-ark/*;

Verse by Verse Ministry:
https://www.versebyverseministry.org/bible-answers/how-long-did-noah-take-to-build-the-ark; Bodie Hodge, "How Long Did It Take for Noah to Build the Ark?" (June 1, 2010; last featured May 23, 2018): *https://answersingenesis.org/bible-timeline/how-long-did-it-take-for-noah-to-build-the-ark/*

[131] Previous similar versions (in fragmentary form) exist that have been dated earlier.

[132] Thanks to Jeffrey Tomkins, Ph.D., Jerry Bergman Ph.D., and Brian Thomas, M.S. for this section.

[133] Jonathan Silvertown (ed), *99% Ape: How Evolution Adds Up* (University of Chicago Press, 2009): 4.

[134] Bruce Bagemihl, *Biological Exuberance: Animal Homosexuality and Natural Diversity* (1999). St. Martins Press. New York.

[135] R.J. Rummel, "Statistics of Democide: Genocide and Mass Murder Since 1900," *School of Law, University of Virginia* (1997).

[136] Jerry Bergman, *Hitler and the Nazis Darwinian Worldview: How the Nazis Eugenic Crusade for a Superior Race Caused the Greatest Holocaust in World History*, (Kitchener, Ontario, Canada: Joshua Press, 2012).

[137] J. Tomkins, "Separate Studies Converge on Human-Chimp DNA Dissimilarity." *Acts & Facts* 47 (11) (2018): 9.

[138] See: *http://useast.ensembl.org/Homo_sapiens/Info/Annotation*

[139] Many attempts have been made and all have failed. See Kirill Rossiianov, "Beyond Species: Ii'ya Ivanov and His Experiments on Cross-Breeding Humans with Anthropoid Apes." *Science in Context.* 15 (2) (2002): 277–316.

[140] See the U.S. Department of Health and Human Services (*https://optn.transplant.hrsa.gov/*) (February 1, 2016).

[141] Credit: Wikipedia

[142] Tomkins, 2018.

[143] Various sources will show minor differences in these comparisons. These are for example only.

[144] S. Kakuo, K. Asaoka, and T. Ide, "Human is a unique species among primates in terms of telomere length." *Biochemistry Biophysics Research Communication*, 263 (1999): 308–314

[145] N. Archidiacono, C.T. Storlazzi, C. Spalluto, A.S. Ricco, R. Marzella, M. Rocchi, "Evolution of chromosome Y in primates." *Chromosoma* 107 (1998): 241–246.

[146] Answers in Genesis: "What about the Similarity Between Human and Chimp DNA?" *www.answersingenesis.org/articles/nab3/human-and-chimp-dna* (January 14, 2014).

[147] J. Bergman & J. Tomkins, "Is the Human Genome Nearly Identical to Chimpanzee? A Reassessment of the Literature" *Journal of Creation* 26 (2012): 54–60.

[148] Ibid.

[149] J. Tomkins, "How Genomes are Sequenced and why it Matters: Implications for Studies in Comparative Genomics of Humans and Chimpanzees," *Answers Research Journal* 4 (2011): 81–88.

[150] I. Ebersberger, D. Metzler, C. Schwarz, & S. Pääbo, "Genomewide Comparison of DNA Sequences between Humans and Chimpanzees," *American Journal of Human Genetics* 70 (2002): 1490–1497.

[151] "Human-Chimp Genetic Similarity: Is the Evolutionary Dogma Valid?" Institute for Creation Research: *www.icr.org/article/6197/*

[152] Chimpanzee Sequencing and Analysis Consortium, "Initial Sequence of the Chimpanzee Genome and Comparison with the Human Genome," *Nature* 437 (2005): 69–87.

[153] J. Tomkins, "Genome-Wide DNA Alignment Similarity (Identity) for 40,000 Chimpanzee DNA Sequences Queried against the Human Genome is 86–89%," *Answers Research Journal* 4 (2011): 233–241.

[154] J. Prado-Martinez, et al. "Great Ape Genetic Diversity and Population History," *Nature* 499 (2013): 471–475.

[155] J. Tomkins, & J. Bergman. "Genomic Monkey Business—Estimates of Nearly Identical Human-Chimp DNA Similarity Re-evaluated using Omitted Data," *Journal of Creation* 26 (2012), 94–100; J. Tomkins, "Comprehensive Analysis of Chimpanzee and Human Chromosomes Reveals Average DNA Similarity of 70%," *Answers Research Journal* 6 (2013): 63–69.

[156] Nathaniel T. Jeanson, "Purpose, Progress, and Promise, Part 4*," Institute for Creation Research: http://www.icr.org/article/purpose-progress-promise-part-4* (September 2, 2015).

[157] Tomkins & Bergman, 63–69.

[158] Tomkins, 2011.

[159] R. Buggs, "How similar are human and chimpanzee genomes?" Posted on Richardbuggs.com July 14, 2018, accessed August 9, 2018.

[160] Tomkins & Bergman, 63–69.

[161] Subsequent analyses revealed an anomaly in the BLASTN algorithm used for determining the 70% figure and the revised estimate (88%) has been included in this chapter. See: Jeffrey P. Tomkins, "Documented Anomaly in Recent Versions of the BLASTN Algorithm and a Complete Reanalysis of Chimpanzee and Human Genome-Wide DNA Similarity Using Nucmer and LASTZ," (October 7, 2015), Answers in Genesis: *https://answersingenesis.org/genetics/dna-similarities/blastn-algorithm-anomaly/*

[162] Tomkins, 2011.

[163] E. Wijaya, M.C. Frith, P. Horton & K. Asai, "Finding Protein-coding Genes through Human Polymorphisms," *PloS one* 8 (2013).

[164] New Genome Comparison Finds Chimps, Humans Very Similar at the DNA Level, 2005, National Human Genome Research Institute (*www.genome.gov/15515096*)

[165] Christine Elsik. et al. The Genome Sequence of Taurine Cattle: A Window to Ruminant Biology and Evolution. *Science*. 324:522-528.

[166] Source is Pontius, Joan. et al., 2007. Initial Sequence and Comparative Analysis of the Cat Genome. *Genome Research*. 17:1675–1689 (*www.eupedia.com/forum/threads/25335-Percentage-of-genetic-similarity-between-humans-and-animals*).

[167] Background on Comparative Genomic Analysis (December, 2002) (*www.genome.gov/10005835*).

[168] NIH/National Human Genome Research Institute. "Researchers Compare Chicken, Human Genomes: Analysis of First Avian Genome Uncovers Differences Between Birds and Mammals." ScienceDaily (December 10, 2004).

[169] M. J. Hangauer, I.W. Vaughn & M. T. McManus, "Pervasive Transcription of the Human Genome Produces Thousands of Previously Unidentified Long Intergenic Noncoding RNAs," *PLoS genetics* 9 (2013).

[170] S. Djebali, et al. "Landscape of Transcription in Human Cells," *Nature* 489 (2012): 101–108.

[171] M. D. Paraskevopoulou, et al. "DIANA-LncBase: Experimentally Verified and Computationally Predicted MicroRNA Targets on Long Non-coding RNAs," *Nucleic Acids Research* 41 (2013): 239–245.

[172] J. J Yunis & O. Prakash, "The Origin of Man: A Chromosomal Pictorial Legacy," *Science* 215 (1982): 1525–1530.

[173] J. W. Ijdo, A. Baldini, D.C. Ward, S. T. Reeders & R. A. Wells, "Origin of Human Chromosome 2: An Ancestral Telomere-telomere Fusion," *Proceedings of the National Academy of Sciences of the United States of America* 88 (1991): 9051–9055.

[174] J. Bergman & J. Tomkins, "The Chromosome 2 Fusion Model of Human Evolution—Part 1: Re-evaluating the Evidence," *Journal of Creation* 25 (2011): 110–114.

[175] J. Tomkins, "Alleged Human Chromosome 2 'Fusion Site' Encodes an Active DNA Binding Domain Inside a Complex and Highly Expressed Gene—Negating Fusion," *Answers Research Journal* 6 (2013): 367–375.

[176] Y. Fan, E. Linardopoulou, C. Friedman, E. Williams & B.J. Trask, "Genomic Structure and Evolution of the Ancestral Chromosome Fusion Site in 2q13-2q14.1 and Paralogous Regions on other Human Chromosomes," *Genome Research* 12 (2002): 1651–1662; Y. Fan, T. Newman, E. Linardopoulou, & B.J. Trask, "Gene Content and Function of

248

the Ancestral Chromosome Fusion Site in Human Chromosome 2q13-2q14.1 and Paralogous Regions," *Genome Research* 12 (2002): 1663–1672.

[177] Y.Z. Wen, L. L. Zheng, L.H. Qu, F. J. Ayala & Z.R. Lun, Z. R, "Pseudogenes are not Pseudo Any More," *RNA Biology* 9 (2012): 27–32.

[178] J. Tomkins, "The Human Beta-Globin Pseudogene Is Non-Variable and Functional," *Answers Research Journal* 6 (2013): 293–301.

[179] M. Y. Lachapelle, & G. Drouin, "Inactivation Dates of the Human and Guinea Pig Vitamin C Genes," *Genetica* 139 (2011): 199–207.

[180] J. Sanford, *Genetic Entropy and the Mystery of the Genome,* 3rd ed (FMS Publications, 2010).

[181] J. Tomkins & J. Bergman, "Incomplete Lineage Sorting and Other 'Rogue' Data Fell the Tree of Life," *Journal of Creation* 27 (2013): 63–71.

[182] Brian Thomas, "Where Are All the Human Fossils?" (August 31, 2018). Institute for Creation Research: *www.icr.org/article/where-are-all-the-human-fossils/* (November 5, 2018).

[183] Dinosaur Provincial Park-World Heritage Site (*www.albertaparks.ca/media/4499676/dinosaur_pp_-_fact_sheet.pdf*) (November 5, 2018).

[184] Fossilworks.org as of October 19, 2018.

[185] J.D. Morris, *Is the Big Bang Biblical*? (Green Forest, AR: Master Books, 2003): 108–109; and J.D. Morris, *The Young Earth* (Green Forest, AR: Master Books, 1994): 70. Statistics provided by paleontologist Kurt P. Wise, Ph.D. Geology (Paleontology).

[186] T.L. Clarey & D.J. Werner, "Use of sedimentary megasequences to re-create pre-Flood geography." In Proceedings of the Eighth International Conference on Creationism (ed. J.H. Whitmore) Pittsburgh, Pennsylvania: Creation Science Fellowship (2018): 351–372.

[187] T.L. Clarey, "Local Catastrophes or Receding Floodwater? Global Geologic Data that Refute a K-Pg (K-T) Flood/post-Flood Boundary." *Creation Research Society Quarterly*, 54 (2) (2017): 100-120.

[188] Michael J. Oard, "Are the Greenland and the Antarctic Ice Sheets old?" Creation.com: *http://creation.com/ice-sheet-age* (November 5, 2018).

[189] Jake Hebert, "Ice Cores, Seafloor Sediments, and the Age of the Earth, Part 1." Institute for Creation Research: *www.icr.org/article/8130/*

[190] Jake Hebert, "Ice Cores, Seafloor Sediments, and the Age of the Earth, Part 2." Institute for Creation Research: *www.icr.org/article/8181/*

[191] Oard, 2018.

[192] Jake Hebert, "WWII Plane Found Frozen in Greenland Ice," (September 11, 2018). Institute for Creation Research.

[193] Glacier Girl. Lewis Air Legends. Posted on lewisairlegends.com. K. Jensen, "Glacier Girl: The Back Story." (1993). Originally published as Iced Lightning. Smithsonian Air & Space magazine. Posted on airspacemag.com (July 2007) (August 28, 2018).

[194] Hebert, Ibid.

[195] National Geographic, "Animal Photo Ark: Eastern Gray Kangaroo," Nationalgeographic.com: (*www.nationalgeographic.com/animals/mammals/e/eastern-gray-kangaroo/?user.testname=none*) (October, 2018).

[196] Image credit: National Geophysical Data Center (NGDC) at NOAA. Image caption: "During the last Ice Age (above) sea level was at least 394 feet (120 m) lower than it is today (below), exposing much more area on the continents."

[197] Australian Institute of Marine Science, "Big Bank Shoals of the Timor Sea: An environmental resource atlas." (2001): *www2.usgs.gov/climate_landuse/glaciers/glaciers_sea_level.asp* (November 5, 2018); K. Lambeck, Y. Yokoyama, & A. Purcell, "Into and out of the Last Glacial Maximum: sea-level change during Oxygen Isotope Stages 3 and 2," *Quaternary Science Reviews*, vol. 21 (2002): 343–360.

[198] See comments by: Jim Allen of La Trobe University, Australia and Peter Kershaw of Monash University, Australia; in: Straus, L.G. et al., Humans at the End of the Ice Age, Plenum Press, New York, London, 1996, p. 175; reported by: Hancock, ref. 12, p. 56.

[199] S. Oppenheimer, Eden in the East, The Drowned Continent of Southeast Asia (Weidenfeld and Nicolson, London, 1998): 147–148 (see Ref. 13).

[200] Image Credit: *https://commons.wikimedia.org/wiki/File:Map_of_Sunda_and_Sahul_2.png*

[201] Brian C. Howard, "Australia Is Drifting So Fast GPS Can't Keep Up: A significant correction must be made by the end of the year for navigation technology to keep working smoothly." (September 23, 2016). Nationalgeographic.com: *https://news.nationalgeographic.com/2016/09/australia-moves-gps-coordinates-adjusted-continental-drift/?user.testname=none* (Accessed October 24, 2018).

[202] A.C. McIntosh, T. Edmondson, & S. Taylor, "Genesis and Catastrophe: the Flood as the Major Biblical Cataclysm," TJ 14(1) (2000):101–109 (see pp. 106–107 and their Ref. 30).

[203] *Scientific American*, January 1993, p. 90.

[204] Thanks to Dr. Andrew Snelling of Answers in Genesis for contributions to this section.

[205] Pigs were first introduced in the 1500's by Spanish Explorer, Hernando DeSoto. "In the centuries following European exploration and colonization of the eastern U.S., free-range livestock management practices and escapes from enclosures resulted in the establishment of wild pig populations and promoted their spread," David Pimentel, Lori Lach, Rodolfo Zuniga, and Doug Morrison, "Environmental and Economic Costs Associated with Non-

Indigenous Species in the United States," College of Agriculture and Life Sciences, Cornell University (Ithaca, New York), June 12, 1999.
[206] Image Credit: Wikipedia: "Rhino - Big Game Hunt mosaic - Villa Romana del Casale - Italy 2015."
[207] Osborne, Hannah, "First Humans in Australia Arrived Thousands of Years Earlier than we Thought," (July 19, 2017), Newsweek.com: *www.newsweek.com/humans-arrived-australia-thousands-years-thought-638914* (Accessed October 24, 2018); See also: *https://news.nationalgeographic.com/2017/07/australia-aboriginal-early-human-evolution-spd/?user.testname=none*
[208] Genographic Project (Migration to Australia). Nationalgeographic: *https://genographic.nationalgeographic.com/migration-to-australia/*
[209] Emily DeMarco, "Indigenous Australian stories reveal sea level rise from 7000 years ago," (September 16, 2015), *www.sciencemag.org/news/2015/09/indigenous-australian-stories-reveal-sea-level-rise-7000-years-ago* (October 24, 2018); John Upton, "Ancient Sea Rise Tale Told Accurately for 10,000 Years: Aboriginal stories of lost islands match up with underwater finds in Australia," Climate Central (January 26, 2015): Scientificamerican.com: *www.scientificamerican.com/article/ancient-sea-rise-tale-told-accurately-for-10-000-years/* (October 24, 2018).
[210] Some areas, however, were subject to major Ice Age related flooding.
[211] Since not all the family lines are listed in Genesis 10 and a few more are listed in Genesis 11, it's likely that between 78 and 100 languages were divinely given at Babel. See: Bodie Hodge, "Was the Dispersion at Babel a Real Event?" (August 19, 2010) (Chapter 28). Answers in Genesis: https://answersingenesis.org/tower-of-babel/was-the-dispersion-at-babel-a-real-event/ (November 5, 2018).
[212] Ethnologue: Summary by language size (available: https://www.ethnologue.com/statistics/size)
[213] Image Credit: *https://en.wikipedia.org/wiki/List_of_languages_by_number_of_native_spea kers*
[214] Bill Cooper, *After the Flood: The Early Post-flood History of Europe Traced Back to Noah*, (New Wine Press: West Sussex, England). Available: *www.creationism.org/books/CooperAfterFlood/index.htm#CooperAF_TOC* (November 5, 2018).
[215] See several sources: *www.icr.org/article/human-languages-fit-young-earth-model* *www.icr.org/article/scientists-get-glimpse-into-infant* *www.icr.org/article/human-language-all-or-nothing-proposition*
[216] Brian Thomas, "Was Leviathan Real?) (Acts & Facts, January 30, 2015), Institute for Creation Research: *www.icr.org/article/was-leviathan-real/*

[217] Ed Yong, "How This Beetle Creates 500 Explosions Per Second in Its Bum," (April 30, 2015). *www.nationalgeographic.com/science/phenomena/2015/04/30/how-this-beetle-creates-500-explosions-per-second-in-its-bum/* (November 5, 2018).

[218] Adam Hoffman, Photo by Charles Hedgcock: "How the Bombardier Beetle Packs Its Punch: Researchers have figured how a toxin-spraying beetle packs its pulsing punch." May 20, 2015 by *www.sciencefriday.com/articles/picture-of-the-week-bombardier-beetle/* Photo on right: Eisner & Aneshansley 1999 (PNAS).

[219] Source: *www.thoughtco.com/how-do-fireflies-light-1968122* (November 5, 2018).

[220] Brian Thomas, Ibid.

[221] Dr. John Sanford, Jim Pamplin & Christopher Rupe, "Genetic Entropy Recorded in the Bible?" (FMS Foundation, 2014).

[222] Ibid.

[223] Creation Ministries International: Who wrote Genesis? (December 18, 2013): *https://www.youtube.com/watch?v=KLzRDKDcJ_E*

[224] Image Credit: Tamar Hayardeni (Wikimedia).

[225] Image Credit: Dr. John Baumgardner.

[226] Answers in Depth, Vol. 5 (2010). *www.answersingenesis.org/doc/articles/aid/v5/catastrophic_plate_tectonics.pdf* (November 5, 2018).

[227] See: "Noah's Flood and Catastrophic Plate Tectonics (from Pangea to Today)" (Genesis Apologetics) (Available: *https://youtu.be/zd5-dHxOQhg*).

[228] Continental Sprint: A Global Flood Model for Earth History *https://youtu.be/0RLlbUBpzr0*

[229] Chandler Burr, "The Geophysics of God: A scientist embraces plate tectonics—and Noah's flood." U.S. News & World Report. pp. 55–8. Archived from the original on August 10, 2007 (Original published June 8, 1997).

[230] Thanks to Dr. John Baumgardner for contributing this section (personal communication, May 21, 2018).

[231] Plate Tectonics Theory, National Park Service: for Teachers Scalera, Giancarlo (December 2, 2009). "Roberto Mantovani (1854–1933) and his ideas on the expanding Earth, as revealed by his correspondence and manuscripts." Annals of Geophysics. 52 (6): 617.

[232] AlteredQualia: *https://alteredqualia.com/xg/examples/earth_bathymetry.html*

[233] Image Credit: National Geographic

[234] "Ring of Fire." USGS. 2012-07-24. Retrieved 2013-06-13; "Where do earthquakes occur?" USGS. 2013-05-13. Archived from the original on 2014-08-05. Retrieved June 13, 2013.

[235] Wikipedia.

[236] S. H. Kirby (1983) "Rheology of the lithosphere," Reviews of Geophysics and Space Physics 25, 1219–1244.

[237] J. R. Baumgardner (2003) "Catastrophic plate tectonics: the physics behind the Genesis Flood," in Proceedings of the Fifth International Conference on Creationism, R. L. Ivey, Jr., Editor, Creation Science Fellowship, Pittsburgh, PA, 113-126.

[238] J. R. Baumgardner (2018). Understanding how the Flood sediment record was formed: The role of large tsunamis. In Proceedings of the Eighth International Conference on Creationism, ed. J.H. Whitmore, 287–305. Pittsburgh, Pennsylvania: Creation Science Fellowship.

[239] Ibid.

[240] Ibid.

[241] J. R. Baumgardner (2018). "The Importance of the Genesis Flood to a Correct Understanding of the Earth's Past" (PowerPoint Presentation).

[242] Image Credit: John D. Morris, 2012. The Global Flood: Unlocking Earth's Geologic History. Dallas, TX: Institute for Creation Research.

[243] Carl Werner, "Evolution the Grand Experiment," The Grand Experiment: *www.thegrandexperiment.com/index.html* (January 1, 2014).

[244] There is disagreement in the paleontology field as to whether the "dinosaur death pose" is due to choking while dying from drowning, or due to strong water currents arching the neck back after death. See: Reisdorf, Achim G. & Wuttke, Michael. "Re-evaluating Moodie's Opisthotonic-Posture Hypothesis in Fossil Vertebrates Part I: Reptiles—the taphonomy of the bipedal dinosaurs Compsognathus longipes and Juravenator starki from the Solnhofen Archipelago (Jurassic, Germany)," Palaeobiodiversity and Palaeoenvironments 92 (2012):119-168. Their findings stated, "From what has been presented above, it can be concluded that the formation of the 'opisthotonic posture' in subaquatically deposited carcasses of long-necked and longtailed reptiles is the result of a postmortem process…this posture must be seen as a normal phenomenon that occurs during subaquatic gradual embedding of these sorts of carcasses." See discussion: Drwile.com, "Arched Necks In Dinosaur Fossils: Is Water to Blame?" *www.blog.drwile.com/?p=7118* (February 16, 2016).

[245] Liu, L., S. Spasojevi & M. Gurnis (2008), Reconstructing Farallon Plate Subduction Beneath North America back to the Late Cretaceous, *Science*, 322, 934-938; Spasojevi, S., L. Liu & M. Gurnis (2009), Adjoint Convection Models of North America Incorporating Tomographic, Plate motion and Stratigraphic Constraints, Geochem., Geophy., Geosys. 10, Q05W02; G. A. Bond, Geology 4, 557 (1976); Timothy A. Cross & Rex H. Pilger Jr, "Tectonic controls of late Cretaceous sedimentation, western interior, USA," Nature, Volume 274, 653–657 (1978).

[246] Thanks to Dr. John Baumgardner for contributing this section (personal communication, May 21, 2018).

[247] Image Credit: *https://www.canyonministries.org/bent-rock-layers/*

[248] T.L. Clarey and D.J. Werner (2018). Use of sedimentary megasequences to re-create pre-Flood geography. In Proceedings of the Eighth International Conference on Creationism, ed. J.H. Whitmore, pp. 351–372. Pittsburgh, Pennsylvania: Creation Science Fellowship. Note: the literature on this topic reports 1,500 bore holes, but this has since increased to 2,000.

[249] Courtesy of Dr. Nathaniel Jeanson.

[250] Image Credit: Clarey and D.J. Werner (2018).

[251] Andrew A. Snelling, "How Did We Get All This Coal?" (April 1, 2013; last featured April 1, 2014): *https://answersingenesis.org/biology/plants/how-did-we-get-all-this-coal/*

[252] These estimates are based on the smaller cubit size.

[253] Answers in Genesis: Created Kinds (Baraminology): *https://answersingenesis.org/creation-science/baraminology/*

[254] R. M. Nowak, *Walker's Mammals of the World* (6th ed. 2 Vols, Baltimore, Maryland: The Johns Hopkins University Press (1999).

[255] Wilson & Reeder, *Mammal Species of the World* (3rd ed. 2005).

[256] Jean K. Lightner, "Mammalian Ark Kinds," *Answers Research Journal* 5 (2012):151–204. *Answers in Genesis*: *www.answersingenesis.org/arj/v5/mammalian-ark-kinds.pdf* (November 5, 2018).

[257] Dr. Nathaniel T. Jeanson, "Which Animals Were on the Ark with Noah? Stepping Back in Time." (May 28, 2016) Answers in Genesis: *https://answersingenesis.org/creation-science/baraminology/which-animals-were-on-the-ark-with-noah/* (November 5, 2018).

[258] Ronald J. Litwin, Robert E. Weems, and Thomas R. Holtz, Jr. *Dinosaurs Fact and Fiction* (*https://pubs.usgs.gov/gip/dinosaurs/types.html* and *https://pubs.usgs.gov/gip/dinosaurs/* (November 5, 2018).

[259] Answers in Genesis: "Putting the Ark into Perspective" (January 23, 2014): *https://answersingenesis.org/noahs-ark/putting-the-ark-into-perspective/*

[260] Michael Belknap and Tim Chaffey, "How Could All the Animals Fit on the Ark?" (April 2, 2019): *https://answersingenesis.org/noahs-ark/how-could-all-animals-fit-ark/*

[261] John Woodmorappe, "Chapter 5: How Could Noah Fit the Animals on the Ark and Care for Them? (October 15, 2013; last featured March 2, 2014): *https://answersingenesis.org/noahs-ark/how-could-noah-fit-the-animals-on-the-ark-and-care-for-them/*

[262] Dr. Hong earned his Ph.D. degree in applied mechanics from the University of Michigan, Ann Arbor.

[263] S.W. Hong, S. S. Na, B.S. Hyun, S.Y. Hong, D.S. Gong, K.J. Kang, S.H. Suh, K.H. Lee, & Y.G. Je, "Safety investigation of Noah's Ark in a seaway," Creation.com: *www.creation.com/safety-investigation-of-noahs-ark-in-a-seaway* (January 1, 2014).

[264] John Whitcomb, *The World that Perished* (Grand Rapids, Michigan: Baker Book House, 1988): 24.

[265] Y. Eyüp Özveren Shipbuilding, 1590–1790, Vol. 23, No. 1, Commodity Chains in the World-Economy, 1590–1790 (2000), 15–86.

[266] Genesis 10 provides a listing of most of these families. Since not all the family lines are listed in Genesis 10 and a few more are listed in Genesis 11, it's likely that between 78 and 100 language groups were involved.

[267] Ibid, Australian Institute of Marine Science (2001) & Lambeck, et al., (2002).

[268] Ibid, Cooper, 2018.

[269] Paul F. Taylor, "Chapter 11: How Did Animals Spread All Over the World from Where the Ark Landed?" October 18, 2007; last featured February 17, 2014. Answers in Genesis: *https://answersingenesis.org/animal-behavior/migration/how-did-animals-spread-from-where-ark-landed/* (October 24, 2018).

[270] It should be noted that different types of vegetation grew back after the Flood based on soil conditions, the different rates of the receding floodwaters in various places, etc.

[271] Luis Villazon, "How far can dandelion seeds travel? Make a wish… a dandelion parachute can go further than you would think." *www.sciencefocus.com/nature/how-far-can-dandelion-seeds-travel/* (November 5, 2018).

[272] Susan Feldkamp, *Modern Biology* (2006): 618.

[273] H. F. Howe & J. Smallwood (1982). "Ecology of Seed Dispersal," *Annual Review of Ecology and Systematics* 13: 201–228.

[274] Ginger Allen, "How Did Plants Survive and Disperse after the Flood?" (February 28, 2017). Answers in Genesis: *https://answersingenesis.org/biology/plants/how-did-plants-survive-and-disperse-after-flood/*

[275] See 2 Peter 3:6; Genesis 1; and Romans 8:22.

[276] See Romans 5:12 and 1 Corinthians 15:22.

[277] Dr. Andrew A. Snelling, "Noah's Lost World," (May 3, 2015)/ (*https://answersingenesis.org/geology/plate-tectonics/noahs-lost-world/*) (January 26, 2017).

[278] *The New Defender Study Bible* (Nashville, TN: World Publishing, 2006) states, "9:13 my bow. The rainbow, requiring small water droplets in the air, could not form in the pre-diluvian world, where the high vapor canopy precluded rain (Genesis 2:5). After the Flood, the very fact that rainfall is now possible makes a worldwide rainstorm impossible, and the rainbow "in

the cloud" thereby becomes a perpetual reminder of God's grace, even in judgment." Several other Biblical Creation resources hold this view.

[279] Catherine Brahic, *New Scientist Daily News* (April 24, 2007). "Mystery prehistoric fossil verified as giant fungus": (*www.newscientist.com/article/dn11701-mystery-prehistoric-fossil-verified-as-giant-fungus/#.Uea7Qo2G18E*) (January 26, 2017).

[280] *Guinness World Book of Records 2014,* (The Jim Pattison Group, 2014): 27.

[281] Image Credit: Wikipedia.

[282] Gregory S. Paul, *Dinosaurs of the Air: The Evolution and Loss of Flight in Dinosaurs and Birds* (Johns Hopkins University Press, 2002): 472. See also: M.P. Witton and M.B. Habib. "On the Size and Flight Diversity of Giant Pterosaurs, the Use of Birds as Pterosaur Analogues and Comments on Pterosaur Flightlessness." *PLoS ONE*, 5(11) (2010). Other estimates place a range the weight range between 440 and 570 pounds: "That said, most mass estimates for the largest pterosaurs do converge, using multiple methods, around a 200–260kg [440–570lb] range at present, which represents decent confidence." (Ella Davies, BBC Earth, May 9, 2016) and "The biggest beast that ever flew had wings longer than a bus." (*www.bbc.com/earth/story/20160506-the-biggest-animals-that-ever-flew-are-long-extinct*) (January 26, 2017).

[283] Larry O' Hanlon, November 8, 2012. "This pterodactyl was so big it couldn't fly, scientist claims." *www.nbcnews.com/id/49746642/ns/technology_and_science-science/#.WH-U2_krKUn* (January 26, 2017).

[284] Mark P. Wilton, *Pterosaurs: Natural History, Evolution, Anatomy.* (Princeton University Press, 2013).

[285] Ian Anderson, "Dinosaurs Breathed Air Rich in Oxygen," *New Scientist*, vol. 116, 1987, p. 25.

[286] Image Credit: Wikipedia.

[287] "No giants today: tracheal oxygen supply to the legs limits beetle size," was presented October 10-11 at Comparative Physiology 2006: Integrating Diversity (Virginia Beach). The research was carried out by Alexander Kaiser and Michael C. Quinlan of Midwestern University, Glendale, Arizona; J. Jake Socha and Wah-Keat Lee, Argonne National Laboratory, Argonne, IL; and Jaco Klok and Jon F. Harrison, Arizona State University, Tempe, AZ. Harrison is the principal investigator.

[288] Geological Society of America. "Raising giant insects to unravel ancient oxygen." *Science Daily*, October 30, 2010. *www.sciencedaily.com/releases/2010/10/101029132924.htm* (January 26, 2017). See also: Gauthier Chapelle & Lloyd S. Peck (May 1999). "Polar gigantism dictated by oxygen availability." *Nature*. 399 (6732): 114–115. This article argues that higher oxygen supply (30–35%) may also have led to

256

larger insects during the Carboniferous period: A.N. Nel, G. Fleck, R. Garrouste, and G. Gand, "The Odonatoptera of the Late Permian Lodève Basin (Insecta)." *Journal of Iberian Geology* 34 (1) (2008): 115–122.
[289] Colin Schultz, "Long Before Trees Overtook the Land, Earth Was Covered by Giant Mushrooms," Smithsonian.com (July 17, 2013). *www.smithsonianmag.com/smart-news/long-before-trees-overtook-the-land-earth-was-covered-by-giant-mushrooms-13709647/* (January 26, 2017).
[290] University of Chicago News Office. "Prehistoric mystery organism verified as giant fungus 'Humongous fungus' towered over all life on land" *www.news.uchicago.edu/releases/07/070423.fungus.shtml* (April 23, 2007) (January 26, 2017).
[291] Simon J. Braddy, Markus Poschmann, and O. Erik Tetlie, "Giant claw reveals the largest ever arthropod," *Biological Letters.* (2008) 4 106–109 (Published February 23, 2008).
[292] M. G. Lockley & Christian Meyer. "The tradition of tracking dinosaurs in Europe," *Dinosaur Tracks and Other Fossil Footprints of Europe.* (Columbia University Press, 2013), pp. 25–52. See also: Donald R. Prothero, *Bringing Fossils to Life: An Introduction to Paleobiology.* Third Edition. (New York: Columbia University Press, 2015), p. 381.
[293] Jerry Bergman, Ph.D.
[294] Gerhard Meisenberg & William Simmons, *Principles of Medical Biochemistry* (New York: Mosby, 2006).
[295] Susan Chavez Cameron and Susan Macias Wycoff, "The Destructive Nature of the Term 'Race': Growing Beyond a False Paradigm," *Journal of Counseling & Development,* Volume 76, no. 3 (Summer 1998): 277–285. The article cites information from L. Luca Cavalli-Sforza, Paolo Menozzi, and Alberto Piazza, *The History and Geography of Human Genes* (Princeton, NJ: Princeton University Press, 1994): 279.
[296] Credit: Dreamstime.
[297] Credit: Shutterstock.
[298] Darwin, *Descent of Man, and Selection in Relation to Sex.*
[299] Darwin, *Descent of Man, and Selection in Relation to Sex,* Volume 1, 201.
[300] Stephen Jay Gould, *Ontogeny and Phylogeny* (Cambridge, MA: Harvard University Press, 1977): 127.
[301] Darwin, *Descent of Man, and Selection in Relation to Sex,* Volume 2, 327.
[302] Darwin, *Descent of Man, and Selection in Relation to Sex,* Volume 2, 328.
[303] Kenneth R. Miller and Joseph S. Levine, *Biology.* (Boston, MA.: Pearson, 2006), p. 466.
[304] This section was written by Roger Sigler and was carried over from: Daniel A. Biddle (editor), *Creation V. Evolution: What They Won't Tell You*

in Biology Class (Xulon Press). Roger Sigler, M.S. is a licensed professional geoscientist in the State of Texas and has taught and published in the field of Biblical Creation since 1989.

[305] Gunter Faure, *Principles of Isotope Geology,* 2nd ed. (John Wiley & Sons, 1986), 41, 119, 288.

[306] A.O.Woodford, *Historical Geology.* (W.H. Freeman and Company, 1965): 191–220.

[307] Judah Etinger, *Foolish Faith.* (Green Forest, AR.: Master Books, 2003): Chapter 3.

[308] C.S. Noble and J.J. Naughton, *Science,* 162 (1968): 265–266.

[309] Data compiled and modified after Snelling (1998): Andrew Snelling, "The Cause of Anomalous Potassium-Argon 'Ages' for Recent Andesite Flows at Mt. Ngauruhoe, New Zealand, and the Implications for Potassium-argon Dating," in Robert E. Walsh (ed.), *Proceedings of the Fourth International Conference on Creationism* (1998), p. 503–525. See also: Andrew A Snelling, "Excess Argon": The "Archilles' Heel" of Potassium-Argon and Argon-Argon "Dating" of Volcanic Rocks. *www.icr.org/article/excess-argon-achillies-heel-potassium-argon-dating/* (February 3, 2016); Steve Austin, "Excess argon within mineral concentrates from the new dacite lava dome at Mount St Helens volcano," *J. Creation* 10 (3) (1996): 335–343 (see: *www.creation.com/lavadome).* (February 3, 2016).

[310] Andrew Snelling, "Radiocarbon Ages for Fossil Ammonites and Wood in Cretaceous Strata near Redding, California." *Answers Research Journal.* 2008 1: 123-144. *www.answersingenesis.org/geology/carbon-14/radiocarbon-ages-fossils-cretaceous-strata-redding-california/.* (February 3, 2016).

[311] Ibid.

[312] See earlier endnote regarding biblical genealogies and dating Creation and the Flood.

[313] World Wide Fund for Nature, "What do Pandas eat? The simple answers is: bamboo," Pando.org: *www.wwf.panda.org/what_we_do/endangered_species/giant_panda/panda/what_do_pandas_they_eat/* (February 13, 2017).

[314] Nathaniel T. Jeanson, "Did Lions Roam the Garden of Eden?" ICR.org: *www.icr.org/article/did-lions-roam-garden-eden/* (February 13, 2017).

[315] Image Credit: https://upload.wikimedia.org/wikipedia/commons/thumb/5/5c/The_Scientific_Method_as_an_Ongoing_Process.svg/2000px-The_Scientific_Method_as_an_Ongoing_Process.svg.png (spelling errors corrected on original, side text and shaded boxes added).

[316] Danny Faulkner, "A Proposal for a New Solution to the Light Travel Time Problem." Answersingenesis.com. February 23, 2014.

[317] See for example: _https://web.archive.org/web/20140401081546_ and _http://cosmologystatement.org/_ and _http://creation.com/crisis-in-cosmology-continues-with-conference-of-big-bang-dissidents_

[318] We are grateful to Astronomer Jason Lisle and his presentation on Distant Starlight with Answers in Genesis (Creation Library) for these salient points.

[319] Ken Ham, _The New Answers Book 1_ (Green Forest, AR: Master Books, 2006): 251–253.

[320] _Guide to Creation Basics_ (Institute for Creation Research, Dallas, TX, 2013): 51–59.

[321] Hugh Ross, "Species Development: Natural Process or Divine Action," Creation and Time Audiotape, Tape 2, Side 1 (Pasadena, CA: Reasons to Believe, 1990).

[322] Overview Eric Hovind and Paul Taylor welcome special guest Dr. G. Charles Jackson in the August 18, 2011 episode of Creation Today.

[323] John MacArthur, "Creation: Believe It or Not, Part 2 (90–209)": _www.gty.org/resources/sermons/90-209/creation-believe-it-or-not-part-2_ (March 28, 1999) (January 27, 2017).

[324] See: _www.en.wikipedia.org/wiki/Tiktaalik_ (February 16, 2016).

[325] Z. Johanson, J.A. Long, J.A. Talent, P. Janvier, J.W. Warren, "Oldest coelacanth, from the Early Devonian of Australia," _Biology Letters_ 2 (3) (2006): 443–6

[326] See: _www.en.wikipedia.org/wiki/File:Fishapods.png_

[327] Shubin N. et al., "Pelvic girdle and fin of Tiktaalik roseae," Proceedings of the National Academy of Sciences (13 January 2014); see also: _www.answersingenesis.org/extinct-animals/did-tiktaaliks-pelvis-prepare-fish-to-walk-on-land/_ (February 16, 2016).

[328] Neil Shubin, "Tiktaalik roseae fossil analysis provides new details on the origin of vertebrate legs," (University of Chicago, January 13, 2014). Phys.org: _www.phys.org/news/2014-01-discovery-tiktaalik-roseae-fossils-eveals.html#jCphttp://phys.org/news/2014-01-discovery-tiktaalik-roseae-fossils-reveals.html_ (November 5, 2018).

[329] Philippe Janvier & Gaël Clément, "Palaeontology: Muddy tetrapod origins," Nature 463, 40–41 (January 7, 2010).

[330] Smith C. Lavett, Charles S. Rand, Bobb Schaeffer, James W. Atz, "Latimeria, the Living Coelacanth, is Ovoviviparous," _Science_ 190 (4219) (1975): 1105–6.

[331] Credit: _www.cecwisc.org/Content/files/2013/09/Coelacanth-1.jpg_

[332] See: _www.dinofish.com/discoa.htm_

[333] S. Ebbert, & M. Sangiorgio, "Facing the dreaded third molar," _Prevention_, 43(7) (1991):108–110.

[334] Jerry Bergman, "Are wisdom teeth (third molars) vestiges of human evolution?" Creation.com: *https://creation.com/are-wisdom-teeth-third-molars-vestiges-of-human-evolution* (Accessed October 25, 2018).

[335] A.J. MacGregor, "The Impacted Lower Wisdom Tooth," (Oxford University Press, New York, 1985).

[336] MacGregor, 1985, p. 16

[337] J.W. Friedman, "The Prophylactic Extraction of Third Molars: A Public Health Hazard," *Am J Public Health* 97(9) (September, 2007): 1554–1559.

[338] Fiona MacDonald, "Evidence Is Mounting That Routine Wisdom Teeth Removal Is a Waste of Time," (October 28, 2016), Sciencesource.com: *www.sciencealert.com/no-you-probably-don-t-need-to-get-your-wisdom-teeth-removed-ever* (Accessed October 25, 2018).

[339] E. Rozkovcová, M. Marková, J. Dolejší, "Studies on agenesis of third molars amongst populations of different origin." *Sborník lékařský* 100 (2) (1999): 71–84.

[340] M.K. Sujon, M.K. Alam, S.A. Rahman, "Prevalence of Third Molar Agenesis: Associated Dental Anomalies in Non-Syndromic 5923 Patients." PLoS ONE 11(8) (2016): e0162070.

[341] A. Olze, P. van Niekerk, T. Ishikawa, B.L. Zhu, R. Schulz, H. Madea, A. Schmeling, "Comparative study on the effect of ethnicity on wisdom tooth eruption." *Int J Legal Med,* 121 (2007): 445–448.

[342] C. Stringer, "Human evolution and biological adaptation in the Pleistocene," In R. Foley, *Hominid evolution and community ecology* (New York: Academic Press, 1984).

[343] Homo Neanderthalensis—the Neanderthals. Australian Museum: *https://australianmuseum.net.au/homo-neanderthalensis*

[344] J.W. Cuozzo, "Neanderthal children's fossils: Reconstruction and interpretation distorted by assumptions," *Creation Ex Nihilo Technical Journal* 8, no. 2 (1994): 166–178

Made in USA - Kendallville, IN
75232_9781727870305
05.05.2022 0920